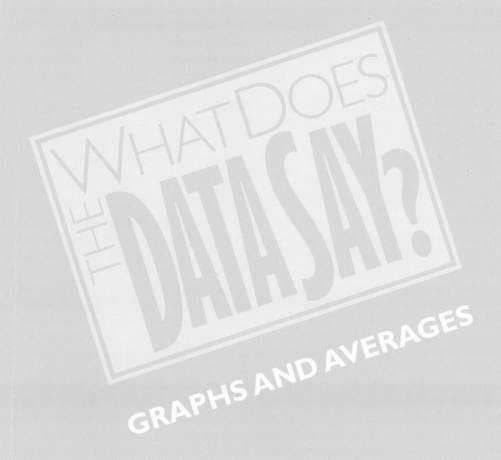

WHAT DOES THE DATA SAY?

GRAPHS AND AVERAGES

STUDENT GUIDE

WHAT DOES THE DATA SAY?

GRAPHS AND AVERAGES

MathScape
SEEING AND THINKING MATHEMATICALLY

Super Data Company collects data, shows data on graphs, and analyzes data. As an apprentice statistician, you will conduct a survey, create a graph of the data you collect, and analyze it. These are important skills for statisticians to know.

How can we use data to answer questions about the world around us?

WHAT DOES THE DATA SAY?

PHASE**TWO**
Representing
and Analyzing Data

You will explore bar graphs.
You will create single bar graphs
and identify errors in several
bar graphs. You will also
investigate how the scale on a
bar graph can affect how the
data is interpreted. At the end
of the phase, you will conduct a
survey of two different age
groups. Then you will make a
double bar graph to represent
the data and compare the
opinions of the two groups.

PHASE**THREE**
Progress over Time

Start off with a Memory Game
in which you find out if your
memory improves over time
and with practice. You will
create a broken-line graph to
show your progress. Then you
will analyze the graph to see if
you improved, got worse, or
stayed the same. The phase ends
with a project in which you
measure your progress at a skill
of your choice.

PHASE**FOUR**
Probability and Sampling

You will investigate the chances
of choosing a green cube out
of a bag of green and yellow
cubes. Then you will explore
how changing the number of
cubes in the bag can change the
probability of picking a green
cube. At the end of the phase,
you will apply what you've
learned so far by helping one
of Super Data Company's
clients solve the Jelly Bean Bag
Mix-Up.

PHASE ONE

To: Apprentice Statisticians
From: President, Super Data Company

Welcome to Super Data Company! In your new job as an apprentice statistician, you will conduct and analyze surveys for our many customers. There are different kinds of questions that you can ask in a survey. There is also a lot of information that you can get from the results of surveys. In your first assignment, you will conduct a survey and collect data about your classmates.

A statistician collects and organizes data. Surveys, questionnaires, polls, and graphs are tools that statisticians use to gather and analyze the information.

In Phase One, you will begin your new job as an apprentice statistician by collecting data about your class. You will learn ways to organize the data you collect. Then you will analyze the data and present your findings to the class.

Measures of Central Tendency

WHAT'S THE MATH?

Investigations in this section focus on:

COLLECTING DATA

- Conducting surveys to collect data
- Collecting numerical data

GRAPHING

- Making and interpreting frequency graphs

ANALYZING DATA

- Finding the mean, median, mode, and range of a data set
- Using mean, median, mode, and range to analyze data

1 Class Survey

How well do you know your class? Taking a survey is one way to get information about a group of people. You and your classmates will answer some survey questions. Then you will graph the class data and analyze it. You may be surprised by what you find out about your class.

Find the Mode and Range

How can you find the mode and range for a set of data?

The data your class tallied from the Class Survey Questions is a list of numbers. The number that shows up most often in a set of data like this is called the *mode*. The *range* is the difference between the largest number and the smallest number in a set of data. For the data in the Class Frequency Graph you see here, the mode is 10. The range is 9.

Look at the frequency graph your class created for Question A. Find the mode and the range for your class data.

How Many Glasses of Soda We Drink

```
                                    X
                                    X
        X                           X
        X                           X
        X               X           X
        X               X           X
        X       X       X           X
        X       X       X           X
        X       X       X           X
  X  X  X       X           X       X
 ─────────────────────────────────────
  1  2  3  4  5  6  7  8  9  10
         Number of glasses
```

Analyze the Class Data

Your teacher will give your group the class's responses for one of the survey questions you answered at the beginning of the lesson. Follow these steps to find out everything you can about your class.

1 Create a frequency graph of the data.

    a. Include everyone's answer on your graph.

    b. Don't forget to label the graph and give it a title.

2 Analyze the data from your graph.

    a. Find the mode.

    b. Find the range.

How can you use mode and range to analyze data?

Write About the Class Data

Write a summary that clearly states what you learned about your class from the data. Be sure to include answers to the following questions:

- What does the data tell you about the class? Make a list of statements about the data. For example, "Only one student in the class has 7 pets."

- What information did you find out about the class from the mode and range?

hot **words** | mode
            | range

Homework

page 36

2 Name Exchange

One of the questions often asked about a set of data is, "What is typical?" You have learned to find the mode of a list of numbers. Two other measures of what's typical are the *mean* and the *median*. Here you will use mean, median, and mode to analyze data on the names in your class.

Find the Mean

How can you find the mean length of a name in the class?

One way to find the mean length of a set of first names is to do the Name Exchange. Follow these steps to find the mean, or average, length of the first names of members in your group.

1 Write each letter of your first name on a different sheet of paper.

2 Members of your group should exchange just enough letters so that either:

  a. each member has the same number of letters, or

  b. some group members have just *one* letter more than other members.

You may find that some members of the group do not need to change their name at all.

3 Record the mean, or average, length of the first names in your group.

> There are 5 girls in the group and these are their names.
> sherry   Lorena   Natasha   Daniella   Ann
>   6   6   7   8   3
> Natasha and Daniella gave letters to Ann, so everyone
> would have 6 letters.
> sherry   Lorena   Natash-a   Daniel-la   Ann-ala
>   6   6   6   6   6
> The mean length for the group is 6.

How does the mean for your group compare to the mean for the class?

Find the Median

When the numbers in a set of data are arranged in order from smallest to largest, the number in the middle is the median. If there is an even number of numbers in a set of data, the median is the mean of the two middle numbers. Use the frequency graph your class made for the lengths of names to answer these questions.

How can you find the median for a data set?

- What is the median length of a first name for your class?

- What does the median tell you?

How does the mean compare to the median for the class?

Write About the Class Data

You have learned about the mean, median, mode, and range. Think about what you have learned to answer the following questions about your class:

- What do each of the measures (mean, median, mode, and range) tell you about the lengths of the first names in the class?

- Which of the measures (mean, median, or mode) do you think gives the best sense of what is typical for the class? Why?

- What are some situations where it would be helpful to know the mean, median, mode, or range for the class?

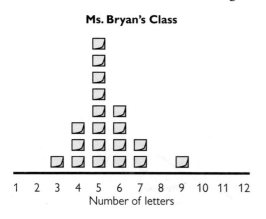

Ms. Bryan's Class

Number of letters

hot **words** | mean
median

Homework

page 37

3 TV Shows

INVESTIGATING RATINGS AND DISTRIBUTIONS

Rating scales are often used to find out about people's opinions. After your class rates some television shows, you will look at some data on how another group of students rated other television shows. Then you will apply everything you have learned so far to conduct and analyze a survey of your own.

Analyze Mystery Graphs

What information can you get by analyzing the distribution of data in a graph?

The graphs below show how some middle school students rated four TV shows. Use the information in the graphs to answer the following questions:

- Overall, how do students feel about each show?
- Do the students agree on their feelings about each show? Explain your answer.
- Which TV shows that *you* watch might give the same results if your classmates rated the shows?

Mystery Graphs

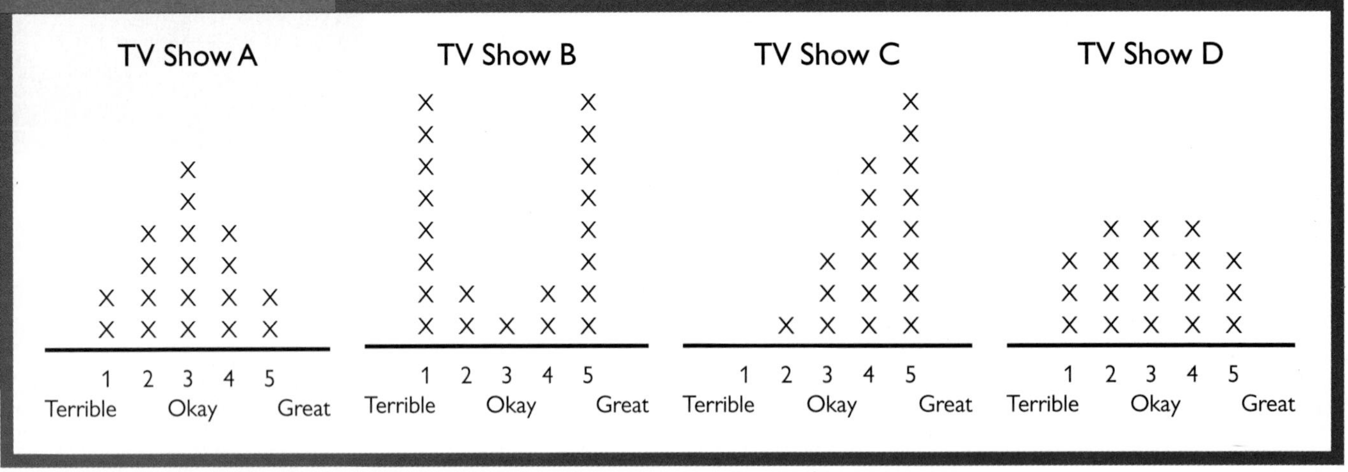

TV Show A
TV Show B
TV Show C
TV Show D
1 2 3 4 5
Terrible
Okay
Great

Collect and Analyze Data, Part 1

Now it's your turn! You will apply what you have learned about collecting, representing, and analyzing data to find out about a topic of your choice. Follow these steps.

1 Make a data collection plan

Choose a topic	On what topic would you like to collect data?
Choose a population to survey	Who do you want to survey? For example, do you want to ask 6th graders or 1st graders? How will you find at least 10 people from your population to survey?
Write survey	Write four different survey questions that can be answered with numbers. At least one of the questions should use a rating scale. Make sure that the questions are easy to understand.
Identify an audience	Who might be interested in the information you will collect? Why might they be interested?

2 Collect and represent data

Collect data	Collect data for just one of the survey questions. Ask at least 10 people from the population you chose. Record your data.
Graph data	Create an accurate frequency graph of your data.

3 Analyze the data

Write a report that answers these questions:	What are the mean, median, mode, and range? How would you describe the distribution, or shape, of the data? What did you find out? Make a list of statements that are clearly supported by the data.

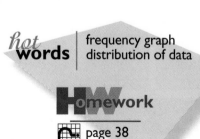

hot **words** frequency graph
distribution of data

Homework

page 38

PHASE TWO

Centimeter Grid Paper

Average speed of some animals

Speed (miles per hour)

AVERAGE

Centipede
House spider
Shrew
House rat
Pig
Type

To: Apprentice Statisticians
From: President, Super Data Company

I hope you are enjoying your work with Super Data
Company!

Super Data Company is working on a new exhibit
for the local zoo. The exhibit will make it easy for
visitors to find out and compare interesting facts
about animals. A bar graph is a useful way to
represent data. In your next assignment, you will
make bar graphs about zoo animals.

In this phase, you will investigate and create bar graphs. You will also learn how the scales on a bar graph can affect how the information is interpreted.

Graphs are used to represent information about many things, such as advertisements, test results, and political polls. Where have you seen bar graphs? What type of information can be shown on a bar graph?

Representing and Analyzing Data

WHAT'S THE MATH?

Investigations in this section focus on:

COLLECTING DATA

- Conducting surveys to collect data
- Collecting numerical data

GRAPHING

- Making and interpreting single and double bar graphs

ANALYZING DATA

- Comparing data to make recommendations

4 Animal Comparisons

INVESTIGATING BAR GRAPHS AND SCALES

Graphs are used in many different ways, like showing average rainfall or describing test results. Here you will explore how the scale you choose changes the way a graph looks as well as how it affects the way people interpret the data.

Represent Data with Bar Graphs

How can you choose scales to accurately represent different data sets in bar graphs?

1. Choose two sets of data about zoo animals to work with.

2. Make a bar graph for each set of data you chose. Follow the guidelines below when making your graphs:

   a. All the data must be accurately represented.

   b. Each bar graph must fit on an $8\frac{1}{2}$ by 11 sheet of paper. Make graphs large enough to fill up at least half the paper.

   c. Each bar graph must be labeled and easy to understand.

3. After you finish making the bar graphs, describe how you chose the scales.

What is important to remember about showing data on a bar graph?

Animal	Weight (pounds)
Sea cow	1,300
Saltwater crocodile	1,100
Horse	950
Moose	800
Polar bear	715
Gorilla	450
Chimpanzee	150

Animal	Weight (ounces)
Giant bat	1.90
Weasel	2.38
Shrew	3.00
Mole	3.25
Hamster	4.20
Gerbil	4.41

Animal	Typical Number of Offspring (born at one time)
Ostrich	15
Mouse	30
Python	29
Pig	30
Crocodile	60
Turtle	104

Animal	Speed (miles per hour)
Centipede	1.12
House spider	1.17
Shrew	2.5
House rat	6.0
Pig	11.0
Squirrel	12.0

Investigate Scales

The scale you choose can change the way a graph looks. To show how this works, make three different graphs for the data in the table.

Number of Visitors per Day at the Zoo

Zoo	Visitors per Day
Animal Arc Zoo	1,240
Wild Animal Park	889
Zooatarium	1,573

How does changing the scale of a graph affect how people interpret the data?

1 Make one graph using a scale that gives the most accurate and fair picture of the data. Label this Graph A.

2 Make one graph using a scale that makes the differences in the numbers of visitors look smaller. Label this Graph B.

3 Make one graph using a scale that makes the differences in the numbers of visitors look greater. Label this Graph C.

Write About Scales

Look at the three graphs you made for Number of Visitors per Day at the Zoo.

- Explain how you changed the scale in Graphs B and C.

- Describe some situations where someone might want the differences in data to stand out.

- Describe some situations where someone might want the differences in data to be less noticeable.

- List tips that you would give for choosing accurate scales when making a graph.

- Explain how you check a bar graph to make sure it accurately represents data.

hot **words** | bar graph
scale

Homework

page 39

5 Double Data

CREATING AND
INTERPRETING
DOUBLE BAR
GRAPHS

A double bar graph makes it easy to compare two sets of data. After analyzing a double bar graph, you will make recommendations based on the data shown. Then you will be ready to create and analyze your own double bar graph.

Analyze the Double Bar Graph

How can you use a double bar graph to compare two sets of data?

The student council at Brown Middle School surveyed forty-six students and forty-six adults to find out about their favorite lunches. The double bar graph shows the results.

- What is the most popular lunch for students? for adults?

- What is the least popular lunch for students? for adults?

- Why is there no bar for adults where hamburgers are shown?

Make Recommendations

Use the data in the double bar graph to make recommendations to the student council about what to serve for a parent-student luncheon. Be sure to use fractions to describe the data.

- What would you recommend that the student council serve at the parent-student luncheon?

- What other things should the student council think about when choosing food for the luncheon?

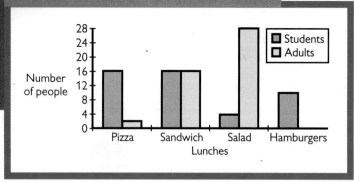

Favorite Lunches of Middle School Students and Adults

Make Double Bar Graphs

The table shown gives data on the number of hours people in different age groups sleep on a typical night.

Hours of Sleep	6-Year-Olds	12-Year-Olds	14-Year-Olds	Adults
5	0	0	3	9
6	0	2	7	15
7	0	16	24	20
8	0	19	36	20
9	3	25	5	9
10	4	12	5	3
11	31	4	0	4
12	37	2	0	0
13	5	0	0	0

1 Choose two columns from the table.

2 Make a double bar graph to compare the data. Be sure your graph is accurate and easy to read.

3 When you finish, write a summary of what you found out.

How can you create a double bar graph to compare two sets of data?

Write About Double Bar Graphs

Students in Ms. Taylor's class came up with this list of topics.

Answer these questions for each topic:

- Could you make a double bar graph to represent the data?

- If it is possible to make a double bar graph, how would you label the axes of the graph?

A: Number of students and teachers at our school this year and last year.

B: Heights of students in the same grade.

C: Time students spend doing homework and time they spend playing sports.

D: Number of hours students watch television and number of televisions in their homes.

E: Number of miles students travel to school.

hot words | double bar graph

Homework page 40

6 Across the Ages

MAKING
COMPARISONS AND
RECOMMENDATIONS

Do you think middle school students and adults feel the same about videos? In this lesson, you will analyze the results of a survey about videos. Then you will conduct your own survey to compare the opinions of two age groups.

How can you use double bar graphs to compare the opinions of two age groups?

Compare Opinion Data from Two Age Groups

The parent-student luncheon was a huge success. The student council has decided to hold a parent-student video evening. They surveyed 100 middle school students and 100 adults to find out their opinions of four videos. The double bar graphs on the handout Video Rating Scale show how students and adults rated each video. Use the graphs to answer these questions:

- How do middle school students feel about each video? Adults?

- Which video do students and adults disagree about the most? Explain your thinking.

- Which video do students and adults agree about the most? Explain your thinking.

Make Recommendations

Make recommendations to the Student Council at Brown Middle School. Be sure the data supports your recommendations.

- Which video should the council choose for a students-only video evening? Why?

- Which video should the council choose for an adults-only video evening? Why?

- Which video should the council choose to show at a parent-student video evening? Why?

Collect and Analyze Data, Part 2

In Lesson 3, you conducted your own survey. This time you will conduct the survey again, but you will collect data from a different age group. Then you will compare the results of the two surveys. You will need your survey from Lesson 3 to complete this activity.

How can you compare data from two different groups?

1 Choose a new age group.

  a. What age group do you want to survey?

  b. How will you find people from the new age group to survey? In order to fairly compare the two groups, you will need to use the same number of people as you did for the first survey.

2 Make a prediction about the results.

  a. How do you think people in the new group are likely to respond to the survey?

  b. How similar or different do you think the responses from the two groups will be?

3 Collect and represent the data.

  a. Collect data from the new group. Ask the same question you asked in Lesson 3. Record your data.

  b. Create a single bar graph to represent the data from the new group.

  c. Create a double bar graph to compare the data from the two groups.

  d. Explain how you chose the scales for the two graphs.

4 Analyze the data.

Write a report that includes the following information:

  a. What are the mean, median, mode, and range for the new age group? What do these measures tell you?

  b. How do the responses for the two groups compare? Make a list of comparison statements that are clearly supported by the data.

  c. How do the results compare with your predictions?

hot **words** | survey
double bar graph

Homework

page 41

PHASE THREE

To: Apprentice Statisticians
From: President, Super Data Company

You have been doing a great job conducting surveys and making graphs. Next, you are going to analyze progress over time.

When people learn new skills, like typing or playing a musical instrument, they need to practice a lot. It's hard work, so they want to know whether the practicing is paying off. Statistics can help measure progress. In your next assignment, you will collect data and analyze your performance at several skills.

Have you ever tried to learn a new skill, such as typing, juggling, or making free throws? How can you tell if you are improving? How can you tell if you are getting worse?

In Phase Three, you will measure your progress at some skills. Then you will use statistics to help you see whether you have been improving, staying the same, going up and down, or getting worse.

Progress over Time

WHAT'S THE MATH?

Investigations in this section focus on:

DATA COLLECTION

- Collecting numerical data

GRAPHING

- Making and interpreting broken-line graphs
- Using broken-line graphs to make predictions

DATA ANALYSIS

- Finding mean, median, mode, and range in a data set
- Using mean, median, mode, and range to analyze data

7 Are You Improving?

USING STATISTICS TO MEASURE PROGRESS

Learning new skills takes a lot of practice. Sometimes it's easy to tell when you are improving, but sometimes it's not. Statistics can help you measure your progress. To see how this works, you are going to practice a skill and analyze how you do.

The Memory Game

How to play:

1. You will be given 10 seconds to look at pictures of 9 objects.

2. After the 10 seconds are up, write down the names of the objects you remember.

3. When you look at the pictures again, record the number you remembered correctly.

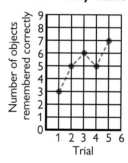

Sample Broken-Line Graph for the Memory Game

Graph and Analyze the Data

How can a broken-line graph help you see whether you improved from one game to the next?

After you play the Memory Game with your class, make a broken-line graph to represent your data.

1 For each game, or trial, plot a point to show how many objects you remembered correctly. Connect the points with a broken line.

2 When your graph is complete, analyze the data. Find the mean, median, mode, and range.

3 Write a summary of your findings. What information do the mean, median, mode, and range tell you about your progress? Overall, do you think you improved? Use data to support your conclusions. How do you predict you would do on the 6th game? the 10th one? Why?

Compare Data

Two students played 5 trials of the Memory Game. In each trial, they looked at pictures of 9 objects for 10 seconds. The table shows their results. Use the table to compare Tomiko's and Bianca's progress.

How can you compare two sets of data?

1 Make broken-line graphs to show how each student did when playing the Memory Game.

2 Find the mean, median, mode, and range for each student.

3 Analyze the data by answering the following questions:

   a. Which student do you think has improved the most? Use the data to support your conclusions.

   b. How many objects do you think each student will remember correctly on the 6th game? the 10th game? Why?

Tomiko's and Bianca's Results

Number of Objects Remembered Correctly

Trial Number	Tomiko	Bianca
1	3	4
2	3	6
3	4	5
4	6	9
5	8	7

Design an Improvement Project

Now it's time to apply what you have learned. Think of a skill you would like to improve, such as juggling, running, balancing, or typing. The Improvement Project handout will help you get started.

1 Write a plan for a project in which you will practice the skill (see Step 1 on the handout).

2 Over the next 5 days, practice the skill and record your progress (see Step 2 on the handout).

hot **words** | broken-line graph
predict

Homework

page 42

8 How Close Can You Get?

In the last lesson, you kept track of your progress in the Memory Game. Now you will play an estimation game in which you try to get closer to the target with each turn. You will keep track of your progress and graph your errors to see if you improved.

Graph and Analyze Progress

How can you represent your errors so you can easily see the progress you have made?

After you play the Open Book Game, make a broken-line graph to represent your data. Be sure to label both axes.

1 For each trial, plot a point to represent the error. Connect the points with a broken line.

2 When your graph is complete, analyze the data. Find the mean, median, mode, and range.

3 Write a summary of your progress. What information do the mean, median, mode, and range tell you about your progress? Overall, do you think you improved? Make sure to use data to support your conclusions. How do you predict you would do on the 6th game? the 10th one? Why? How would you describe your progress from game to game?

The Open Book Game

How to play:

1. Your partner will tell you a page to turn to in the book. Try to open the book to that page without looking at the page numbers.

2. Record the page number you tried to get (Target) and the page you opened the book to (Estimate).

3. Figure out and record how close you were to the target page (Error).

4. For each trial, your partner will tell you a different page number. After 5 trials, switch roles.

Investigate Mixed-up Data

Kim loves to run and wants to get faster. Every day for 20 days she ran around her block and timed how long it took. She kept track of her progress on a broken-line graph and wrote about it in her journal. Unfortunately, her journal fell apart, and all the entries are out of order. Can you figure out which journal entry goes with which days?

How can you use what you have learned about graphing to sort out some mixed-up information?

Kim's Journal Entries

A *Practicing is paying off. I'm making steady progress.*

B *I'm disappointed because I'm not making progress. At least I'm not getting worse.*

C *Wow. I've made my biggest improvement yet.*

D *I've been doing worse. I hope it's because I have a bad cold.*

E *I don't know what's going on. The time it takes me to run has been going up and down from one day to the next.*

Kim's Progress

Seconds (y-axis): 30, 60, 90, 120, 150, 180, 210, 240, 270, 300
Day (x-axis): 0, 2, 4, 6, 8, 10, 12, 14, 16, 18, 20

Read over the entries and examine the graph to help you answer these questions:

- Which days do you think each journal entry describes? Why? Tip: Each entry describes Kim's progress over 2 or more days.

- How did you figure out which entry went with which days on the graph?

- How would you describe Kim's overall progress for 20 days?

- How do you think Kim would do on days 21, 22, 23, and 24? Why? If you were Kim, what would you write in your journal about your progress on those days?

hot **words** | broken-line graph predict

Home**work**

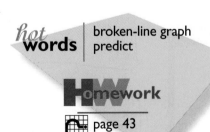

page 43

9 Stories and Graphs

INTERPRETING MULTIPLE REPRESENTATIONS OF DATA

Can you look at a graph and figure out what story it tells?
In this lesson, you will interpret unlabeled graphs to figure out which ones match different people's descriptions of learning skills. Then you will compare and analyze graphs of progress and predict future performance.

Match Descriptions to Graphs

How can you figure out what stories a graph might represent?

Six students worked on improving their skills. They measured their progress by timing themselves. Then they wrote descriptions of their progress. They also graphed their data, but forgot to put titles on their graphs. Read the descriptions and study the graphs on the handout of Graphs of Students' Progress.

- Figure out which graph goes with which student. Explain your reasoning.

- Write a title for each graph.

- The extra graph belongs to Caitlin. Choose a skill for Caitlin. Then write a description of her progress.

Descriptions of Students' Progress

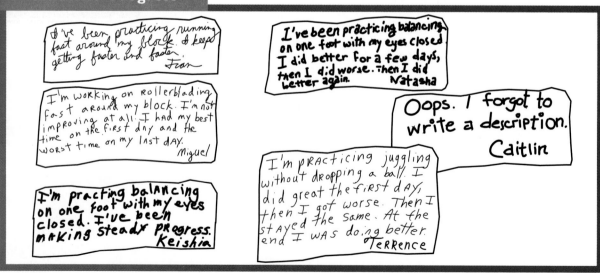

I've been practicing running fast around my block. It keeps getting faster and faster.
Fran

I'm working on rollerblading fast around my block. I'm not improving at all. I had my best time on the first day and the worst time on my last day.
Miguel

I'm practicing balancing on one foot with my eyes closed. I've been making steady progress.
Keishia

I've been practicing balancing on one foot with my eyes closed. I did better for a few days, then I did worse. Then I did better again.
Natasha

Oops. I forgot to write a description.
Caitlin

I'm practicing juggling without dropping a ball. I did great the first day, then I got worse. Then I stayed the same. At the end I was doing better.
Terrence

WHAT DOES THE DATA SAY? LESSON 9

26 © Creative Publications • MathScape

Analyze Data from the Improvement Project

Now it's time to look at the data you've been collecting for the last 5 days. You will need the Improvement Project handout. Enter your data for each day in the table on your handout. Then analyze the data.

- Complete the table by entering the range, mean, mode, and median for each day's data.

- Look at your completed table. Use data you choose from the table to make two graphs. For example, you may want to graph the mean, or the highest score, or the total score each day.

After practicing a skill for 5 days, how can you tell if you improved?

Write About the Improvement Project

Write a report to share your project with the class. Include answers to the following questions in your report:

- How did you decide which data to graph? Does one graph show more improvement than the other?

- Describe your progress from day to day.

- Overall, do you think you improved? Use the data to support your conclusions.

- How do you think you will do on the 6th day? Why?

- What mathematics did you use in the project?

hot **words** | predict
broken-line graph

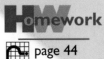

Homework
page 44

PHASE FOUR

To: Apprentice Statisticians
From: President, Super Data Company

I hope you have enjoyed your work at Super Data
Company so far!

People often talk about the likelihood of things
happening (there's an 80% chance of rain; the Lions
are favored to win). Being able to predict the
probability that a particular event will occur can be
very useful. In your next assignment, you will find
the probability of picking a green cube out of a bag of
colored cubes. You will need to use your data-
collection and analysis skills in the investigation.

Have you ever decided to wear a raincoat because the weather report said it was likely to rain? Have you ever bought a raffle ticket because you thought your chances of winning were good? If you have, then you were basing your decisions on the probability that a specific event would occur.

Probability is the mathematics of chance. In this phase, you will investigate probability by playing some games of chance.

Probability and Sampling

WHAT'S THE MATH?

Investigations in this section focus on:

DATA COLLECTION

- Collecting and recording data
- Sampling a population

DATA ANALYSIS

- Using the results of sampling to make a hypothesis
- Using bar graphs to make an informed prediction

DETERMINING PROBABILITY

- Describing probabilities
- Calculating theoretical and experimental probability

10 What Are the Chances?

Probability is the mathematics of chance. Raffles involve chance. The tickets are mixed together, and one ticket is picked to be the winner. Here you will play a game that is similar to a raffle. Then you will figure out the probability of winning.

Analyze Data from a Game of Chance

How can you use data to predict the probability of picking a green cube?

The Lucky Green Game is a game of chance. The chances of winning could be very high or very low. You will conduct an investigation to find out just how good the chances of winning really are.

1 Play the game with your group. Be sure each player takes 5 turns. Record the results in a table like the one shown.

2 After each player has taken 5 turns, answer the following questions:

   a. How many greens do you think are in the bag? Use your group's results to make a hypothesis. Be sure to explain your thinking.

   b. Which of these words would you use to describe the probability of picking a green cube?

   Never • Very Unlikely • Unlikely • Likely • Very Likely • Always

   How can you analyze the class results?

The Lucky Green Game

Your group will be given a bag with 5 cubes in it. Do not look in the bag! Each player should do the following steps 5 times.

1. Pick one cube from the bag without looking.

2. If you get a green, you win. If you get a yellow, you lose. Record your results.

3. Put the cube back and shake the bag.

Analyze Data for a Different Bag of Cubes

Ms. Ruiz's class did an experiment with a bag that had 100 cubes in two different colors. Each group of students took out 1 cube at a time and recorded the color. Then they put the cube back in the bag. Each group did this 10 times. The groups put their data together in a class table shown on the handout, A Different Bag of Cubes. Help Ms. Ruiz's class analyze the data by answering these questions:

What conclusions can you draw from another class's data?

1 What are the mode, mean, median, and range for each color?

2 Based on the whole class's data, what is the experimental probability of picking each color?

3 Here is a list of bags that the class might have used in the experiment. Which bag or bags do you think the class used? Explain your thinking.

a. 50 red, 50 blue	**b.** 20 red, 80 blue
c. 80 red, 20 blue	**d.** 24 red, 76 blue
e. 70 red, 30 blue	**f.** 18 red, 82 blue

Types of Probabilities

Experimental probabilities describe how likely it is that something will occur. Experimental probabilities are based on data collected by conducting experiments, playing games, and researching statistics in books, newspapers, and magazines.

The experimental probability of getting a cube of a particular color can be found by using this formula:

$$\frac{\text{Number of times a cube of a particular color was picked}}{\text{Total number of times a cube was picked}}$$

Theoretical probabilities are found by analyzing a situation, such as looking at the contents of the bag.

The theoretical probability of getting a cube of a particular color can be found by using this formula:

$$\frac{\text{Number of cubes of that color in the bag}}{\text{Total number of cubes in the bag}}$$

 hot **words** | experimental probability theoretical probability

 Homework

 page 45

11 Changing the Chances

Does having more cubes in the bag improve your chances of winning? In this lesson, you will change the number of green and yellow cubes. Then you will play the Lucky Green Game to see if the probability of winning has gotten better or worse.

How does changing the number of cubes in the bag change the probability of winning?

Compare Two Bags of Cubes

In Lesson 10, you found the probability of winning the Lucky Green Game. Now, you'll conduct an experiment to see how changing the number of cubes in the bag changes the chances of winning. Follow these steps to find out:

1 Change the number of cubes in the bag you used in Lesson 10 (Bag A), so that it contains 6 green cubes and 4 yellow cubes. Call this new bag, Bag B.

2 Make a hypothesis about which bag (Bag A or Bag B) gives you a better chance of picking a green cube. Explain your reasoning.

3 Collect data by playing the Lucky Green Game (see page 30). Make sure each player takes 5 turns! Record your results on the handout, Changing the Chances.

Summarize the Data

After your group finishes the experiment, write a summary of your data that includes the following information:

- What were the range, mode, and mean number of greens?

- What was the experimental probability of picking a green cube?

- Did your results support your hypothesis about which bag (A or B) gives you a better chance of picking a green cube? Why or why not?

Rank the Bags

Mr. Chin's class wants to investigate the chances of winning with more bags of cubes. The table below shows the number of cubes in the different bags Mr. Chin's class plans to use.

More Bags of Cubes

Bag	Green Cubes	Yellow Cubes	Total Number of Cubes
B	6	4	10
C	7	13	20
D	14	6	20
E	13	27	40
F	10	30	40

1. Choose one of the bags (except Bag B). If you picked a cube from that bag 100 times, how many times do you think you would get a green cube? Why?

2. For each bag, find the theoretical probability of picking a green cube. Explain how you figured it out.

3. Rank the bags from the best chance of getting a green cube to the worst chance of getting a green. (Best = 1, Worst = 5) Be sure to explain your answer.

4. After you finish ranking the bags, make a new bag of cubes that will give you a better chance of getting a green than the second-best bag, but not as good as the best bag. How many green and yellow cubes are in the new bag? Explain.

Make Generalizations

Use the results of your data to answer these questions:

- A class did an experiment with one of the bags shown in the table. In 100 turns, they got 32 yellow cubes. Which bag or bags do you think it is most likely that they used? Why?

- What generalizations would you make about how to determine which bag of cubes gives you a better chance of picking a green cube?

hot**words** | chance probability

Homework

page 46

12 Which Bag Is Which?

APPLYING
PROBABILITY AND
STATISTICS

In the last two lessons, you used a method called *sampling* when you made predictions. Here you will use sampling again to predict what's in the bag, but this time you will need to share your findings with the rest of the class in order to be sure.

Investigate the Jelly Bean Bag Mix-Up

How can you use what you have learned about sampling to make predictions?

The graphs on the handout Jelly Bean Bag Combinations show how many jelly beans are in each bag. Each group in your class will get one of the bags to sample. Can you tell which graph matches your bag?

1 Collect data by sampling your bag.

2 Compare your data to the bar graphs on Jelly Bean Bag Combinations. Which bag do you think you have? Write down why you think your group has that bag. If you are not sure, explain why.

Sampling the Jelly Bean Bags

How to sample:

Each student should do the following steps 6 times (that is, take 6 samples):

1. Pick one cube from the bag without looking.

2. Record which color you got in a table like the one shown.

3. Put the cube back and shake the bag before taking the next sample.

Student	Cherry (Red)	Blueberry (Blue)	Lemon (Yellow)	Lime (Green)
Marie Elena	I	I I I	I	I
Ricardo	I I	I I I	I	
Myra	I	I I	I I	I
Ursula	I	I I	I	I I

Analyze and Compare Bags of Cubes

After the class has solved the Jelly Bean Bag Mix-up, write about the investigation by answering these questions.

1 Write about your group's bag of cubes.

   a. Which bag did your group have? What strategies did your group use to try to figure this out?

   b. Use your group's data to figure out the experimental probability of picking a cube of each color from the bag.

   c. What is the theoretical probability of picking a cube of each color from the bag?

2 Compare the five bags of cubes.

   a. Rank the five bags from best to worst theoretical probability of picking a red cube. (Best = 1, Worst = 5)

   b. Rank the five bags from best to worst theoretical probability of picking a green cube. (Best = 1, Worst = 5)

   c. Explain how you figured out how to rank the bags.

   d. Fiona took many samples from one of the bags. She got 62 reds, 41 blues, 8 yellows, and 9 greens. Which bag or bags do you think she had? Why?

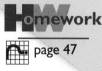

hot **words** | sampling with replacement probability

Homework

page 47

Class Survey

Applying Skills

In items **1–5,** find the range and mode (if any) for each set of data. Be sure to express the range as a difference, not as an interval.

1. 14, 37, 23, 19, 14, 23, 14

2. 127, 127, 117, 127, 140, 133, 140

3. 93, 40, 127, 168, 127, 215, 127

4. 12, 6, 23, 45, 89, 31, 223, 65

5. 1, 7, 44, 90, 6, 89, 212, 100, 78

6. Mr. Sabot's class took a survey in which students were asked how many glasses of water they drink each day. Here are the results:

Glasses of Water Students Drink
X = one student's response

```
                    X
            X   X   X
            X   X   X
        X   X   X   X   X
        X   X   X   X   X
        X   X   X   X   X   X
    0   1   2   3   4   5   6   7   8   9   10
                Glasses per day
```

What are the range and mode of the data?

7. Ms. Feiji's class took a survey to find out how many times students had flown in an airplane. Below is the data. Make a frequency graph for the survey and find the mode and range.

- Nine students had never flown.
- Ten students had flown once.
- Six students had flown twice.
- One student had flown five times.

Extending Concepts

8. Ms. Olvidado's class took this survey, but they forgot to label the graphs. Decide which survey question or questions you think each graph most likely represents. Explain your reasoning.

Question 1: How many hours do you sleep on a typical night?

Question 2: How many times do you eat cereal for breakfast in a typical week?

Question 3: In a typical week, how many hours do you watch TV?

Mystery Graph 1
X = one student's response

```
                    X
                X   X
                    X
        X   X   X
        X   X   X
        X   X   X
        X   X   X
    X   X   X   X
    X   X   X   X   X
    X   X   X   X   X
    0  1  2  3  4  5  6  7  8  9  10  11
```

Mystery Graph 2
X = one student's response

```
                X
                X       X
        X       X       X
        X       X   X   X   X
        X   X   X   X   X   X
    0   1   2   3   4   5   6   7
```

Writing

9. Answer the letter to Dr. Math.

> Dear Dr. Math:
> We tried to survey 100 sixth graders to find their preferences for the fall field trip, but somehow we got 105 responses. Not only that, some kids complained that we forgot to ask them. What went wrong? Please give us advice on how to conduct surveys.
> Minnie A. Rohrs

Name Exchange

Applying Skills

Find the mean and median of each data set.

1. 10, 36, 60, 30, 50, 20, 40

2. 5, 8, 30, 7, 20, 6, 10

3. 1, 10, 3, 20, 4, 30, 5, 2

4. 18, 22, 21, 10, 60, 20, 15

5. 29, 27, 21, 31, 25, 23

6. 3, 51, 45, 9, 15, 39, 33, 21, 27

7. 1, 4, 7, 10, 19, 16, 13

8. 10, 48, 20, 22, 57, 50

A study group has the following students in it:

Girls: Alena, Calli, Cassidy, Celina, Kompiang, Mnodima, and Tiana

Boys: Dante, Harmony, J. T., Killian, Lorn, Leo, Micah, and Pascal

9. Find the mean and median number of letters in the girls' names.

10. Find the mean and median number of letters in the boys' names.

11. Find the mean and median number of letters in *all* the students' names.

12. Find the mean and median numbers of pretzels in a bag of Knotty Pretzels, based on this graph of the results of counting the number of pretzels in 10 bags.

Knotty Pretzels
X = one bag

```
                X
                X
                X       X
X   X   X   X   X   X
148 149 150 151 152 153
   Number of pretzels
```

Extending Concepts

Professor Raton, a biologist, measured the weights of capybaras (the world's largest rodent) from four regions in Brazil.

Weights of Capybaras

Region	Weights (kg)
A	6, 21, 12, 36, 15, 12, 27, 12
B	18, 36, 36, 27, 21, 48, 36, 33, 21
C	12, 18, 12, 21, 18, 12, 21, 12
D	30, 36, 30, 39, 36, 39, 36

13. Find the mean and median weight of the capybaras in each region.

14. Find the mode and range of each data set. For each set explain what the range tells us that the mode doesn't.

Writing

15. Answer the letter to Dr. Math.

Dear Dr. Math:

When we figured out the mean, median, mode, and range for our survey, some answers were fractions or decimals, even though we started with whole numbers. Why is this? If the numbers in the data set are whole numbers, are any of those four answers sure to be whole numbers?

Frank Shun and Tessie Mahl

TV Shows

Applying Skills

Jeff conducted a survey rating TV shows on a scale of 1 ("bo-o-o-oring") to 5 ("Excellent, dude!"). Here are the results:

Show 1

Rating	Number of Students
1	0
2	3
3	7
4	3
5	7

Show 2

Rating	Number of Students
1	2
2	2
3	4
4	7
5	5

1. Draw a frequency graph of the results of each survey.

2. Find the mode(s) for the ratings, if any, of each survey.

3. Find the median rating for each survey.

Lara's class took a survey asking students to rate four different activities on a scale of 1 ("Yuck!") to 5 ("Wowee!").

Activity A
X = one student's response

Activity B
X = one student's response

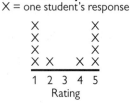

Activity C
X = one student's response

Activity D
X = one student's response

4. Find the median rating for each survey.

5. Find the mean rating for each survey.

Extending Concepts

Statisticians describe graphs of data sets by using four different types of distributions.

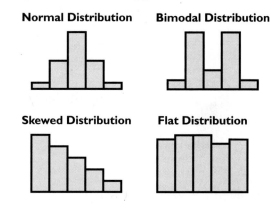

Normal Distribution   Bimodal Distribution

Skewed Distribution   Flat Distribution

6. Describe the shape of each graph showing the data from Lara's class.

7. Here are four activities: going to the dentist, listening to rap music, taking piano lessons, and rollerblading. Tell which activity you think goes with each graph for Lara's class, and why.

Animal Comparisons

Applying Skills

Here is some information about dinosaurs. "MYA" means "Millions of Years Ago."

Dinosaur	Length (ft)	Height (ft)	Lived (MYA)
Afrovenator	27	7	130
Leaellynasaura	2.5	1	106
Tyrannosaurus	40	18	67
Velociraptor	6	2	75

1. Make a bar graph showing the length of each dinosaur.

2. Make a bar graph showing the height of each dinosaur.

3. Make a bar graph showing how many millions of years ago the dinosaurs lived.

Here are one student's answers to items 1–3:

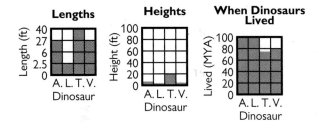

4. What is wrong with the bar graph of the dinosaurs' lengths?

5. What is wrong with the bar graph of the dinosaurs' heights?

6. What is wrong with the graph showing how long ago the dinosaurs lived?

Extending Concepts

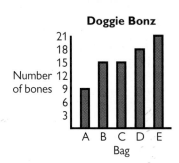

Doggie Bonz

7. Use the graph that shows the number of dog bones in five different bags of Doggie Bonz to make a table of the data.

8. Find the range, mean, and median number of bones in a bag of Doggie Bonz.

Making Connections

Some scientists think that the size of the largest animals on land has been getting smaller over many millions of years. Here are the weights of the largest *known* animals at different periods in history.

Animal	MYA	Estimated Weight (tons)
Titanosaur	80	75
Indricothere	40	30
Mammoth	3	10
Elephant	0	6

9. Draw a bar graph of this information.

10. Does the graph seem to support the conclusion that the size of the largest animals has been getting smaller? What are some reasons why this conclusion might *not* actually be true?

Double Data

Applying Skills

Forty middle school students and 40 adults were asked about their favorite activities. Here are the results of the survey.

Adults' and Students' Favorite Activities

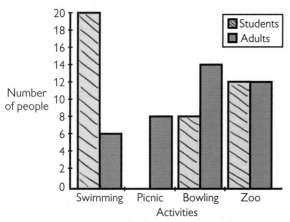

1. Show the survey results in a table (like the one for items 5–7 below).

2. What is the most popular activity for students?

3. What is the most popular activity for adults?

4. Why is there no student bar for Picnic?

Eighty 6-year-olds and eighty 12-year-olds were asked how many hours a day they usually watch TV. Here are the results.

Hours	6-Year-Olds	12-Year-Olds
0	16	4
1	23	9
2	26	15
3	15	38
4	0	14

5. Make a double bar graph of the data.

6. Calculate the mean, median, and mode for the number of hours each group watches TV.

7. Which group on average watches more TV?

Extending Concepts

Signorina Cucina's cooking class rated pies made with 1 cup of sugar, 2 cups of sugar, or 3 cups of sugar. Here are the results.

	Yucky	OK	Yummy
1 cup	2	4	14
2 cups	7	9	4
3 cups	11	6	3

8. Make a triple bar graph of the results. Label the *y*-axis *Number of Students* and the *x*-axis *Number of Cups*.

9. Now make another triple bar graph with the survey results. This time, label the *y*-axis *Number of Students* and the *x*-axis *Yucky*, *OK*, and *Yummy*.

Writing

10. Tell whether you could make a double bar graph for each set of data. If you *could* make one, tell what the labels on the axes would be. If not, explain why not.

    a. Heights of students at the beginning of the year and at the end of the year.

    b. Ages of people who came to see the school show.

Across the Ages

Applying Skills

Here are the ratings given to two different bands by 100 students and 100 adults.

Band A

Rating	Number of Students	Number of Adults
Terrible	3	1
Bad	5	3
OK	40	27
Good	43	60
Great	9	9

Band B

Rating	Number of Students	Number of Adults
Terrible	2	26
Bad	10	22
OK	14	20
Good	21	18
Great	53	14

1. Make a double bar graph for the ratings of Band A. Use different colors for students and adults.

2. Make a double bar graph for the ratings of Band B. Use different colors for students and adults.

3. Make a double bar graph for the ratings by students. Use different colors for Band A and Band B.

4. Which band would be best for a party for students?

5. Which band would be best for a party for adults?

6. Which band would be best for a party for students and adults?

Extending Concepts

7. Here are the results of a survey a student did on the number of glasses of milk 35 sixth graders and 35 adults drink in a typical week. Describe what's wrong with the graph and make a correct one.

Glasses per Week	Number of 6th Graders	Number of Adults
0	2	7
1	1	0
2	0	1
3	2	7
4	1	0
5	4	7
6	5	4
7	10	6
8	4	2
9	6	1

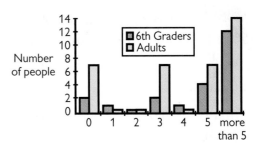

Number of glasses of milk per week

Writing

8. Pat wanted to compare how many seventh graders and kindergartners have pets. She found that of 25 seventh graders, 15 had pets. She didn't know any kindergartners, so she questioned 5 younger brothers and sisters of the seventh graders. Two of them had pets. What do you think about Pat's survey?

Are You Improving?

Applying Skills

Our Data for the Memory Game

Trial	Number of Objects Remembered	
	Ramir	Anna
1	3	6
2	4	5
3	6	5
4	7	8
5	8	7

The table shows how Ramir and Anna did when they played the Memory Game.

1. Draw a broken-line graph to show each student's progress. Use a different color to represent each student.

Find the following information for Ramir and Anna.

2. Find the median number of objects remembered correctly.

3. Find the mean.

The graph shows Caltor's progress while playing the Memory Game.

Caltor's Data for the Memory Game

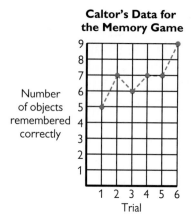

4. How many objects did Caltor remember correctly on Trial 3?

5. How many more objects did Caltor remember correctly on the 6th trial than on the 1st trial?

6. What is the mode?

Extending Concepts

Katia is trying to learn Spanish. Her teacher gave her worksheets with pictures of 20 objects. She has to write the Spanish word for each object. Then she checks to see how many words she got correct. The graph shows her progress.

Katia's Data for Learning Spanish Words

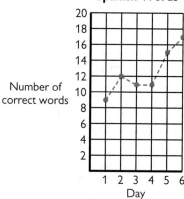

7. Create a table of the data.

8. Find the mean, median, mode, and range for Katia's data.

Writing

9. Give examples of five different types of data for which you might use a broken-line graph. Tell how you would label the x-axis and the y-axis for each graph.

How Close Can You Get?

Applying Skills

The table below shows the results for a student who played the Open Book Game five times.

Dolita's Data for the Open Book Game

Trial	Target	Estimate	Error
1	432	334	
2	112	54	
3	354	407	
4	247	214	
5	458	439	

1. Complete the table by finding the Error for each trial.

2. Make a broken-line graph of Dolita's errors.

3. Find the mean, median, mode (if any), and the range of Dolita's errors.

Every day for 12 days, Tomas runs down the block and times how long it takes.

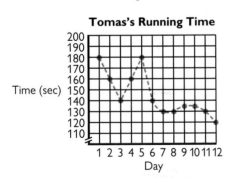

4. Use the graph to figure out the mode, median, and range for Tomas's running times.

5. Use a calculator to figure out Tomas's mean time for running down the block.

6. Make a prediction for how fast you think Tomas would run on Day 15. Explain how you made your prediction.

7. Look at the data for the first 5 days only. On which days did Tomas get faster?

8. On which day(s) did Tomas run the fastest?

Extending Concepts

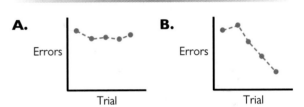

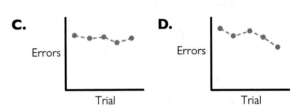

9. The graphs shown represent four students' progress in the Open Book Game. For each graph, write a description of the student's progress.

10. Which graph shows the least improvement? Explain.

11. Which graph shows the most improvement? Explain.

Writing

12. Dottie noticed that when her scores in the Memory Game improved, her graph kept going up. But when she played the Open Book Game, her graph went down, although she was sure she was improving. Explain to Dottie how to read a broken-line graph.

Stories and Graphs

Applying Skills

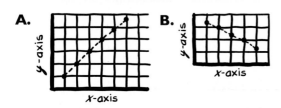

A.

B.

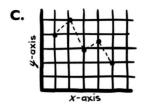

C.

D.

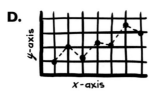

Match each description with the appropriate graph. Then tell how you would label the *x*-axis (across) and the *y*-axis (up and down).

1. "I've made steady improvement in the Memory Game."

2. "I've been running faster every day."

3. "My errors for the Open Book Game have been going up and down. Overall, I've gotten better."

4. "My swimming speed has been going up and down. Overall, I don't seem to be improving!"

5. "I've been timing how long I can stand on my head. I've had good days and bad days, but mostly I've increased my time."

Extending Concepts

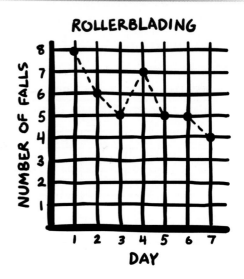

6. Make a table for the data represented on the graph "Rollerblading."

7. Calculate the mean, median, mode (if any), and range for number of falls.

8. Did this student improve at rollerblading? Write a sentence to describe his progress.

Writing

9. Answer the letter to Dr. Math.

Dear Dr. Math,
I'm confused. I don't know how you can look at a broken-line graph that has no numbers and figure out whether it shows that a student is or isn't improving.
Reada Graph

What Are the Chances?

Applying Skills

Each student picked a cube from a bag twenty times. After each turn, the cube was returned to the bag. Results for each student were recorded in the table.

Data From Our Experiment

Students	Number of Greens	Number of Yellows
Anna	15	5
Bina	18	2
Carole	12	8
Dan	16	4
Elijah	14	6

Use the data on green and yellow cubes to find the following values for each color.

1. mode　　　　　**2.** range

3. mean　　　　　**4.** median

Use fractions to describe each student's experimental probability of getting a **green cube.**

Example: Anna: $\frac{15}{20}$

5. Bina　　　**6.** Carole　　　**7.** Dan

8. Elijah

Use fractions to describe each student's experimental probability of getting a **yellow cube.**

9. Anna　　　**10.** Bina　　　**11.** Carole

12. Dan　　　**13.** Elijah

14. Combine the data for the whole group. What is the whole group's experimental probability for picking a **green cube?**

Extending Skills

Here is a list of bags that the students might have used to collect the data shown in the table. For each bag, decide whether it is **likely, unlikely,** or **impossible** that students used that bag. Explain your thinking.

15. 28 green, 12 yellow

16. 10 green, 30 yellow

17. 8 green, 2 yellow

18. 16 green, 4 blue

19. 15 green, 15 yellow

20. If students used a bag with 100 cubes in it, how many green and yellow cubes do you think it contained? Explain your thinking.

Making Connections

21. Frequently on TV the weather reporter gives the chance of rain as a percentage. You might hear, "There's a 70% chance of rain for tomorrow afternoon, and the chances increase to 90% by tomorrow night." What does this mean? Why do you think this kind of language is used to talk about weather? In what other situations do people talk about the chances of something happening?

Changing the Chances

Applying Skills

Bag	Blue	Red	Total Number of Cubes	Theoretical Probability of Picking Blue	Theoretical Probability of Picking Red
A	9	1	10	$\frac{9}{10}$	$\frac{1}{10}$
B	7	13			
C	16	4			
D	15	15			
E	22	8			
F	30	10			

1. Copy the table and fill in the missing information. Use the first row as an example.

2. Which bag gives you the highest probability of getting a blue cube?

3. Which bag gives you the highest probability of getting a red cube?

4. Which bag gives you the same chance of picking a blue or a red cube?

5. Yasmine has a bag with 60 cubes that gives the same probability of picking a blue cube as Bag C. How many blue cubes are in her bag?

6. How many red cubes are in Yasmine's bag?

7. Rank the bags from the best chance of getting a blue cube to the worst chance of getting a blue cube.

Extending Concepts

Students did experiments with some of the bags shown in the table. The results of these experiments are given below. For each of the results, find the indicated experimental probability. Which bag or bags do you think it is most likely that the students used? Why?

8. In 100 turns, we got 20 reds.

9. We got 44 blues and 46 reds.

10. In 100 turns, we got 75 blues.

11. In 5 turns, we got 0 reds.

Writing

12. Suppose Sandy's bag has 2 purple cubes out of a total of 3 cubes and Tom's bag has 8 purple cubes out of 20 cubes. Explain how to figure out which bag gives you the best chance of picking a purple cube if you pick without looking.

Homework 12

Which Bag Is Which?

Applying Skills

This bar graph shows the number of cubes of different colors that are in a bag of 20 cubes.

Cubes in a Bag

Number of cubes

	Purple	White	Orange	Gray	Brown
	5	4	1	7	3

Color

Use the graph to figure out the theoretical probability of picking each color. Be sure to write the probability as a fraction.

1. a purple cube   **2.** a white cube

3. an orange cube   **4.** a grey cube

5. a brown cube

Students each took 10 samples from the bag and recorded their data in the table shown.

Data From Our Experiment

Student	Purple Cubes	White Cubes	Orange Cubes	Gray Cubes	Brown Cubes
Miaha	2	2	0	4	2
Alec	3	1	1	5	0
Dwayne	3	2	1	3	1
SooKim	2	3	0	3	2

6. Combine the data for all the students to figure out the group's **experimental probability** of picking each color. Write the probability as a fraction.

7. For each color, find the mean number of times it was picked.

Extending Skills

8. A box of Yummy Chewy Candy has 30 pieces of candy. The pieces of candy are blue, green, red, and pink. The probability of picking a blue piece is $\frac{1}{3}$, a green piece is $\frac{1}{6}$, and a red piece is $\frac{1}{5}$. How many pieces of pink candy are in the box? Explain.

Writing

9. Answer the letter to Dr. Math.

> Dear Dr. Math,
> I was looking at the results of the Jelly Bean Supreme Investigation and I'm confused. The theoretical probability of picking a blueberry from Bag A is $\frac{7}{12}$. My group picked 24 times from Bag A and got 16 blueberries. Is that more or less blueberries than you would expect? Why didn't our results match the theoretical probability exactly?
> Beanie

STUDENT GALLERY

The Seeing and Thinking Mathematically project is based at Education Development Center, Inc. (EDC), Newton, MA, and was supported, in part, by the National Science Foundation Grant No. 9054677. Opinions expressed are those of the authors and not necessarily those of the National Science Foundation.

CREDITS: Photography: Chris Conroy, Donald B. Johnson • Beverley Harper (cover) • © Image Club Graphics, Inc.: 16, 17 • Greg Stadler: pp. 36, 37, 44, 47 • Courtesy of KTVU-TV (Bill Martin): pp. 3TR, 28a. Illustrations: Marlow Markus: pp. 8, 17, 25, 26

Creative Publications and MathScape are trademarks or registered trademarks of Creative Publications.

© 1998 Creative Publications
1300 Villa Street, Mountain View, California 94041

Printed in the United States of America.

0-7622-0203-3

1 2 3 4 5 6 7 8 9 10.02 01 99 98 97

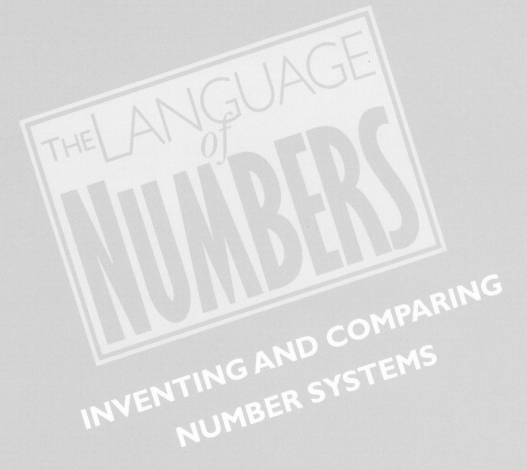

THE LANGUAGE of NUMBERS

INVENTING AND COMPARING NUMBER SYSTEMS

STUDENT GUIDE

THE LANGUAGE of NUMBERS

INVENTING AND COMPARING NUMBER SYSTEMS

MathScape™ SEEING AND THINKING MATHEMATICALLY

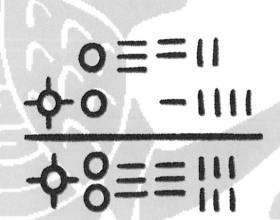

How is our current number system like an ancient number system?

LANGUAGE
OF
NUMBERS

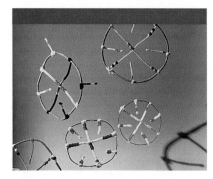

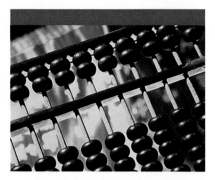

PHASE**ONE**
Mystery Device

Our everyday number system is one of humanity's greatest inventions. With just a set of ten simple digits, we can represent any amount from 1 to a googol (1 followed by 100 zeros) and beyond. But what if you had to create a new system? In Phase One, you will investigate the properties of a number system. To do this, you will be using a Mystery Device™ to invent a new system.

PHASE**TWO**
Chinese Abacus

The Chinese abacus is an ancient device that is still used today. You will use the abacus to solve problems such as: What 3-digit number can I make with exactly three beads? You will compare place value in our system to place value on the abacus. This will help you to better understand our number system.

PHASE**THREE**
Number Power

In this phase, you will test your number power in games. This will help you see why our number system is so amazing. You will explore systems in which place values use powers of numbers other than 10. You will travel back in time to decode an ancient number system. Finally, you will apply what you have learned to create the ideal number system.

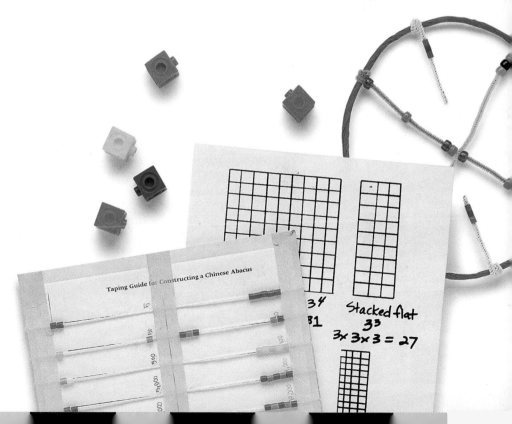

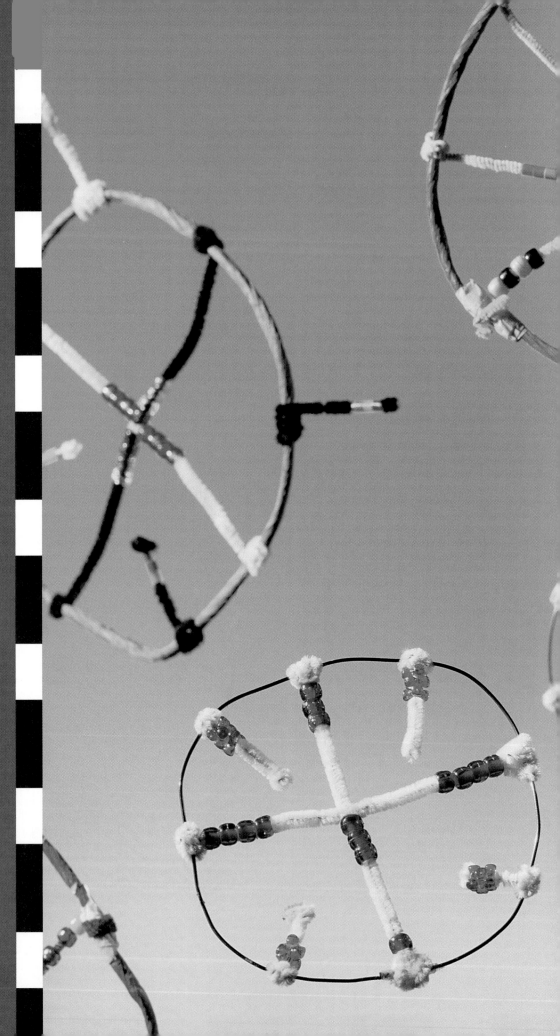

PHASE ONE

Imagine a mysterious number-making device has been discovered. The device does not work with our everyday number system. Only you can unlock the secrets of the Mystery Device.

What do computer programmers and experts in cracking codes have in common? For people in these careers, understanding number systems is an important skill. Can you think of other careers in which number systems are important?

Mystery Device

WHAT'S THE MATH?

Investigations in this section focus on:

PROPERTIES of NUMBER SYSTEMS

- Identifying different properties of a number system

- Analyzing a new number system, and comparing it to our everyday number system

- Making connections between number words and a number system's rules

- Describing a number system as having symbols, rules, and properties

NUMBER COMPOSITION

- Using expanded notation to show how numbers are made in different systems

- Writing arithmetic expressions for number words

- Recognizing that the same number can be written in different ways

- Finding arithmetic patterns in number words

1 Inventing a Mystery Device System

Some pipe cleaners and beads are all you need to make your own Mystery Device. You will use it to invent your own system for making numbers. Can you make rules so that others will be able to use your system?

Create a Mystery Device

What would you need to invent a number system?

Use the Mystery Device Assembly page to make your own Mystery Device. Your Mystery Device will look like this when it is complete. Make sure that the short "arms" can be turned outward as well as inward.

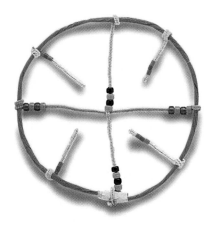

Make Numbers Using the Mystery Device

Find a way to make all the numbers between 0 and 120 on your Mystery Device. See if you can create one set of rules for making all of the numbers on the Mystery Device. Use the following questions to test your new system.

■ How does my system use the beads to make a number? Does the size of a bead or the position of a bead or an arm make a difference?

■ Does my system work for large numbers as well as small numbers? Do I have to change my rules to make any number?

■ How could I explain to another person how to use my system? Would it make a difference which part of the device was at the top?

How can we use a Mystery Device to represent numbers?

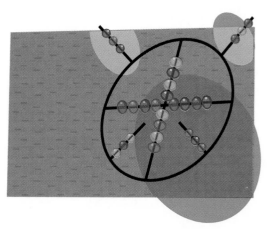

Describe the Invented Number System

Describe the rules for your Mystery Device number system. Use drawings, charts, words, or numbers. Explain your number system so that someone else could understand it and use it to make numbers.

1 Explain in words and drawings how you used your system to make each of the following numbers: 7, 24, 35, 50, 87, and 117.

2 Explain in words and pictures how you made the largest number it is possible to make in your system.

3 Explain how you can use expanded notation to show how you composed a number in your system.

How is your system different from the other systems in the classroom?

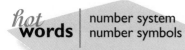

hot **words** | number system
number symbols

Homework

 page 34

2 Comparing Mystery Device Systems

What are the "building blocks" of a number system? To find out, you will make different numbers on the Mystery Device. You will invent your own way to record them. See how the building blocks of your Mystery Device system compare to those in our number system.

Explore Expanded Notation

How can you use expanded notation to show how you made a number in your system?

Use your Mystery Device to make these numbers. Come up with a system of expanded notation to show how you made each number on the Mystery Device.

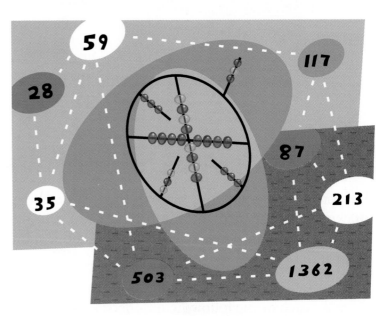

Why is it important for the class to agree on one method of expanded notation?

Investigate the Building Blocks of Number Systems

Figure out the different numbers you can make on your Mystery Device using 3 beads. The beads you use can change from number to number, but you must use only 3 for each number. Keep a record of your work using expanded notation.

What numbers can you make using 3 beads?

- What do you think is the smallest number you can make with only 3 beads? the largest?

- If you could use any number of beads, could you make a number in more than one way?

- Do you think there are numbers that can be made in only one way?

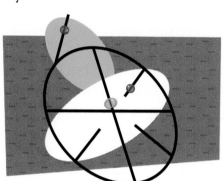

$20 + 4 + 1 = 25$

Compare Number Systems

Answer the five questions below to compare your Mystery Device system to our number system. Then make up at least three of your own questions for comparing number systems.

1. Can you make a 3-bead number that can be written with exactly 3 digits in our number system?

2. Can you make a 3-bead number with more than 3 digits?

3. Can you make a 3-bead number with fewer than 3 digits?

4. What are the building blocks of the Mystery Device system?

5. What are the building blocks of our number system?

hot **words** | arithmetic expressions
expanded notation

 page 35

3 Number Words in Many Languages

FINDING
ARITHMETIC
PATTERNS

Patterns in the number words of other languages can help you see how numbers can be made. Here you will search for patterns in number words from different languages. This will help you understand the arithmetic behind some English number words.

Find Patterns in Number Words from Fulfulde

What can you learn about number systems from looking at number words in many languages?

Look at the Fulfulde words for 1–100. Figure out how each of the Fulfulde number words describe how a number is made. Beside each number word, write an arithmetic expression that shows the building blocks for that number. The *e* shows up in many of the number words. What do you think *e* means?

Number Words in Fulfulde (Northern Nigeria)			
1	go'o	15	sappo e joyi
2	didi	16	sappo e joyi e go'o
3	tati	17	sappo e joyi e didi
4	nayi	18	sappo e joyi e tati
5	joyi	19	sappo e joyi e nayi
6	joyi e go'o	20	noogas
7	joyi e didi	30	chappan e tati
8	joyi e tati	40	chappan e nayi
9	joyi e nayi	50	chappan e joyi
10	sappo	60	chappan e joyi e go'o
11	sappo e go'o	70	chappan e joyi e didi
12	sappo e didi	80	chappan e joyi e tati
13	sappo e tati	90	chappan e joyi e nayi
14	sappo e nayi	100	teemerre

How are Fulfulde number words similar to English number words?

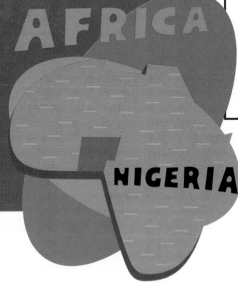

Decode Number Words from Another Language

Work as a group to complete each of the following steps. Decode the number words using either a Hawaiian, Mayan, or Gaelic number words chart.

1 Write an arithmetic expression for each word on the number chart.

2 Predict what the number words would be in the new language for 120, 170, 200, and 500.

3 Write arithmetic expressions for each new number word and explain how you created the new number word.

What do the different languages have in common in the way they make number words?

> **How can you use arithmetic expressions to compare number words in different languages?**

Create a Mystery Device Language

Invent a Mystery Device language that follows the rules of at least one number system you have decoded. Use the chart as an example. Make up number words for 1–10 in your own Mystery Device language.

1 Using your new Mystery Device language, try to create words for the numbers 25, 43, 79, and 112. The words should describe how these numbers would be made on your Mystery Device.

2 Write an arithmetic expression to show how you made each number.

1	en
2	sessi
3	soma
4	vinta
5	tilo
6	chak
7	bela
8	jor
9	drona
10	vinta

hot **words** | multiple pattern

Homework

page 36

4 Examining Alisha's System

ANALYZING A NEW NUMBER SYSTEM

How well does the number system invented by Alisha work? You will use what you have learned to analyze Alisha's number system and language. See if Alisha's system works well enough to become the Official Mystery Device System!

How does Alisha's system work?

Analyze Alisha's Mystery Device System

Use this chart to figure out Alisha's system. As you answer each question, make a drawing and write the arithmetic expression next to it. Only show the beads you use in each drawing.

1 How would you make 25 in Alisha's system, using the least number of beads?

2 Choose two other numbers between 30 and 100 that are not on the chart. Make them, using the least number of beads.

3 What is the largest number you can make?

Alisha's Mystery Device System

All small beads = 1.

Small beads pointing up = 20.

Beads are counted when they are pushed into the middle, or out to the end of an arm.

All large beads = 4.

This shows 11.

Make Number Words in Alisha's System

How is Alisha's system like our number system?

Alisha also made up number words to go with her Mystery Device system. They are shown in the table. Answer the questions below to figure out how Alisha's system works.

1 Tell what number each number word represents and write the arithmetic expression.

   a. soma, sim-vinta, en   **b.** set-soma, vintasim

   c. sim-soma, set   **d.** vinta-soma, set-vinta

   e. vintaen-soma, set-vinta, sim

2 Write the word in Alisha's system for 39, 95, and 122.

1	en	11	set-vinta, sim	30	soma, set-vinta, set
2	set	12	sim-vinta	40	set-soma
3	sim	13	sim-vinta, en	50	set-soma, set-vinta, set
4	vinta	14	sim-vinta, set	60	sim-soma
5	vintaen	15	sim-vinta, sim	70	sim-soma, set-vinta, set
6	vintaset	16	vinta-vinta	80	vinta-soma
7	vintasim	17	vinta-vinta, en	90	vinta-soma, set-vinta, set
8	set-vinta	18	vinta-vinta, set	100	vintaen-soma
9	set-vinta, en	19	vinta-vinta, sim		
10	set-vinta, set	20	soma		

Evaluate Number Systems

Use these questions to evaluate your Mystery Device system and Alisha's system. Decide which one should become the Official Mystery Device System. Explain your reasons.

- What are two things that an Official Mystery Device Language System would need to make it a good number system?

- Which of the two things you just described does Alisha's system have? Which of them does your system have? Give examples to show what you mean.

- What is one way you would improve your system to make it the Official Mystery Device System?

hot **words** | rule
arithmetic expressions

Homework

page 37

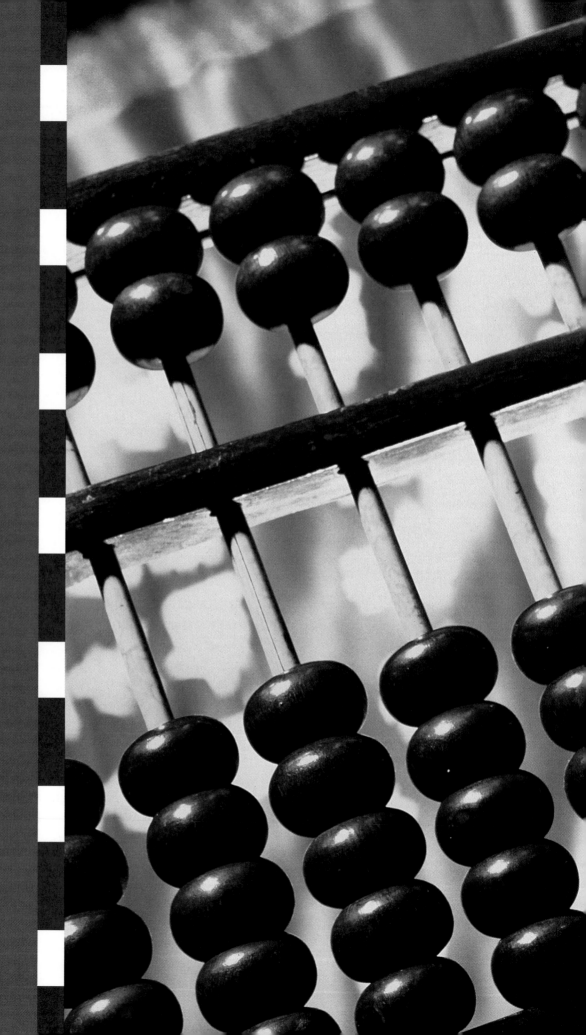

PHASE TWO

This counting instrument is called *choreb* in Armenian. The Russians call it a *s'choty*. In Japanese, it is a *soroban,* and the Turks know it as the *coulba*. The Chinese call it a *suan pan* or *sangi*. Most of us know it by the Latin name *abacus*.

Different forms of the abacus have developed in different cultures around the world over many centuries. Many are still widely used today. You may be familiar with the Chinese, Japanese, Russian, or other abaci. The abacus helps us to see how place value works in a number system.

Chinese Abacus

WHAT'S THE MATH?

Investigations in this section focus on:

PROPERTIES of NUMBER SYSTEMS

- Representing and constructing numbers in a different number system

- Investigating and contrasting properties of number systems

- Understanding the use and function of place value in number systems

NUMBER COMPOSITION

- Understanding the connection between trading and place value in number systems

- Recognizing patterns in representing large and small numbers in a place-value system

- Understanding the role of zero as a place holder in our own place-value number system

5 Exploring the Chinese Abacus

As on the Mystery Device, you move beads to show numbers on the Chinese abacus. But you will find that in other ways the abacus is more like our system than the Mystery Device. Can you find the ways that the abacus system is like our system?

Make Numbers on a Chinese Abacus

How does an abacus make numbers?

The columns on this abacus are labeled so that you can see the values. See if you can follow the Chinese abacus rules to make these numbers: 258; 5,370; and 20,857.

Chinese Abacus Rules

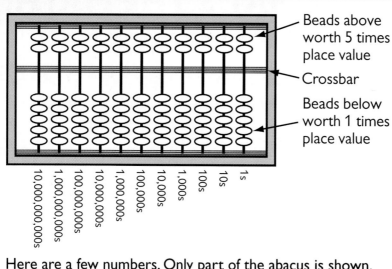

Beads above worth 5 times place value

Crossbar

Beads below worth 1 times place value

- Each column on the Chinese abacus has a different value.

- A crossbar separates the abacus into top and bottom sections.

- Each bead above the crossbar is worth 5 times the value of the column if pushed toward the crossbar.

- Each bead below the crossbar is worth 1 times the value of the column if pushed toward the crossbar.

- A column shows 0 when all the beads in the column are pushed away from the crossbar.

Here are a few numbers. Only part of the abacus is shown.

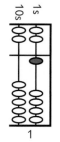 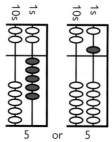 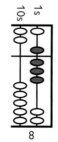 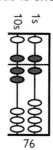

1   5   or   5   8   76

Investigate the Chinese Abacus

For each investigation below, explore different ways to make numbers on your abacus. Use both a drawing and an arithmetic notation to show how you made each number.

1 Make each of these numbers on the abacus in at least two different ways.

    a. 25   **b.** 92   **c.** 1,342   **d.** 1,000,572

2 Use any 3 beads to find these numbers. You can use different beads for each number, but use exactly three beads.

    a. the largest number you can make

    b. the smallest number you can make

3 Find some numbers we write in our system with 3 digits that can be made with exactly 3 beads.

    a. Find at least five different numbers that you can make with 3 beads.

    b. Make at least one number using only the first two columns of the abacus.

How is place value on a Chinese abacus like place value in our system? How is it different?

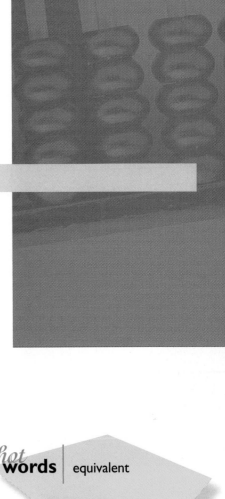

Define Place Value

Our number system uses place value. Each column has a value, and 0 is used as a place holder, so that 3 means 3 ones, 30 means 3 tens, 300 means 3 hundreds, and so on. How is the use of place value on the Chinese abacus like its use in our system? How is it different?

■ Write a definition for place value that works for both the Chinese abacus and our system.

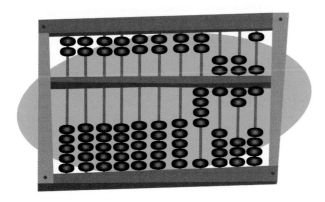

hot **words** | equivalent

Homework

page 38

6 How Close Can You Get?

TRADING AND PLACE VALUE

How close can you get to a target number using a given number of beads? In this game you will explore trading among places on the Chinese abacus. You can use what you discover in playing the game to compare the Chinese abacus to our system.

Investigate Trading Relationships

How close can you get to 6,075 using exactly 14 beads?

Follow these steps to play the game How Close Can You Get. Try to get as close as possible to the target number using the given number of beads. If you can't make the number exactly, get as close as you can.

How Close Can You Get? Game Rules

1. One player picks a target number between 1,000 and 9,999.

2. Another player picks a number of beads, from 7 to 16. You must use the exact number of beads selected.

3. All players write down the group's challenge for the round: How close can you get to _____ using exactly _____ beads?

4. When all players have made a number, compare answers. The player or players who come closest to the target number score one point.

5. Continue playing, with different players picking the target number and number of beads. When someone reaches 10 points, the game is over.

When do we use trading in our number system?

Solve the Mystery Number Puzzles

Here are four mystery number puzzles. To solve each puzzle, you need to figure out which part of the abacus might be shown and give at least one number that the beads might make. Use drawings and expanded notation to show your answers. Beware! One of the mystery number puzzles is impossible to solve, and some puzzles can be solved in more than one way.

Puzzle A

What number might be shown?

Clues:
- All the beads used to make the number are shown.
- One of the columns is the 10,000s column.
- The 10s column is not shown at all.

Puzzle B

What number might be shown?

Clues:
- All the beads used to make the number are shown.
- One of the columns is the 100s column.
- The number is between 100,000 and 10,000,000.

Puzzle C

What number might be shown when you add the missing bead?

Clues:
- All the columns used to make the number are shown.
- One bead is missing from the figure.
- When we write the target number in our system, there is a 1 in the 1,000,000s place.

Puzzle D

What number might be shown when you add the missing beads?

Clues:
- All the columns used to make the number are shown.
- There are two beads missing from the figure.
- Beads are used only in the top part of the abacus to make the number.
- When we write the target number in our system, the only 5 used is in the 1,000s place.

What trades can you make on the Chinese abacus to make both 5,225 and 5,225,000 with only 12 beads?

hot **words** | equivalent expressions

Homework

page 39

7 Additive Systems

**EXAMINING A
DIFFERENT KIND
OF SYSTEM**

An additive system does not use place value. You simply add together the values of individual symbols to find the value of the number. For example, if △ equals 1 and □ equals 7, then □ □ △ equals 7 + 7 + 1 = 15. Do you think a number system like this would be easier or harder to use than our system?

What if place value was not used at all in a number system?

Investigate How Additive Systems Work

Figure out how your additive system works by making the following numbers. Record how you made each number on a chart. Write arithmetic expressions for the three largest numbers.

1 Make the numbers 1 through 15.

2 Make the largest number possible with three symbols.

3 Make five other numbers greater than 100.

Number in our System	Number in Additive System	Arithmetic Expression (for three largest numbers only)
10	□△△△	7+1+1+1=10

What are the patterns in your system?

Compare the Three Systems

In our system, three-digit numbers are always greater than two-digit numbers. For example, 113 has three digits. It is greater than 99, which has two digits. In the system you are investigating, are numbers that have three symbols always greater than numbers that have two symbols? Explain why or why not.

Improve the Number Systems

Improve your additive number system by making up a new symbol. The new symbol should make the system easier to use or improve it in some other way.

How does a new symbol improve the system?

1 Give the new symbol a different value than the other symbols in the system.

2 Make at least five numbers with your improved system. Write them on your recording sheet.

Analyze the Improved Additive Systems

Work with a partner who investigated a different system. See if you can figure out how each other's improved systems work. Compare the largest numbers you can make with three symbols and with four symbols. Answer the following questions.

- Which system lets you make larger numbers more easily? Why?

- Which patterns of multiples are easy to recognize in each system? Are they the same? Why or why not?

- Can you find other ways in which the two systems are alike?

- Can you find other ways in which they are different?

- In what ways are these number systems like our system?

hot **words** | additive systems
Roman numerals

 page 40

8 The MD System

IDENTIFYING THE PROPERTIES OF NUMBER SYSTEMS

It's time to get out your Mystery Device and learn a new number system: the MD system. As you learn to use the MD system, you will investigate making numbers in more than one way. To do this, you will play How Close Can You Get?

Decode the MD Number System

How would you make 25 using the MD system?

This illustration shows how much the beads are worth in the MD system. The Mystery Device here shows 0—all of the beads are away from the center. To make numbers, you push beads toward the center of the Mystery Device. Always keep the short arms inside the hoop.

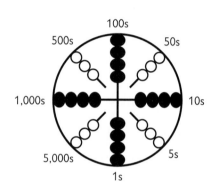

Create Multiple Representations of Numbers

Can you make numbers in more than one way in the MD system?

Use the MD system to make each of the following numbers on the Mystery Device.

1. Make a 4-digit number with 0 in one of the places.

2. Make a 3-digit number that can be made in at least two ways.

3. Make a number that can be shown in only one way.

Investigate Trading Relationships in the MD System

Jackie is playing How Close Can You Get? and she needs help. She has made 6,103 with 6 beads, but she doesn't know what to do next to get to 12 beads. Write a hint to Jackie using words, drawings, or arithmetic notation. Be careful not to give away the answer.

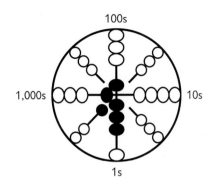

How close can you get to 6,103 with exactly 12 beads using the MD number system?

Compare the MD System to Other Systems

Make a chart like the one shown. Fill in the chart to compare the MD number system to your Mystery Device system, the abacus system, the additive system you investigated in Lesson 7, and our own number system.

How is the MD number system similar to each of the other systems?

Comparison Questions	MD System	My Mystery Device System	Chinese Abacus	Additive System Investigated	Our Number System
What are the kinds of symbols used to make numbers?					
What are the building blocks?					
Is there a limit on the highest number possible?					
Is there more than one way to show a number?					
How does the system use place value?					
How does the system use trading?					
How does the system use zero?					
What are the patterns in the system?					
How is the system additive?					

hot **words** | place value

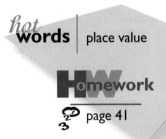

Homework

page 41

PHASE THREE

Our system for representing numbers was developed over thousands of years. People from cultures all over the world have had a part in making it such a powerful tool for working with numbers.

Imagine that you have been asked to investigate different number systems to help improve our number system. How would you create a "new and improved" number system?

Number Power

WHAT'S THE MATH?

Investigations in this section focus on:

PROPERTIES of NUMBER SYSTEMS

- Understanding that number systems are efficient if every number can be represented in just one way and only a few symbols are used

- Describing in detail the features of our number system

- Identifying and describing a mathematically significant improvement to a number system

NUMBER COMPOSITION

- Writing an arithmetic expression using exponents

- Learning how to solve terms with exponents, including the use of 0 as an exponent

- Developing number sense with exponents

9 Stacks and Flats

WRITING
ARITHMETIC
EXPRESSIONS USING
EXPONENTS

Our number system is a base 10 place-value system. You can better understand our system by exploring how numbers are shown in other bases. As you explore other bases, you will learn to use exponents to record the numbers you make.

How can you show a number using the least amount of base 2 pieces?

Make Numbers in the Base 2 System

Make a set of pieces in a base 2 system. Use your base 2 pieces to build the numbers 15, 16, 17, 26, and 31. Write an arithmetic expression using exponents for each number. You may need to make more pieces to build some numbers.

1 Fill in your Stacks and Flats Recording Sheet with the amount of pieces you used to make each number. Write 0 for the pieces you do not use.

2 Write an arithmetic expression using exponents for each number you make.

How does the pattern of exponents in base 2 compare to the pattern of exponents in base 10?

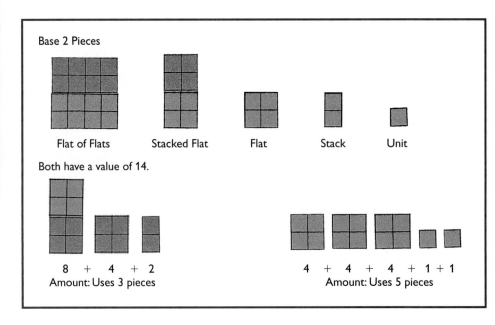

Base 2 Pieces

Flat of Flats · · · Stacked Flat · · · Flat · · · Stack · · · Unit

Both have a value of 14.

8 + 4 + 2
Amount: Uses 3 pieces

4 + 4 + 4 + 1 + 1
Amount: Uses 5 pieces

Investigate a Base 3 or Base 4 Number System

Choose whether you will work in base 3 or base 4. Make a new set of pieces for the base you have chosen. Your set should include at least 5 units, 5 stacks, 5 flats, 3 stacked flats, and 3 flats of flats.

Make at least four different numbers in your base using the least amount of pieces.

How can you use what you know about patterns of exponents to create a set of pieces for a different base?

Write a Report About the Different Base

Once you have created and investigated your set of base 3 or base 4 pieces, write a report about your set. Attach to your report one of each kind of piece from the base you chose.

1 Describe the patterns you find in your set, including what your base number to the zero power equals.

2 On a new Stacks and Flats Recording Sheet, write arithmetic expressions for, and record how you made, the numbers 11, 12, 35, and 36.

3 Figure out the next number after 36 that would have a 0 in the units column. Describe how you figured this out.

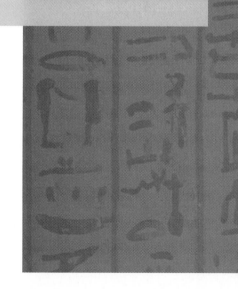

hot **words** | base two system
binary system

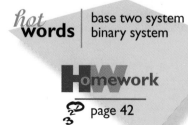

omework

page 42

10 Power Up Game

EVALUATING EXPRESSIONS WITH EXPONENTS

Do you think switching the base and exponent will result in the same number? Can a small number with a large exponent be greater than a large number with a small exponent? Play the Power Up game and find out.

Explore Exponents with the Power Up Game

How can you use 3 digits to make the greatest possible expression using exponents?

Play the Power Up game with a partner. Make a chart like the one on this page to record the numbers you roll, the expression you write, what the expression equals, and whether you score a point on the turn.

Power Up Game Rules

1. Each player rolls a number cube four times and records the digit rolled each time. If the same digit is rolled more than two times, the player rolls again.

2. Each player chooses three of the four digits rolled to fill in the boxes in this arithmetic expression: $(\square + \square)^{\square}$

3. Players then solve their expressions. The player whose expression equals the larger number gets one point.

What did you learn about exponents from the Power Up game?

Evaluate Arithmetic Expressions with Exponents

Choose three of the four letters to Dr. Math that you want to answer. Write answers using words, drawings, and arithmetic expressions. Make sure that you describe how you solved each problem. Do not just give the answer.

Can you describe the effect of exponents on numbers in different ways?

Dear Dr. Math,

We're studying exponents in math class. I was asked to draw a picture that showed what 4^3 means. I drew this:

(□□□□) (□□□□) (□□□□)

I drew 3 sets of 4 because 4 gets multiplied 3 times. But I know that $4 \times 4 \times 4 = 64$, so I don't understand why my picture shows 12. Why doesn't it show 64, even though it shows 4^3? Can you explain what's happening with my picture? How would I draw a picture of 4^3?

Exasperated with Exponents

Dear Dr. Math,

Isn't it true that $8 \times 3 = 3 \times 8$? I know I learned this! And aren't exponents a way of showing multiplication? But 8^3 does not $= 3^8$! This is really confusing. Can you explain to me why this doesn't work? Is there ever a time when it does work to switch the two digits?

Bambfoozled in Boston

Dear Dr. Math,

Something is wrong with my calculator! I think that 3^6 should be much smaller than 5^4, because after all, 3 is smaller than 5. And 6 is not that much bigger than 4. So I don't understand why my calculator tells me that the answer for 3^6 is bigger than the answer for 5^4. I think it needs a new battery; what do you think? Why can't I tell which of two numbers is bigger by comparing the base numbers?

Crummy Calculator

Dear Dr. Math,

One of the problems I had to do for homework last night was to figure out what 10^0 was equal to. I called my friend to ask him, and he thought it was 0. He said it means that 10 is multiplied by itself 0 times, so you have nothing. I thought it was 1, but I don't remember why that works. Which of us is right? And can you please explain to me why?

Zeroing In

hot **words** | exponent
power

page 43

11 Efficient Number Systems

COMPARING THE FEATURES OF DIFFERENT SYSTEMS

Some number systems use a base, and others do not.
Here you will decode different place-value systems. You will see that some systems work better than others. Your decoding work will help you think about the features that make different systems work and that make a number system easy to use.

Decode Three Place-Value Systems

How are bases used in a place-value system?

Each of the number systems shown uses a different place-value system. See if you can use the numbers on this page and on the Decoding Chart to decode each system.

1. Figure out what goes in the place-heading boxes (▢) to decode the system.

2. Choose two numbers that are not on the chart. Write an arithmetic expression that shows how the numbers are made in each system. Make sure you label each expression with the name of the system.

Our System	Hand System Place Values				
30		1	0	1	0
35		1	0	2	2
40		1	1	1	1
50		1	2	1	2
60		2	0	2	0
101	1	0	2	0	2

Our System	Crazy Places Place Values				
30			1	0	0	0
32			1	0	0	2
40		1	0	0	0	0
47		1	0	0	0	7
53	1	0	0	0	0	3

Our System	Milo's System Place Values			
30		●	★	★	★
34		●	★	●	●
58		●	◆	◆	◆
105	●	★	★	●	◆

THE LANGUAGE OF NUMBERS   LESSON 11
30   © Creative Publications • MathScape

Compare the Features of Many Number Systems

What features make a number system efficient?

Use the features from class discussion to make a chart that compares some of the systems you have learned in this unit. Include at least one system that is additive, one that uses a base, and one that uses place value.

1 Make a list of at least six different features of a number system.

2 Choose at least six different number systems and describe how they use each feature.

3 Create your own chart format. Leave an empty column so you can add our system to your chart later.

Feature	MD	Chinese Abacus	Milo's System
Place Value	Yes, large beads are worth 10. Small beads = 1.	5 is on top. 1 is on bottom. Yes.	No, because the system use symbols.
base system	Yes, 1, 10, 100.	Base of 5. 5, 50, 500, 5,000 Base of 1. 1, 10, 100, 1,000	Yes, it have base. 1, 3, 10, 30, 100
#s represented in more than one way	Yes, you can use 10 small bead or 1 big bead to make 10.	Yes, you can use 5 ones or 1 5's to make 5.	Yes, you can use U and make 2.

Check Whether Our System Is Efficient

What makes some number systems more efficient than others? Use your chart to check whether our system is efficient or not. Explain your reasoning in writing and use your chart as an example.

hot **words** | base (Number) place value

Homework

page 44

12 A New Number System

FINAL PROJECT

You have decoded many different types of number systems and looked at their features. Now it is time to improve one of the systems by bringing together the best of each. You will start by taking a look at the ancient Egyptian system.

How does the ancient Egyptian system work?

Decode the Egyptian Number System

Use what you have learned about decoding systems to figure out the value of each symbol on your Ancient Egyptian Reference Sheet. On a separate sheet of paper, write the value of each symbol.

1. Choose four numbers that are not on the chart. Write each number in the ancient system.

2. Write arithmetic expressions to show how each of the four numbers is made.

1,024... ...50

Analyze the Ancient Number System

Describe the features of the Egyptian system. What are its disadvantages? Find at least one way to improve the ancient system.

What are the ways in which the ancient system is like our system?

Revise a Number System

Choose one of the following number systems. Find a way to make it more efficient. Present your revised system clearly with words, drawings, and arithmetic expressions, so that others could use it.

1 Revise either Alisha's (Lesson 4), Yumi's (Lesson 7), Milo's (Lesson 11), or your own Mystery Device system.

2 Find a more efficient way to make all the numbers between 0 and 120, using words or symbols. Show how at least four numbers are made using arithmetic expressions.

3 Describe how your system uses the following features:

a. place value   **b.** base system

c. symbols   **d.** rules

e. a way to show zero   **f.** trading

g. range (highest and lowest number)   **h.** making a number in more than one way

4 Compare your system to our system and describe the differences and similarities.

> **What features would a number system need to be efficient?**

Evaluate the Efficiency of an Improved System

A good way to evaluate a number system is to ask questions about the different properties of the system. What are the building blocks of the system? Does it use base or place value? Can a number be made in more than one way? Come up with at least three more questions and use them to explain why your partner's system is or is not efficient. Make sure your explanation talks about the mathematical features of the system.

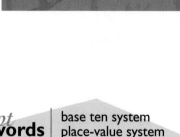

hot **words** | base ten system
place-value system

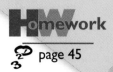

page 45

Inventing a Mystery Device System

Applying Skills

1. $3(7) + 5(2) = ?$

2. $6(5) + 3(2) + 7(8) = ?$

3. $4(25) + 6(15) + 2(10) = ?$

4. $9(100) + 4(10) + 4(1) = ?$

5. $5(1,000) + 3(100) + 2(10) + 9(1) = ?$

6. $6(1,000) + 3(10) + 4(1) = ?$

George's Mystery Device System
• Large beads = 10
• Small beads with arms pointing in = 1
• Small beads with arms pointing out = 5

Show each number in George's system. Draw only the beads you need for each number. Remember to draw the diagonal arms either in or out. Use the fewest beads you can.

7. Draw 128 in George's system.

8. Draw 73 in George's system.

9. Draw 13 in George's system.

10. What is this number?

11. What is this number?

12. What is this number?

Extending Concepts

13. What is the largest number you can make with this system? Explain how you know.

14. Can you find a number you can make in more than one way? Can you find a number that can be made in more than two ways?

15. Is there a number you can make in only one way in George's system? What is the arithmetic expression? What would the arithmetic expression be for that same number written in our system?

Writing

16. Answer the letter to Dr. Math.

> Dear Dr. Math,
>
> In my Mystery Device system, for numbers larger than 100, large beads mean 100, small beads with the arms pointing out are 20, and small beads with the arms pointing in are 10. To make numbers less than 100, large beads are 10, small beads with the arms pointing in are 5, and small beads with the arms pointing out are 1. My friends get confused using my system. How should I change it?
>
> B. D. Wrong

Comparing Mystery Device Systems

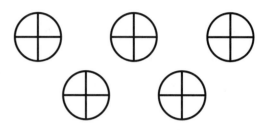

Applying Skills

Write each number in arithmetic expressions.

1. 6,782   **2.** 9,015

3. 609   **4.** 37,126

5. 132,056   **6.** 905,003

What number do these arithmetic expressions represent?

7. $8(100,000) + 7(10,000) + 6(1,000) + 3(100) + 2(10) + 1(1)$

8. $3(10,000) + 1(1,000) + 6(100) + 3(1)$

9. $5(100,000) + 2(1,000) + 3(100)$

10. $7(1,000,000) + 5(100,000) + 6(10,000) + 2(1,000) + 4(100) + 3(10)$

Remember George's system from Lesson 1.

George's Mystery Device System
- Large beads = 10
- Small beads with arms pointing in = 1
- Small beads with arms pointing out = 5

11. Using only 3 beads, draw at least seven numbers in George's system. Only draw the beads that count.

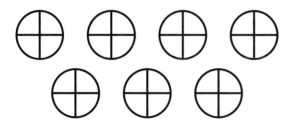

Extending Concepts

12. Using George's system, draw 32 in at least five different ways. Only draw the beads that count.

13. Can you think of an explanation for why you can make numbers so many ways in this system but not in our own?

Making Connections

14. Look at the way you solved items **11** and **12.** Did you just keep thinking of different solutions or did you try to use a pattern? Describe the pattern you used or one you might try next time.

Number Words in Many Languages

Applying Skills

Number Words in Fulfulde		
1 go'o	11 sappo e go'o	30 chappan e tati
2 ɗiɗi	12 sappo e ɗiɗi	40 chappan e nayi
3 tati	13 sappo e tati	50 chappan e joyi
4 nayi	14 sappo e nayi	60 chappan e joyi e go'o
5 joyi	15 sappo e joyi	70 chappan e joyi e ɗiɗi
6 joyi e go'o	16 sappo e joyi e go'o	80 chappan e joyi e tati
7 joyi e ɗiɗi	17 sappo e joyi e ɗiɗi	90 chappan e joyi e nayi
8 joyi e tati	18 sappo e joyi e tati	100 teemerre
9 joyi e nayi	19 sappo e joyi e nayi	
10 sappo	20 noogas	

Number	Fulfulde Word	Arithmetic Expression	English Word	Arithmetic Expression
25	a.	b.	c.	d.
34	e.	f.	g.	h.
79	i.	j.	k.	l.
103	m.	n.	o.	p.

1. Copy and complete the chart above.

2. What building blocks does Fulfulde use that English also uses?

3. What building blocks does Fulfulde use that English does not use?

4. Write the Fulfulde number words that match these arithmetic expressions, and tell what each number equals:

   a. $(10)(5 + 3) + 1(1)$

   b. $(10)(4) + 1(5) + 3(1)$

   c. $1(100) + 1(20) + 1(5) + 4(1)$

5. What are the arithmetic expressions for the English number words used in item 4?

Extending Concepts

6. In Fulfulde, the arithmetic expression for chappan e joyi is 5(10). In English, the arithmetic expression for 50 is also 5(10). Find another Fulfulde number word that has the same arithmetic expression as the matching English number word.

Writing

7. How are the Fulfulde number words and arithmetic expressions like the English number words and arithmetic expressions? How are they different?

Examining Alisha's System

Applying Skills

Alisha's Mystery Device System
- Large beads = 4
- Small beads with arms pointing in = 1
- Small beads with arms pointing straight up = 20

Make a chart like the one below and use Alisha's system to show each number on the Mystery Device. Remember to draw in the diagonal arms in the correct position. Next, write the number in Alisha's number language. Then write the arithmetic expression for the number.

Number	Sketch	Number Word	Arithmetic Expression
65	**1.**	**2.**	**3.**
143	**4.**	**5.**	**6.**
180	**7.**	**8.**	**9.**
31	**10.**	**11.**	**12.**

13. How would you commonly write the number word for 36? What is the arithmetic expression for this number?

Alisha's Number Language			
1 en	15 sim-vinta, sim
2 set	16 vinta-vinta
3 sim	17 vinta-vinta, en
4 vinta	18 vinta-vinta, set
5 vintaen	19 vinta-vinta, sim
6 vinta, set	20 soma
7 vinta, sim	30 soma, set-vinta, set
8 set-vinta	40 set-soma
9 set-vinta, en	50 set-soma, set-vinta, set
10 set-vinta, set	60 sim-soma
11 set-vinta, sim	70 sim-soma, set-vinta, set
12 sim-vinta	80 vinta-soma
13 sim-vinta, en	90 vinta-soma, set-vinta, set
14 sim-vinta, set	100 vintaen-soma

Extending Concepts

14. What is the largest number in the system that you can make in more than one way? Find all the different ways you can make the number and write an arithmetic expression for each one.

15. What is the smallest number you can make in more than one way? Make a different number word for each way to show how the number is made.

Exploring the Chinese Abacus

Applying Skills

Abacus Rules

The beads above the crossbar are worth five times the value of the column if pushed toward the crossbar. Each bead below the crossbar is worth one times the value of the crossbar if pushed toward it. The value of the column is zero when all beads are pushed away from the crossbar.

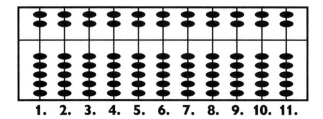

1. 2. 3. 4. 5. 6. 7. 8. 9. 10. 11.

Write the place value using words and numbers for each row marked on the abacus. For example, row 11 = 1 or *the ones place.*

Show each number on the abacus using the fewest beads. Show only the necessary beads. Write the arithmetic notation for each solution.

Number	Sketch	Arithmetic Expression
6,050	**12.**	**13.**
28,362	**14.**	**15.**
4,035,269	**16.**	**17.**

Extending Concepts

18. How is zero shown on the abacus? Why is the zero important? How is zero on the abacus like or unlike zero in our system?

19. Find a number smaller than 100 that you could make on the abacus in more than one way. What is the arithmetic expression for each way you can make the number?

Writing

20. Answer the letter to Dr. Math.

Dear Dr. Math,

It seems like the Chinese abacus system has two different values for each column. Do the columns have the different values or do the beads?

Out O'Place

How Close Can You Get?

Applying Skills

Show different ways you can make this number on the abacus. Write the arithmetic expression for each solution.

Number	Sketch	Arithmetic Expression
852	1.	2.
852	3.	4.
852	5.	6.

What are some different ways you can make 555? How many beads do you use each time? Make a chart putting the number of beads you used in order from smallest to largest.

	Number of Beads Used	Arithmetic Expression
7.		
8.		
9.		
10.		

Extending Concepts

11. What pattern do you see in the number of beads used to make 852 and 555? Why does this pattern work this way? Don't forget to explain how you used trading to make the different numbers.

Writing

12. Answer the letter to Dr. Math.

> Dear Dr. Math,
> To make the number 500, I can use five 100-beads from the bottom, or one 500-bead from on top. Or I can use four 100-beads from the bottom AND two 50-beads from on top. When would it make sense to use a different way to make the number?
> Clu

Additive Systems

Applying Skills

Judy's System Judy invented a new additive system. ◊ = 1 □ = 9 ! = 81

Judy's System	Our Number System	Arithmetic Expression
!!□◊◊◊	**1.**	**2.**
!!!!!□□□□◊◊◊	**3.**	**4.**
□□□◊◊	**5.**	**6.**
!!!!!!!□□□□□◊◊◊◊◊◊◊◊◊◊◊◊◊	**7.**	**8.**
9.	222	**10.**
11.	98	**12.**

What do these numbers in Judy's system represent in our system? How would you make numbers using Judy's system? Complete the chart and write an arithmetic expression for each number.

Extending Concepts

13. Write 1,776 in Judy's system. What number would you add to Judy's system to make writing larger numbers easier? Make sure your number fits the pattern. Write 1,776 using your added symbol.

14. How did you choose your added number?

Writing

15. Answer the letter to Dr. Math.

Dear Dr. Math,

When my teacher asked us to add a new symbol and value to the additive number system we had been using, I added ☆ to represent 0. But when I tried making numbers with it, things didn't turn out the way I planned. When I tried to use it to make the number 90, everyone thought the number was 9. Why didn't people understand? Here's what I did:
□☆

Z. Roe

The MD System

Applying Skills

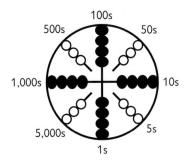

Make the numbers below using the MD system. Use the above illustration of the MD system to help you.

1. 9   **2.** 72   **3.** 665

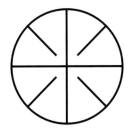

4. Show 7,957 in the MD system using the fewest beads you can.

5. Make the same number with the most beads you can.

Write the arithmetic notation for how you made each number using the MD system.

6. 9   **7.** 72   **8.** 665

9. 7,957   **10.** 7,957

Extending Concepts

11. What is the largest number you can represent in the MD system?

12. How do you know there are not any higher numbers?

13. Can you make all the numbers in order up to that number?

14. What is one change you could make to the system, so that there would be some numbers you could not make?

15. What kind of trades could you make in the MD system?

16. How do you show 0 in the MD system? Is this like having a 0 in our system or is it different? Why?

Writing

17. The MD system and the Abacus system use the same place values. What other similarities do they have? differences? Which do you find easier to use? Explain.

Stacks and Flats

Applying Skills

Make a list of powers through 4 for each number and write the value.

1. $2^0 =$ $2^1 =$ $2^2 =$ $2^3 =$ $2^4 =$

2. $3^0 =$ $3^1 =$ $3^2 =$ $3^3 =$ $3^4 =$

3. $4^0 =$ $4^1 =$ $4^2 =$ $4^3 =$ $4^4 =$

Figure out which base is used in each problem below.

4. $36 = 1(?^3) + 1(?^2)$

5. $58 = 3(?^2) + 2(?^1) + 2(?^0)$

6. $41 = 2(?^4) + 1(?^3) + 1(?^0)$

7. $99 = 1(?^4) + 1(?^2) + 3(?^1)$

Write the arithmetic expression for each number.

8. 25 base 2   **9.** 25 base 3   **10.** 25 base 4   **11.** 78 base 2   **12.** 78 base 3   **13.** 78 base 4

Extending Concepts

14. Describe how you figured out the arithmetic expressions above. Did you use a power higher than 4? Explain why. If you didn't, look for places where you could and explain why.

15. In the base 2 system, how does the pattern continue after 1, 2, 4, 8, 16, …? How is this pattern different from the pattern 2, 4, 6, 8, 10, 12, …?

16. Look at the patterns in the chart below. Fill in the missing numbers for each pattern. Then answer the three questions at the bottom of the chart.

Number	Patterns of Powers	Patterns of Multiples
2	1, 2, 4, 8, 16, __, __, __	2, 4, 6, 8, 10, 12, __, __, __
3	1, 3, 9, 27, __, __, __	3, 6, 9, 12, 15, 18, __, __, __
4	1, 4, 16, 64, __, __, __	4, 8, 12, 16, 20, __, __, __

a. How can you use multiplication to explain the patterns of powers?

b. How can you use addition to explain the pattern of multiples?

c. Do you have another way to explain either pattern?

Power Up Game

Applying Skills

What do these expressions equal?

1. $1(2^4) + 2(2^3) + 2(2^2) + 1(2^1) + 2(2^0)$

2. $2(3^4) + 1(3^3)$

3. $1(4^3) + 2(4^2) + 2(4^0)$

4. $2(3^3) + 2(3^2) + 2(3^1) + 2(3^0)$

5. $2(2^3) + 1(2^1)$

Arrange each set of numbers to make the largest and smallest values for each expression.

6. 3, 6, 5, 2   largest (____ + ____)—
              smallest (____ + ____)—

7. 7, 6, 6, 5   largest (____ + ____)—
              smallest (____ + ____)—

8. 5, 2, 3, 4   largest (____ + ____)—
              smallest (____ + ____)—

9. 1, 2, 3, 4   largest (____ + ____)—
              smallest (____ + ____)—

10. **Powers Puzzle** Figure out the missing value. The sixteen numbers add to 11,104 when you have finished.

Number	To the 2nd Power	To the 5th Power	To the ___ Power	To the ___ Power
3			27	
	16			
6				1,296
		32		

Extending Concepts

11. What conclusion did you reach about the number that goes in the exponents place when you want a large or a small number? Find 2 digits where the larger digit raised to the smaller digit is bigger than the smaller digit raised to the larger digit. Find 2 digits where the larger digit raised to the smaller digit is equal to the smaller digit raised to the larger digit.

Making Connections

12. Earthquakes are rated on a Richter scale from 1 to 10. They are rated to one decimal place; the most powerful earthquake in North America was in Alaska and was rated 8.5. The power of an earthquake increases 10 times from one whole number to the next. An 8.5 earthquake is 10 times more powerful than a 7.5 earthquake. How many times more powerful is a 6.2 earthquake than a 4.2 earthquake?

Efficient Number Systems

Applying Skills

Show how you would write each of these numbers in these systems.

1. Zany Places

	50	40	20	10	5	1
43						
72						
25						
17						

2. Maria's System   ★ = 1 ● = 2 ◆ = 4

	100	20	10	2	1
31					
67					
183					
118					

Write an arithmetic expression for each number.

3. 43, Zany Places

4. 72, Zany Places

5. 25, Zany Places

6. 17, Zany Places

7. 31, Maria's system

8. 67, Maria's system

9. 183, Maria's system

10. 118, Maria's system

Extending Concepts

11. What is the largest single digit in our base ten system? What is the largest single digit in the base 2 system? base 3? base 4? base 9?

12. How does the base of a place value system affect the number of digits/symbols it contains?

13. What numbers cannot be made in Maria's system? Why?

14. Why can you make any number in Zany Places, but not in Maria's system?

15. Which system do you think is easier for writing numbers, Zany Places or Maria's system? Why?

Making Connections

16. The Metric system uses base 10 for measurement. Write the powers of 10 that are used in the measurements below. How is the English system (inches, feet, yards) different from the Metric system? Can you use exponents to describe the English system?

Metric	Number of Units	Exponents
deka	ten	$10^?$
kilo	thousand	$10^?$
giga	billion	$10^?$

Homework 12

A New Number System

Applying Skills

Give one example of a system you've learned about that uses each property, and explain how it works in that system.

1. place value   **2.** base   **3.** zero

4. trading   **5.** building blocks

George's Mystery Device System
- Large beads = 10
- Small beads with arms pointing in = 1
- Small beads with arms pointing out = 5

George's New and Improved Mystery Device System

George decided to add place value to his system. He made each bead on the horizontal arms worth 100 and each bead on the vertical arms worth 10. He didn't change the value for the smaller beads.

- Large beads on vertical arm = 1 ten
- Large beads on horizontal arm = 1 hundred

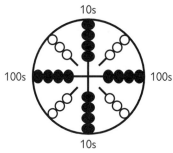

- Small beads with arms pointing in = 1
- Small beads with arms pointing out = 5

Draw each number in George's original system and in his revised system. Beware—some numbers can't be made.

Original

New and improved

6. 32   **7.** 97   **8.** 156   **9.** 371

Extending Concepts

Write the arithmetic expression for each of the numbers you made in both George's original system and his new and improved system.

10. 32   **11.** 97

12. 156   **13.** 371

14. What is the highest number that George is unable to make in his revised system? Are there any numbers lower than this number? Tell why or why not.

15. In what way is George's revised system better than his old system? In what way is George's revised system worse than his old system?

16. What are some ways that George's revised system is different from our system? Name at least 3 differences.

17. Make a list of all the different things in our own number system that make it easy to use. For each thing on your list, write one sentence explaining why.

MORE NUMBER WORDS IN OTHER LANGUAGES

Investigations in this section focus on foreign language.

Number	Arabic	French	Danish	Hebrew
1	wahid	un	én	ekhad
2	ethneyn	deux	to	shtayim
3	thalaathah	trois	tre	shalosh
4	arba'ah	quatre	fire	arbah
5	khamsah	cinq	fem	khameish
6	sittah	six	seks	sheish
7	sab'ah	sept	syv	sheva
8	thamaniyah	huit	otte	shmoneh
9	tis'ah	neuf	ni	teisha
10	ashrah	dix	ti	esseir
11	ehde-ahar	onze	elleve	ekhad-esrei
12	ethna-ashar	douze	tolv	shtaim-esrei
13	thalaatha-ashar	treize	tretten	shalosh-esrei
14	arba'ah-ashar	quatorze	fjorten	arbah-esrei
15	khamsah-ashar	quinze	femten	khameish-esrei
16	sittah-ashar	seize	seksten	sheish-esrei
17	sab'ah-ashar	dix-sept	sytten	shvah-esrei
18	thamaniyah-ashar	dix-huit	atten	shmonah-esrei
19	tis'ah-ashar	dix-neuf	nitten	t'shah-esrei
20	eshreen	vingt	tyve	esreem
30	thalaatheen	trente	tredive	shlosheem
40	arba'yeen	quarante	fyrre	arba-eem
50	khamseen	cinquante	halvtreds	khameesheem
60	sitteen	soixante	tres	sheesheem
70	sab'yeen	soixante-dix	halvfjerds	shvee-eem
80	thamaneen	quatre-vingt	firs	shmoneem
90	tis'yeen	quatre-vingt-dix	havlfems	teesheem
100	mee'ah	cent	hundrede	meia

MORE NUMBER WORDS IN OTHER LANGUAGES

Investigations in this section focus on foreign language.

Mayan							
1	•	11	≡ with dot	21	••• (three stacked dots)	30	=
2	••	12	≡ with two dots	22	dots over bar pattern	40	•• over shell
3	•••	13	≡ with three dots	23	dot/dots over bar	50	•• over two bars
4	••••	14	≡ with four dots	24	dot over four dots	60	••• over shell
5	—	15	≡≡	25	dot over bar	70	••• over two bars
6	• over bar	16	dot over two bars			80	•••• over shell
7	•• over bar	17	•• over two bars			90	•••• over two bars
8	••• over bar	18	••• over two bars			100	— over shell
9	•••• over bar	19	•••• over two bars			200	= over shell
10	=	20	dot over shell			300	≡ over shell

400	shell over shell
500	dot over bar over shell
600	dot over two bars over shell
700	dot over three bars over shell
800	•• over shell over shell
900	•• over bar over shell
1000	•• over two bars over shell
1024	•• over bar over ••••
1200	••• over shell over shell
8000	dot over shell over shell over shell

THE LANGUAGE OF NUMBERS

MORE NUMBER WORDS
IN OTHER LANGUAGES

Investigations in this section focus on foreign language.

Babylonian								
1	▼	11	◀▼	21	◀◀▼	30	◀◀◀	400
2	▼▼	12	◀▼▼	22	◀◀▼▼	40	◀◀◀◀	500
3	▼▼▼	13	◀▼▼▼	23	◀◀▼▼▼	50	◀◀◀◀◀	600
4	▼▼▼	14	◀▼▼▼	24	◀◀▼▼▼	60	▼ ≪	700
5	▼▼▼▼	15	◀▼▼▼▼	25	◀◀▼▼▼▼	70	▼ ◀	800
6	▼▼▼	16	◀▼▼▼			80	▼ ◀◀	900
7	▼▼▼▼	17	◀▼▼▼▼			90	▼ ◀◀◀◀	1000
8	▼▼▼▼	18	◀▼▼▼▼			100	▼ ≪≪	1024
9	▼▼▼▼	19	◀▼▼▼▼			200	▼▼▼ ◀◀	1200
10	◀	20	◀◀			300	▼▼▼ ≪	8000

The Seeing and Thinking Mathematically project is based at Education Development Center, Inc. (EDC), Newton, MA, and was supported, in part, by the National Science Foundation Grant No. 9054677. Opinions expressed are those of the authors and not necessarily those of the National Science Foundation.

© 1998 Creative Publications
1300 Villa Street, Mountain View, California 94041

Printed in the United States of America.

0-7622-0205-X   1 2 3 4 5 6 7 8 9 10.02 01 00 99 98 97

CREDITS: Photographs: Chris Conroy • Beverley Harper (cover) • © Ken Whitmore/Tony Stone Images: pp. 3TC, 14, 15 • © Will & Deni McIntyre/Tony Stone Images: p. 3TL • bar art, pp. 7, 9, 11, 13, 17, 19, 21, 23, 27, 29, 31, 33: Courtesy of the Rosicrucian Egyptian Museum and Planetarium, owned and operated by the Rosicrucian Order, AMORC, San Jose, CA. Illustrator: Doug Ross, pp. 7–10, 12, 13, 17, 28.

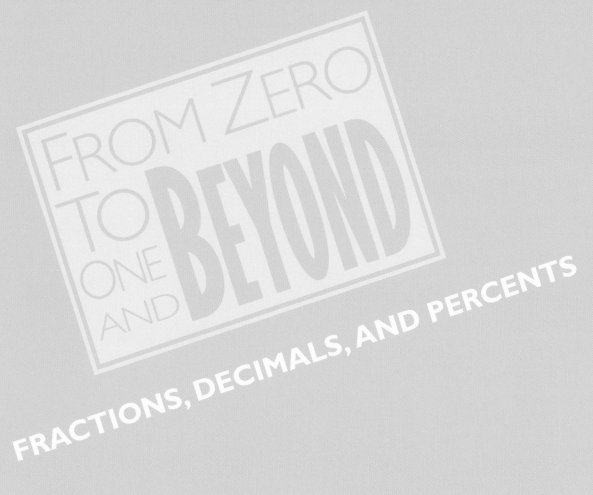

FROM ZERO TO ONE AND BEYOND

FRACTIONS, DECIMALS, AND PERCENTS

FROM ZERO TO ONE AND **BEYOND**

FRACTIONS, DECIMALS, AND PERCENTS

In this phase you will develop your fraction sense so that you are able to recognize and write equivalent fractions, compare fractions, and think about "hard" fractions by using easier fractions that they are close to. You will use what you learn by using fractions to represent data you collect on a topic of your own choice.

FROM ZERO TO ONE AND BEYOND

How are fractions, decimals, and percents related?

PHASE**TWO**
Percents from Zero to One

Percents are another way of representing parts of a whole. You will explore equivalent percents for familiar fractions. By the end of the phase, you will have collected 60 to 90 pieces of data on a topic you have chosen. You will use what you learn to represent the data as percents and display it on a "fraction circle" graph.

PHASE**THREE**
Decimals from Zero to One

In Phase Three, you will develop strategies for renaming a fraction, decimal, or percent in either of the other two ways. You will transform fractions to decimals or percents, percents to fractions or decimals, and decimals to fractions or percents. The secret is in understanding how fractions, decimals, and percents are related.

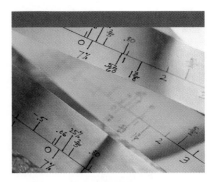

PHASE**FOUR**
Beyond Zero and One

What lies beyond zero and one on the number line? You will see what happens when the number line is extended beyond 0 and 1 in both directions. Then you will zoom in closer and closer on the number line. Some interesting questions will come up as you look deeper and deeper at the numbers between numbers.

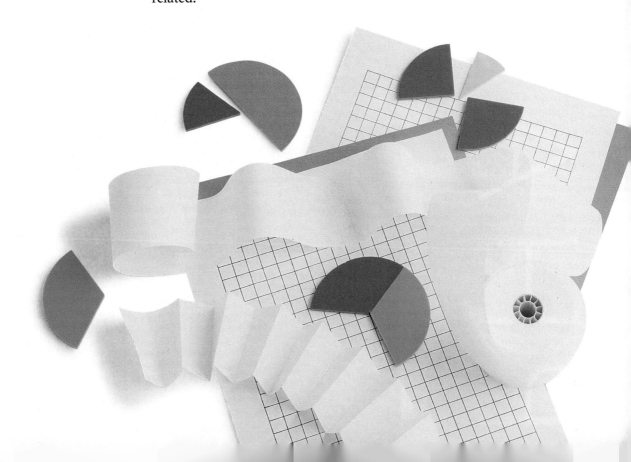

PHASE ONE

Fractions are one way to represent the relationship between a part and a whole. In this phase, you will use fractions to label distances between 0 and 1 on a number line. You also will use fractions to label parts of a circle and describe a set of data.

When you cook from a recipe, write a check, fill a gas tank, or describe the results of a survey, understanding fractions can help you make sense of the world around you.

Fractions from Zero to One

WHAT'S THE MATH?

Investigations in this section focus on:

NUMBER and NUMBER RELATIONSHIPS

- Recognizing and writing equivalent fractions
- Comparing and ordering fractions
- Finding patterns in equivalent fractions

DATA

- Using fractions to describe data
- Sketching fractional parts of a circle to represent data

1 Folding Fractions

You will make a Collections Report about real-world data over the next several weeks. You will describe your data in different ways, starting with fractions. Your exploration of fractions begins with making a fraction strip and looking at fractions that name the same number.

Make a Fraction Strip

What fractions can you show by folding a strip of paper?

A fraction strip is a useful way to show fractions. Follow the steps below to make your own fraction strip using a long strip of paper.

1. Mark 0 on the left corner and 1 on the right corner of the strip as shown.

2. Now, fold your strip *exactly* in half. Unfold the strip and write $\frac{1}{2}$ on the fold.

3. Fold the strip again to show a different fraction. Then unfold the strip and write the fraction that fold represents.

4. Continue folding and labeling your strip to show as many fractions as you can. Be sure to fold carefully—when you fold your strip into fourths, all four parts of your strip should be the same length. Also, don't forget to label each new fraction you make.

Organize Lists of Equivalent Fractions

How are fractions that represent the same number related to each other?

Look at one of the folds on the fraction strip you made. All of the fractions you wrote along the fold are equivalent fractions. Make a list of the equivalent fractions for several folds on your strip.

1 Find the fold on your fraction strip that shows the most fractions. List all of the fractions on this fold in order. Be sure to start with the fraction that has the smallest denominator and end with the fraction that has the greatest denominator.

2 Look for a pattern in the equivalent fractions you listed. Do any fractions seem to be missing? Insert these fractions in the list.

3 Now, extend your list by writing the next two fractions in the pattern.

4 Repeat Steps 1–3 to make lists of equivalent fractions for at least four of the folds on your strip.

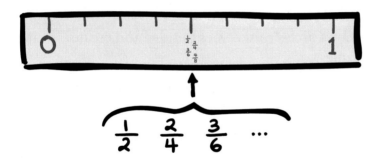

How did you use patterns in equivalent fractions to help fill in and extend your lists?

Write About Equivalent Fractions

Now that you've explored equivalent fractions, write about what you've learned.

- Choose a fraction that is *not* on your fraction strip. List at least four fractions that are equivalent to this fraction. Then explain how you found the equivalent fractions.

- Describe how you could find an equivalent fraction for any fraction you are given.

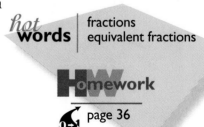

hot **words** | fractions
equivalent fractions

Homework

page 36

2 Fraction Circles

EXPLORING FRACTION EQUIVALENCE AND INEQUALITY

If you have $\frac{5}{8}$ of a stick of butter, can you make a recipe that calls for $\frac{3}{4}$ of a stick of butter? It's important to be able to decide if two fractions are the same size or if one is greater. In this lesson, you'll use Fraction Circles to explore fraction equivalence and inequality.

Find the Greater Fraction

How do you know which of two fractions is greater?

Fraction Circles or sketches can help you decide which of two fractions is greater.

Use Fraction Circles or sketches to solve and create "Which is greater?" questions.

1 Think about each question. Then write a statement using < or > to answer each one.

a. Which is greater: $\frac{3}{4}$ or $\frac{1}{4}$?   b. Which is greater: $\frac{5}{9}$ or $\frac{2}{9}$?

c. Which is greater: $\frac{2}{5}$ or $\frac{3}{5}$?   d. Which is greater: $\frac{3}{8}$ or $\frac{1}{4}$?

e. Which is greater: $\frac{1}{2}$ or $\frac{1}{3}$?   f. Which is greater: $\frac{5}{8}$ or $\frac{5}{6}$?

g. Which is greater: $\frac{3}{5}$ or $\frac{3}{4}$?   h. Which is greater: $\frac{7}{10}$ or $\frac{14}{22}$?

2 Now, write three "Which is greater?" questions of your own. Trade questions with your partner, and answer each other's questions by writing a statement with < or >. When you are done, explain how you knew which fraction was greater.

Inequalities

Inequality signs are used to show how numbers compare. The smaller part of the sign points toward the lesser number.

- We read 5 < 8 as "Five is less than eight."

- We read 3 > 1 as "Three is greater than one."

Make and Solve Fraction Puzzles

In this investigation, you will make and solve fraction puzzles about equivalence and inequalities.

How can you find fractions that are equal to, greater than, or less than other fractions?

1 Create three fractions puzzles about equivalent fractions.

  a. Sketch a fraction on a piece of paper. Write the name of the fraction under the sketch.

  b. Write an equivalence statement for the fraction, but leave either the denominator *or* the numerator blank. (Be sure you can solve the puzzle!)

  c. Exchange puzzles with your partner. Fill in the blank to solve your partner's puzzle. Use Fraction Circles or sketches to show why your answer is correct.

$$\frac{1}{2} = \frac{}{4}$$

2 Write three puzzles using a $<$ or $>$ sign. Exchange puzzles with your partner and solve your partner's puzzles. Use Fraction Circles or a sketch to show that your answer is correct.

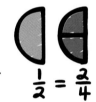

$$\frac{1}{2} = \frac{2}{4}$$

3 Now, write a fraction puzzle that you think will stump the class. Again, be sure that *you* know the answer to your puzzle.

$$\frac{1}{3} < \frac{}{4}$$

Write About Fraction Equivalence and Inequality

Write about what you have learned about fraction equivalence and inequality.

- Write a list of "dos" and "don'ts" for finding equivalent fractions. Be sure to include sketches to illustrate your ideas.

- Tell how you can decide which of two fractions is greater if they have the same denominator and different numerators. What if two fractions have the same numerator and different denominators? Don't forget to explain your thinking.

hot **words** | equivalent fractions
inequality

Homework

 page 37

3 The First Collections Report

Some fractions, such as $\frac{1}{2}$ and $\frac{1}{3}$, are so familiar that most people find it easy to think about them and compare them. Other fractions, such as $\frac{11}{23}$ and $\frac{8}{19}$, are not so familiar. It is easier to think about an unfamiliar fraction if you can identify a familiar fraction that is equivalent or close to it.

Make Fractions More Familiar

How can you make a less familiar fraction easier to think about?

Use what you know about equivalent fractions to find more familiar ways to name unfamiliar fractions.

1 With a partner, find familiar equivalent fractions for at least *four* different fractions.

- Choose a number from the "numerators" list below. Have your partner choose one from the "denominators" list. Then use these numbers to write a fraction.

    Numerators: 3, 6, 9   Denominators: 18, 24, 36

- Rewrite this fraction with the smallest denominator that you can. Make sure that this more familiar fraction is equivalent to the original fraction.

2 For a fraction that does not have a more familiar equivalent, it can be helpful to find a more familiar fraction that is close to it, or approximate. Find approximate fractions for at least *four* different fractions.

- Choose a number from the "numerators" list below. Have your partner choose one from the "denominators" list. Write a fraction using these numbers.

    Numerators: 5, 7, 11 Denominators: 23, 32, 43

- Find a more familiar fraction that is close to this fraction. Then write a sentence explaining how you found this fraction.

Compare Familiar and Unfamiliar Fractions

In each fraction pair listed below, one fraction is familiar and the other is unfamiliar. Pick one pair and decide which of the two fractions is greater. Then explain the strategy used.

a. $\dfrac{1}{2}, \dfrac{11}{23}$ b. $\dfrac{1}{8}, \dfrac{8}{27}$ c. $\dfrac{1}{6}, \dfrac{2}{11}$

> **When two fractions are very close, how can you tell which is greater?**

Make a Collections Report

It's time to write a report about the data you have collected so far. Follow these steps to help you put your report together.

1 Write a summary of your data that answers these questions.

- How did you collect your data?

- How many pieces of data have you collected so far?

- How many categories do you have? What are they?

- How many pieces of data are in each category?

2 Use fractions to describe your data.

- Use a fraction to describe the part of your data in each category.

- For each fraction you used to describe your data, name a more familiar fraction that is *equivalent* (with a smaller denominator) or that is *close to* (approximates) the fraction.

3 Sketch circle pieces to illustrate your results.

- Sketch a fractional part of a circle to represent the data in each of your categories.

- Label each of your sketches with the category and the fraction it represents.

hot **words** | numerator
denominator

page 38

PHASE TWO

1996 U.S. imports from sub-Saharan Africa

Nigeria 38%

Angola 18%

Others 16%

South Africa 15%

Gabon 13%

Total: $15.2 billion
Source: Commerce Department

Percents are another way to represent the relationship between a part and whole. How are percents related to fractions? You will find out as you rename percents as familiar fractions they are close to.

You can see percents all around you—representing data in newspapers, in magazines, on television, even on your favorite cereal box. You will use percents to represent the 60 to 90 pieces of data you collect on a topic of your choice.

Percents from Zero to One

WHAT'S THE MATH?

Investigations in this section focus on:

NUMBER and NUMBER RELATIONSHIPS

- Understanding the meaning of percent
- Finding or estimating the percent of space taken up by a shape
- Comparing and ordering percents
- Finding an exact or approximate percent name for a fraction

DATA

- Using percents to describe data
- Creating circle graphs to represent data

4 Out of One Hundred

A percent describes a portion of a whole quantity that has been divided into 100 equal parts. By investigating the percent of space taken up by a shaded region, you will get a better idea of how the sizes of different percents compare.

Create Percent Designs

What do different percents look like?

You will be given handouts of large and small 10-by-10 grids. Use the blank grids to make designs that meet the following descriptions.

1 Use the small grids to create a design for each description below.

    a. 20% shaded   **b.** 33% green, 67% yellow

    c. 15% red, 30% blue, and 55% yellow   **d.** 25% red, 40% blue, 30% green, 15% yellow

2 Choose your favorite design from the grids you colored in Step 1.

    a. Copy your favorite design onto the large grid handout.

    b. Compare the large and small copies of the same design. Look at the areas that are shaded the same color. How are they alike? How are they different?

Estimate Percents Visually

How well can you estimate percents without a grid?

You found the percent of space covered by different figures on a grid. Now you will estimate percents for shapes of your own that aren't on a grid.

1 Each member of your group should draw a "blob" on the Estimate Percents Visually sheet, and shade it in.

2 As a group, estimate the percent of the paper that each blob takes up. Write this percent on the line "First Estimate."

3 Now put your blobs in order from smallest to largest percent. What do you notice about the percents that go with the blobs?

4 With your group, use a grid transparency to revise the percent estimate for each of your blobs. Do this by placing the grid over your blob and finding the percent of space the blob actually takes up. Write your new estimate on the line "Revised Estimate." Look for patterns in the differences between your first estimates and your revised estimates. For instance, were your original estimates always too high or too low?

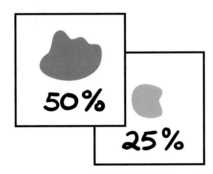

Write About Percents

Imagine this: What if the same size and shape blob you made appeared on a much larger piece of paper?

- Would the percent covered by the blob on the larger paper be equal to, greater than, or less than the percent that you estimated it covered on the smaller paper? Explain your answer.

- Can 50% of something ever be less than 25% of something else? Explain your answer.

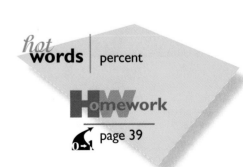

hot **words** | percent

Homework
page 39

5 Percents That Make Sense

RELATING PERCENTS TO FRACTIONS

You used Fraction Circles to explore equivalent fractions for familiar fractions. Here you'll use Fraction Circles to name equivalent percents for familiar fractions. Your knowledge of these percents will help you estimate percents for other fractions.

Label Fraction Circles as Percents

How can you show percents as part of a circle?

For this investigation, you will use Fraction Circles pieces to help you think about percents.

1 Organize your Fraction Circles. Decide what percent each piece represents. (For some pieces, you may want to choose a percent that is close to the right number.)

2 Make sketches of all the Fraction Circles pieces. Label them with their percent names. Be prepared to explain how you decided what percent name to give each color of Fraction Circles piece.

3 Sketch some circle pieces that are not in the set. Label them with their exact or approximate percent names.

Estimate Percent Equivalents for Fractions

How can you estimate the percent name for an unfamiliar fraction?

It's helpful to be able to make a rough estimate of the percent name for a fraction. For instance, knowing that pizza represents $\frac{101}{120}$ of all food-to-go orders may be harder to think about than knowing that about 85% of such orders are for pizza.

Look at the fractions you and your classmates came up with. Work with a partner to do the following:

1 Choose three or four of the fractions.

2 Estimate the percent name for each of the fractions you chose. (Hint: You already know percent names for several familiar fractions. Can these help you begin to make your estimates?)

3 Discuss how you would explain your estimation method to other students. You may be asked to do this when you report your estimates to the class.

Write About Fraction/Percent Equivalence

In your own words, answer the following questions.

- What strategies did you use to find percent names for Fraction Circles pieces?

- Is there a quick way to tell whether or not a fraction is easy to name with an exact percent? If so, describe how.

- How can you estimate the percent name for an unfamiliar fraction?

hot **words** | percent

Home**W**ork

page 40

6 The Final Collections Report

REPRESENTING DATA AS PERCENTS

Many people find it easiest to think about data when it's described as percents. In newspapers and magazines, graphs of data make reports especially easy to understand. Here, you will use percents to report your Collections Report data and to help make circle graphs.

Represent Data on a Circle Graph

How can you use a circle graph to show data?

For her Collections Report, one student gathered data on the different things that her classmates collect. The table below shows her data.

Topic: Student Collections

Category	Number	Approximate Percent
Sports Cards	12	13%
Coins/Stamps	57	61%
Comic Books	12	13%
Stuffed Animals	8	8%
Other	5	5%

1 Find a Fraction Circles piece or combination of pieces that is close to each percent in the table.

2 Try to assemble a circle using these fraction pieces. If you have gaps or overlaps, can you tell where these come from?

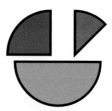

3 Using your Fraction Circles pieces as a guide, sketch a circle graph for the data.

4 Color your graph. Then label each part of the circle with the percent it shows and the name of the category it represents.

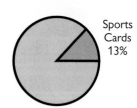

Sports Cards 13%

Use Percents to Make a Collections Report

In your first Collections Report, you described your data using fractions. Now you will make a Collections Report using percents. In this report, you will use what you know about percents and their fraction equivalents to describe the data.

Be sure to include the following in your report.

1 Write a summary of your data that answers these questions:

- How did you collect your data?
- How many pieces of data have you collected?
- How many categories do you have? What are they?
- How many pieces of data are in each category?

2 Use percents to describe your data.

- Use a fraction to describe the part of your data in each category.
- Then, give an exact or approximate equivalent percent for each fraction.

3 Make a circle graph to show your data.

- Choose Fraction Circles pieces to make a circle graph of your data. Some pieces may be exact, some will be approximate.
- Make a sketch to show your circle graph. Label the sketch with both fractions and percents.

How can you use percents to help describe your data?

hot **words** | percent
circle graph

page 41

PHASE THREE

You have seen how to use fractions and percents to name the same number. In this phase you will use a third way to represent part-whole relationships: decimals.

There is no way that is always the "best way" to represent a number. But sometimes one way of representing a number is better in a certain situation. Can you think of different situations in which you would choose to use fractions, decimals, or percents?

Decimals from Zero to One

WHAT'S THE MATH?

Investigations in this phase focus on:

NUMBER and NUMBER RELATIONSHIPS

- Understanding decimal representations of numbers between 0 and 1

- Developing strategies for renaming decimals as percents and percents as decimals

- Using division to rename fractions as decimals

- Understanding how to write a repeating decimal

- Using place value to rename terminating decimals as fractions

- Ordering a mixed set of fractions, decimals, and percents

7 An Important Point

Fractions and percents are two ways to represent numbers between 0 and 1. When you write a part of a dollar, you use a third way to represent a number—a decimal.

Make Fraction/Decimal/Percent Puzzle Pieces

How can you name part of a 10-by-10 grid as a fraction, decimal, or percent?

For this investigation, you will use 10-by-10 grids to explore fractional, percent, and decimal representations for the same number.

1 Cut out the four grids. Take two of them, and leave the other two for your partner.

2 Cut one of your grids into four "puzzle pieces." Cut along the lines, so your pieces are made up of whole squares.

3 On each puzzle piece:

- Write the fraction of the original square that it represents.

- Using the fact that the original square represents 100%, write the percent name for the piece.

- Write the decimal name for the piece.

4 Repeat Steps 2 and 3 for your second grid. Make different-size puzzle pieces than you did the first time.

5 Mix up the eight pieces from your two puzzles. Exchange puzzle pieces with your partner, and assemble each other's puzzles. As you do this, check to be sure that you agree with the fraction, decimal, and percent names on each piece.

Investigate Decimal Equivalence

Earlier in this unit, as you explored fractions, you found patterns that helped you write lists of equivalent fractions. Here you will look at equivalent decimals.

How are decimals that represent the same number related to each other?

1 Cut and label pieces from 10-by-10 grids to show each of the following amounts if the 10-by-10 grid is one.

    a. 0.04   **b.** 0.40   **c.** 0.4   **d.** 0.040

2 Compare the pieces of grid paper you cut and labeled.

- Were any of the decimal amounts equivalent?

- For any equivalents you find, write two more decimals that would also be equivalent. Explain your thinking.

Place Value in Base 10

To be able to give the decimal name for a fraction like $\frac{3}{10}$, $\frac{77}{100}$, or $\frac{833}{1,000}$, you need to know how place value works in decimal numbers.

When we say the number 9,471 aloud, we hear place values: "Nine thousand four hundred and seventy-one." Each step to the right divides the place value by 10.

$$\underline{9},\underline{4}\underline{7}\underline{1}.$$

thousands hundreds tens ones

decimal point (not always shown)

Place value also tells us how to read digits to the right of the decimal point. The 5 in the number 0.542 represents five tenths, the 4 represents four hundredths, and the 2 represents two thousandths. Again, each step to the right divides the place value by 10.

$$0.\underline{5}\underline{4}\underline{2}$$

ones   tenths hundredths

decimal point   thousandths

We use the last digit when we say a decimal number aloud. This number is, "five hundred

hot **words** | decimal system
equivalent

Homework

 page 42

8 Tenths, Hundredths, and More

RENAMING FRACTIONS AS PERCENTS AND DECIMALS

You know the percent and decimal names for some familiar fractions. You also know how to estimate percent names for unfamiliar fractions. In this lesson you will use more exact ways to rename fractions, decimals, and percents.

Rename Some Twelfths and Twentieths

How many percent and decimal names for twelfths and twentieths can you find?

You will be given the handout Twelfths and Twentieths. Use everything you know about equivalent fractions and percent names for familiar fractions to fill in as much of the table as you can.

1 Look at the fractions in the Twelfths and Twentieths table. Do any of these have more familiar equivalent fractions?

   a. List all of the more familiar equivalents you can find in the box with that fraction.

   b. Fill in as many percent names as you can for the fractions in the columns labeled "Percent Names." Circle any percents you write that are approximate.

2 Use what you know about place value to fill in decimal names for fractions on your Twelfths and Twentieths table.

   a. Some of the fractions in your table can be renamed as tenths. Fill in the decimal names for all of these fractions. Be sure to write a 0 to the left of the decimal point.

   b. Now, fill in decimal names for as many of the other fractions in the table as you can.

Fraction Names	Percent Names	Decimal Names	Fraction Names	Percent Names
			$\frac{11}{20}$	
$\frac{1}{20}$			$\frac{7}{12}$	
$\frac{1}{12}$			$\frac{12}{20}$	
$\frac{2}{20}$			$\frac{13}{20}$	
$\frac{3}{20}$			$\frac{8}{12}$	

Complete the Twelfths and Twentieths Table

You can think of a fraction as a division problem. For example, $\frac{3}{4}$ is another way to write $3 \div 4$. Thinking of fractions in this way can help you complete your Twelfths and Twentieths table.

How can you use division to rename a fraction as a decimal?

1 Fill in any missing numbers in the "Decimal Names" columns of your table by using a calculator to divide the numerator of the fraction by its denominator.

2 Find places where you have already written both the decimal and percent names for a fraction. Check to see that these numbers make sense.

3 Now fill in any missing entries in your "Percent Names" columns.

Write About the Renaming Process

So far, you have used a variety of methods to rename fractions, decimals, and percents. Use what you have learned to write about the different methods.

- Write a set of renaming rules for the methods you've investigated.

- Which methods do you think you would choose to use most often? Does it depend on the situation? Tell why.

Repeating Decimals

Some decimal names for fractions have a repeating pattern that goes on forever. For instance,

$\frac{1}{3} = 0.3333333333333333333333333333333$ ... (forever!)

When this happens, you can write the exact decimal name by using a bar to show the repeating digits. Be careful to put the bar only over the digits that repeat.

- $\frac{5}{12} = 0.416666... = 0.41\overline{6}$
- $\frac{3}{11} = 0.272727... = 0.\overline{27}$

hot **words** | repeating decimal equivalent

page 43

9 All Three at Once

You know how to rename fractions as decimals, decimals as percents, and percents as decimals. Now, you will explore ways to rename a decimal as a fraction. Finally, you will use your renaming skills to put a mixed list of fractions, decimals, and percents in order.

Find Fraction Names for Decimals

How can you use familiar fractions to rename decimals?

In this investigation, you will rename decimals as exact fractions and familiar fractions that are easier to think about. Start by making a table with three columns as shown.

1 For each decimal, find an *exact* fraction name, and enter the name in the table.

Decimal Name	Exact Fraction	Familiar Fraction
0.26		
0.71		
0.14		
0.44		
0.08		
0.65		
0.31		
0.86		
0.548		
0.367		

2 Now, find a familiar equivalent fraction (smallest denominator) or a more familiar fraction that is close to each decimal. Add these fractions to the table.

How do you know that your fractions are the *closest*?

Order Fractions, Decimals, and Percents

Here you use what you know about fractions, decimals, and percents to put a mixed group of numbers in order.

1 Cut out the numbers on the handout Ordering Fractions, Decimals, and Percents. Use any strategies that you find helpful to put these numbers in order from least to greatest. As you work, think about ways to convince your classmates that your order is correct.

2 Once you are satisfied with your list, make a written copy of your final ordering.

How can you put a list of fractions, decimals, and percents in order?

hot **words** | equivalent

H⚡omework

page 44

PHASE **FOUR**

Now that you have investigated numbers between zero and one, it's time to go beyond. When you extend the number line in both directions, you will learn about other ways of representing numbers.

Why are there so many ways to show the same number? It's because we need to use numbers in so many different ways. As you learn new ways to show numbers, think about the advantages and disadvantages of all the different ways to represent numbers.

Beyond Zero and One

WHAT'S THE MATH?

Investigations in this phase focus on:

NUMBER and NUMBER RELATIONSHIPS

- Renaming improper fractions as mixed numbers and mixed numbers as improper fractions

- Comparing negative numbers

- Finding exact or approximate square roots

- Calculating powers

- Locating a mix of numbers on a number line, including fractions, decimals, percents, improper fractions, mixed numbers, negative numbers, square roots, and powers

10 Going Beyond

So far in this unit, you've investigated numbers between 0 and 1. Here, you will look at fractions that describe numbers greater than 1. After investigating numbers greater than 1, you will explore negative numbers—numbers that are less than 0.

Investigate Mixed Numbers and Improper Fractions

How can you rename a mixed number as an improper fraction or an improper fraction as a mixed number?

In this investigation, you will look for relationships between mixed numbers and improper fractions.

1 For each number below:

- if it is a mixed number, rename it as an improper fraction.

- if it is an improper fraction, rename it as a mixed number.

(Hint: It may help to use Fraction Circles to represent some of these numbers.)

$$\frac{5}{3} \quad 1\frac{1}{6} \quad \frac{7}{4} \quad 2\frac{3}{8} \quad \frac{37}{10}$$

$$5\frac{1}{2} \quad \frac{38}{5} \quad 4\frac{5}{6} \quad \frac{26}{4} \quad 3\frac{1}{5}$$

2 Use your adding machine tape to make a number line. Mark 0 in the middle of the line. Then add marks for the whole numbers 1 through 10.

3 Now locate each of the numbers in Step 1 on your number line. Write both an improper fraction and a mixed number name for each.

Mixed Numbers and Improper Fractions

There are two different ways to write fractions greater than 1.

- A number that contains both a whole number and a fraction, like $3\frac{1}{3}$, is a mixed number.

- A fraction whose numerator is greater than its denominator, like $\frac{7}{4}$, is an improper fraction.

Play the "Which Is Greater?" Game

All negative numbers are less than 0, but some are "more less" than others! In this investigation, you will think about inequalities involving negative numbers.

How can you write inequalities involving negative numbers?

1 Add the numbers -5 and -10 to your number line.

2 Write a statement using $<$ or $>$ to answer each question. You may want to refer to your class number line as you think about these.

   a. Which is greater: -3 or 9?

   b. Which is greater: 0.01 or -7?

   c. Which is greater: -2 or -8?

   d. Which is greater: -9 or 3?

   e. Which is greater: -6 or -1?

   f. Which is greater: $-2\frac{1}{2}$ or -3?

   g. Which is greater: -8.74 or -8.05?

3 Mark the numbers in these inequalities on your number line.

4 Now, write three "Which is greater?" questions of your own. Trade questions with your partner, and answer each other's questions by writing a statement with $<$ or $>$.

5 With your partner, discuss any rules for ordering negative numbers that you think you have discovered. Be prepared to share your ideas with the class.

Negative Numbers

A number that is less than 0 is a negative number. Every negative number can be thought of as the opposite of a positive number. For example, the opposite of 3 is -3.

hot **words** | improper fractions mixed numbers

Homework

page 45

11 Root for Yourself

When you find the square of a number, you ask, "When I multiply this number by itself, what do I get?" When you look for the *square root* of a number, you ask, "What two numbers, multiplied together, give me my original number?" You will investigate square roots and how to find them.

Investigate Square Roots for Perfect Squares

What is a perfect square?

Complete the tables on the handout Square Roots. Follow these steps to explore why the numbers in the right-hand column of your completed table are called perfect squares.

1 Think of each small square on your 10-by-10 grids handout as a "unit square." Choose a perfect square number from your table. Can you cut a square out of one of your grids that contains this number of unit squares? If you can, cut out the square.

2 Make as many different-size squares as you can with your four grids. (Cut along the lines—no half-squares allowed!)

3 The area of a square is equal to the number of unit squares it contains. Find the area of each of your squares. How does the area of the square compare to its side length?

Squares and Square Roots

Squaring a number means multiplying the number by itself. For example, 5^2 is 5×5, or 25. The square root of 25 is 5. The $\sqrt{}$ sign is called a *square root* (or *radical*) sign. $\sqrt{25}$ asks, "What number, multiplied by itself, equals 25?"

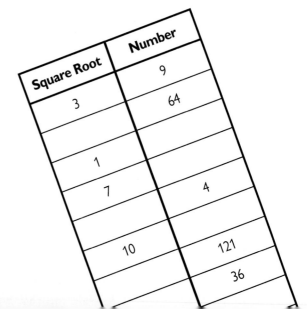

Square Root	Number
3	9
	64
1	
7	4
10	121
	36

"Zoom In" on Square Roots

The numbers below are not perfect squares.

1 Use the "zoom-in" method to locate the square root of each of these numbers. Sketching number lines will help you. For each number, stop when you have "zoomed in" to the hundredths place.

   a. 27   **b.** 48   **c.** 83

   d. 111   **e.** 54.68   **f.** 10

2 Write a short description of how you located each of the square roots.

How can you find the square root of a number that is not a perfect square?

Write About Square Roots

Suppose you are given a number that is not a perfect square. In your own words, explain how you would find its square root to the nearest hundredth.

Zooming In

For numbers that are perfect squares, you can use the "zoom-in" method to locate the square root.

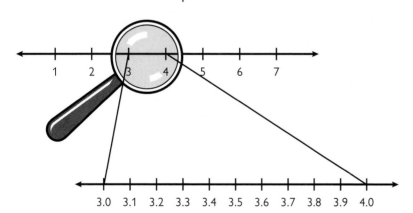

hot **words** | perfect square
square root

 page 46

12 Powering Up

You know that a power describes how many times a number is multiplied by itself. Here, you will investigate how quickly repeated multiplication makes numbers grow. After exploring powers, you will place a mix of different types of numbers on one number line.

Locate Powers on the Number Line

Are powers of a number evenly spaced on a number line?

In this investigation, you will use a strip of adding machine tape to show the part of a number line that goes from 0 to 1,000.

1 Measure or fold your tape so that you can locate the numbers 100, 200, 300, ..., 900 accurately. This is your "power line"!

2 Without calculating any powers, guess the highest power of 2 that fits on this segment of the number line. For instance, is 2^{100} the last power of 2 that is less than 1,000? Or is the real answer more like 2^{30} or 2^{500}?

3 Starting with 2^1, find all of the powers of 2 that fit between 0 and 1,000. When you have found them all, mark them on the number line in the same color. (Hint: Remember that $2^1 = 2$.) How close was your guess from Step 2?

4 Repeat Step 3 for the other whole numbers from 3 to 10. Use different colors to mark the different power families on your power line.

How do powers grow as the exponents increase?

Place Different Numbers on a Number Line

In this unit, you have worked with fractions, decimals, percents, mixed numbers, improper fractions, negative numbers, square roots, and powers. Now you will demonstrate some of what you have learned by placing numbers of each of these types on a number line.

How can you use your knowledge and strategies to place several different types of numbers on a number line?

1 Make a number line that shows the numbers from -10 to 10.

2 Place each of the following numbers on this line. Be sure to show the original form of the number, even if you renamed it in another way to help you see where it belonged.

-8	$\frac{3}{7}$	0.75	50%	-1
$1\frac{1}{5}$	$\frac{7}{3}$	$\sqrt{64}$	2^2	$-5\frac{3}{4}$
$\frac{35}{48}$	0.09	9%	-3	$7\frac{3}{8}$
$\frac{57}{10}$	$\sqrt{22}$	3^2	-0.8	2^3

exponent
powers

page 47

Folding Fractions

Applying Skills

1. Name three equivalent fractions for each fold on the fraction strip shown.

$$0 \quad \frac{1}{8} \quad \frac{1}{3} \quad \frac{1}{2} \quad \frac{3}{4} \quad \frac{14}{16} \quad 1$$

For each fraction listed, give four equivalent fractions. Then place each list in order. Be sure to start with the fraction that has the smallest denominator and end with the fraction that has the greatest denominator.

2. $\frac{2}{3}$ **3.** $\frac{1}{9}$

4. $\frac{3}{8}$ **5.** $\frac{1}{4}$

6. $\frac{7}{8}$ **7.** $\frac{2}{4}$

8. $\frac{4}{11}$ **9.** $\frac{5}{10}$

Provide the next two fractions in each list of equivalent fractions.

10. $\frac{1}{4}, \frac{2}{8}, \frac{3}{12}$ **11.** $\frac{1}{3}, \frac{2}{6}, \frac{3}{9}$

12. $\frac{1}{2}, \frac{2}{4}$ **13.** $\frac{2}{7}, \frac{4}{14}$

14. $\frac{2}{3}, \frac{4}{6}, \frac{6}{9}$ **15.** $\frac{4}{5}, \frac{8}{10}, \frac{12}{15}$

16. $\frac{1}{10}, \frac{2}{20}$ **17.** $\frac{5}{7}, \frac{10}{14}$

Extending Concepts

All of the fractions listed are equivalent to each other except for one. Find the one fraction that does not belong in the list.

18. $\frac{1}{5}, \frac{2}{10}, \frac{4}{12}, \frac{5}{25}, \frac{3}{15}$ **19.** $\frac{1}{8}, \frac{3}{24}, \frac{2}{16}, \frac{5}{30}, \frac{4}{32}$

20. $\frac{2}{3}, \frac{6}{9}, \frac{4}{6}, \frac{8}{10}, \frac{10}{15}$

21. On the fraction strip shown, the fractions in red are correct but several of the fractions listed as equivalent are not. Find each fraction that is not equivalent to the fraction listed in red above it.

0	$\frac{1}{8}$	$\frac{1}{3}$	$\frac{1}{2}$	$\frac{3}{4}$	$\frac{14}{18}$	1
	$\frac{1}{16}$	$\frac{2}{6}$	$\frac{3}{6}$	$\frac{4}{8}$	$\frac{7}{8}$	
	$\frac{2}{16}$	$\frac{3}{8}$	$\frac{4}{8}$	$\frac{6}{7}$	$\frac{8}{9}$	

Writing

22. Name three examples where it would be useful to know equivalent fractions.

23. Answer the letter to Dr. Math.

> Dear Dr. Math,
> My brother said that $\frac{1}{2}$ is equal to $\frac{4}{8}$. I don't see how that could be, since 4 is bigger than 1 and 8 is bigger than 2! Who's right?
> Sincerely,
> Fractured Freddie

Fraction Circles

Applying Skills

Use sketches to solve these "Which is greater?" problems. Then write a statement using < or > to answer each one.

1. $\frac{1}{2}$ or $\frac{1}{4}$ **2.** $\frac{1}{5}$ or $\frac{1}{6}$

3. $\frac{5}{6}$ or $\frac{3}{8}$ **4.** $\frac{1}{4}$ or $\frac{1}{3}$

5. $\frac{2}{16}$ or $\frac{3}{30}$ **6.** $\frac{1}{2}$ or $\frac{4}{6}$

7. $\frac{3}{7}$ or $\frac{1}{2}$ **8.** $\frac{1}{4}$ or $\frac{5}{8}$

9. $\frac{2}{6}$ or $\frac{1}{8}$ **10.** $\frac{2}{3}$ or $\frac{2}{6}$

11. $\frac{1}{10}$ or $\frac{1}{5}$ **12.** $\frac{5}{10}$ or $\frac{4}{12}$

Use sketches to help you solve these fraction puzzles.

13. $\frac{1}{2} = \frac{}{4}$ **14.** $\frac{2}{3} = \frac{}{12}$

15. $\frac{1}{3} = \frac{}{6}$ **16.** $\frac{3}{8} = \frac{}{16}$

17. $\frac{6}{12} = \frac{}{36}$ **18.** $\frac{6}{7} = \frac{}{77}$

Solve these fraction inequalities. Use the < or > signs to indicate greater than or less than.

19. $\frac{1}{3} - \frac{1}{2}$ **20.** $\frac{1}{8} - \frac{1}{9}$

21. $\frac{4}{10} - \frac{2}{3}$ **22.** $\frac{2}{3} - \frac{2}{5}$

23. $\frac{7}{16} - \frac{1}{4}$ **24.** $\frac{5}{8} - \frac{1}{7}$

25. $\frac{7}{12} - \frac{3}{36}$ **26.** $\frac{6}{7} - \frac{7}{8}$

Extending Concepts

Solve these fraction puzzles.

27. $\frac{5}{10} = \frac{}{30}$ **28.** $\frac{7}{9} = \frac{}{45}$

Some of the following statements are true and some are not. Find those that are not true and rewrite them to make them true.

29. $\frac{1}{2} > \frac{2}{4}$ **30.** $\frac{2}{3} > \frac{4}{6}$

31. $\frac{2}{6} > \frac{8}{12}$ **32.** $\frac{2}{84} = \frac{1}{2}$

33. $\frac{15}{45} = \frac{3}{15}$ **34.** $\frac{6}{17} = \frac{12}{34}$

35. $\frac{25}{100} = \frac{1}{3}$ **36.** $\frac{7}{8} = \frac{9}{10}$

Writing

37. Answer the letter to Dr. Math.

> Dear Dr. Math,
> I have three chores to do on Saturdays: empty the trash, take out the newspapers, and clean my room. My dad says that I'm $\frac{2}{3}$ done after I take out the trash and newspapers. I say that I'm not even half done because cleaning my room takes a lot longer than the other two chores. Who's right?
> Sincerely,
> Tidy Tom

The First Collections Report

Applying Skills

Rewrite each fraction with the smallest denominator that you can. Be sure that each fraction you write is equivalent to the original fraction.

1. $\frac{2}{10}$ 2. $\frac{4}{18}$ 3. $\frac{8}{24}$ 4. $\frac{6}{36}$

5. $\frac{6}{24}$ 6. $\frac{8}{28}$ 7. $\frac{4}{10}$ 8. $\frac{2}{36}$

Rewrite each fraction with a more familiar equivalent fraction or a more familiar approximate fraction.

9. $\frac{2}{4}$ 10. $\frac{6}{11}$

11. $\frac{8}{21}$ 12. $\frac{8}{24}$

13. $\frac{12}{48}$ 14. $\frac{3}{21}$

15. $\frac{4}{16}$ 16. $\frac{9}{80}$

Look at the familiar and unfamiliar fraction pairs. For each pair, decide which fraction is greater.

17. $\frac{7}{10}, \frac{5}{20}$ 18. $\frac{3}{8}, \frac{16}{40}$

19. $\frac{27}{81}, \frac{3}{91}$ 20. $\frac{14}{63}, \frac{36}{44}$

21. $\frac{8}{27}, \frac{9}{30}$ 22. $\frac{2}{11}, \frac{11}{21}$

23. $\frac{4}{19}, \frac{6}{26}$ 24. $\frac{1}{6}, \frac{2}{11}$

Extending Concepts

25. For the fractions listed in items **9–16**, explain how you decided if the fractions could be rewritten with a more familiar fraction that is equivalent (with a smaller denominator) or approximate.

26. For each set of fractions, decide which is the greatest.

   a. $\frac{2}{10}, \frac{2}{11}, \frac{3}{12}$ b. $\frac{7}{21}, \frac{7}{22}, \frac{8}{25}$

   c. $\frac{6}{12}, \frac{3}{4}, \frac{2}{10}$ d. $\frac{3}{6}, \frac{2}{4}, \frac{4}{5}$

Making Connections

Dr. Leyva conducted an experiment to see how many orchids would grow in different types of soil. The data he collected is shown in the table.

Soil	Number of Orchids
Moist bark	12
Dry bark	7
Sand	2
Humus	10

27. How many orchids was Dr. Leyva able to grow?

28. Use fractions to tell what portion of the experimental orchids grew in each condition.

Out of One Hundred

Applying Skills

For items 1–4, you will need to refer to the 10-by-10 grid shown.

1. How many squares would you shade in so 50% of the space is shaded?

2. How many squares would you shade in so 20% of the space is shaded?

3. How many squares would you shade in so 10% of the space is orange, 40% of the space is red, 30% of the space is blue, and 5% of the space is purple?

4. How many squares would you shade in so 15% of the space is blue, 30% of the space is red, and 8% is green?

Estimate the percent of space each blob takes up in the squares below.

5.

6.

7.

8.

Extending Concepts

9. What percent of the grid is shaded pink?

10. What percent of the grid is shaded red?

11. What percent of the grid is shaded yellow?

12. What percent of the grid is shaded blue?

13. What percent of the grid is shaded green?

14. What percent of the grid is shaded yellow?

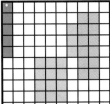

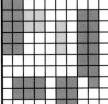

Writing

15. Answer the letter to Dr. Math.

Dear Dr. Math,
My mom says that estimating the percent name for a fraction is a useful thing to know. I told her I can't see where or when I'll ever need to know the percent name of a fraction. Could you help me out?
Sincerely,
D. Uno

Percents That Make Sense

Applying Skills

For each Fraction Circles piece shown, give the percent each piece represents. If there is not an exact whole percent equivalent, write the percent that is closest.

1.   2.

3.   4.

5.   6.

Make a sketch for each fraction in the list below. Then provide the percent name for each fraction. (For some fractions, you may need to estimate the percent name.)

7. $\dfrac{1}{5}$ 8. $\dfrac{4}{30}$

9. $\dfrac{2}{15}$ 10. $\dfrac{6}{25}$

11. $\dfrac{10}{50}$ 12. $\dfrac{12}{23}$

13. $\dfrac{3}{20}$ 14. $\dfrac{44}{49}$

Extending Concepts

Numerators	Denominators
12	20
7	50
13	25
4	80
17	34

15. Use the table to make five fractions.

16. Sketch the fractions and label them with their percent names.

17. What strategies did you use to find the percent names for your sketches?

Making Connections

Mr. Kim owns and operates the food stand for the sporting events at the high school. After the last game, he took inventory to see what sells best. He found that $\frac{9}{10}$ of the hot dogs were sold, while only $\frac{2}{5}$ of the pretzels were sold. He also found that he sold $\frac{4}{5}$ of the lemonade and only $\frac{1}{5}$ of the cola drinks.

18. What percent of the lemonade did he sell?

19. What percent of the cola drinks did he sell?

20. What percent of the pretzels did he sell?

21. What percent of the hot dogs did he sell?

The Final Collections Report

Applying Skills

Maryanne collected data on cat breeds at a cat show. The table shows her data.

Type of Cat	Number
Siamese	20
Calico	12
Himalayan	19
Persian	8
Mixed Breed	39

1. How many cats were at the show?

2. Use fractions to tell what portion of the show was made up of each type of cat.

3. Now give an exact or approximate percent for each fraction.

4. Make a circle graph to show the data.

A team of archaeologists found many items from their last dig. The table shows how they catalogued what they found.

Items Found	Number
furniture	8
clothing	29
cooking utensils	32
other	13

5. How many items did the archaeologists find?

6. Use fractions to describe what portion of the items were of each type.

7. Give an exact or approximate percent for each fraction.

8. Make a circle graph to show the data.

Extending Concepts

A sixth-grade class is baking cookies for a fund raiser. They made a chart to show how many of each type were ordered.

9. Write a fraction to show how many of each type of cookie were ordered.

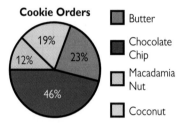

10. If a total of 200 cookies were ordered, how many of each type of cookie will the class have to bake?

11. Because macadamia nuts are expensive, the class would lose money for each macadamia nut cookie they sell. Substituting coconut cookies for orders of macadamia nut cookies, how many coconut cookies will the class need to bake if a total of 100 cookies were ordered?

Writing

12. Answer the letter to Dr. Math.

Dear Dr. Math,
My teacher says that my circle graph should add up to 100%.
I say it should only add up to 64 since I only have 64 pieces of information. Who's right?
Sincerely,
Dotty Data

An Important Point

Applying Skills

Use this grid for items **1–6.**

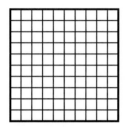

Tell how many squares on the 10-by-10 grid shown you would shade in to represent each decimal amount.

1. 0.08   **2.** 0.80   **3.** 0.8   **4.** 0.080

5. Give the fraction and percent equivalent for each decimal amount in items **1–4.**

6. Copy and complete the table by filling in the fraction, decimal, and percent equivalents.

Fraction	Decimal	Percent
$\frac{5}{10}$		
	0.01	
		10%
$\frac{17}{100}$		
	0.62	
	0.030	
$\frac{50}{1,000}$		

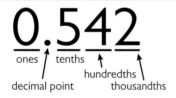

0.542

ones   tenths   hundredths   thousandths
decimal point

Use the diagram to help you answer the following questions.

7. What is the value of the 7 in 0.375?

8. What is the value of the 4 in 362.4835?

Extending Concepts

9. How many squares would you shade in on the 10-by-10 grid to show each of the following?

a. 0.075   **b.** 23%   **c.** 0.80

d. 0.8   **e.** 0.0750   **f.** 18%

g. $\frac{18}{100}$ **h.** $\frac{23}{100}$

10. Write three fraction and decimal equivalents for 0.070.

11. Explain the strategies you used to find the fraction and decimal equivalents for 0.070.

Writing

12. Answer the letter to Dr. Math.

> Dear Dr. Math,
> My tutor was helping me with decimals. She said that 0.80 and 0.8 have the same value, but 0.08 is different. I told her that couldn't be right. Should I find another tutor?
> Sincerely,
> Decimal Weary

Tenths, Hundredths, and More

Applying Skills

In items 1–6, give the percent and decimal equivalent for each fraction. Use the bar notation for repeating decimals.

1. $\frac{2}{20}$ 2. $\frac{3}{12}$ 3. $\frac{3}{20}$

4. $\frac{4}{12}$ 5. $\frac{15}{20}$ 6. $\frac{7}{12}$

Find a decimal equivalent for each fraction below by thinking of each fraction as a division problem. You may use your calculator. Round to the thousandths place if necessary.

7. $\frac{7}{8}$ 8. $\frac{4}{9}$ 9. $\frac{13}{20}$

10. $\frac{121}{400}$ 11. $\frac{18}{33}$ 12. $\frac{9}{83}$

Use your calculator to check each repeating decimal. If it is not written correctly, make the necessary change.

13. $\frac{1}{3} = 0.033\overline{3}$ 14. $\frac{3}{11} = 0.272\overline{7}$

15. $\frac{11}{12} = 0.9\overline{16}$ 16. $\frac{5}{12} = 0.41\overline{6}$

Extending Concepts

17. Find a decimal and percent equivalent for $\frac{200}{323}$. Be sure to round the decimal to the thousandths place.

18. Tell what you did to solve the previous problem. Is your answer exact? Are there any methods that would give a more exact answer?

Making Connections

19. A clothing store is having a sale. The store manager asked one of her employees to make signs indicating the *percent off* for the various items that are on sale. Unfortunately, the employee misunderstood. Correct the signs so they tell the *percent off*.

    a. Shorts: $\frac{1}{3}$ off the original price

    b. Sweaters: $\frac{1}{2}$ off the original price

    c. Shoes: 0.25 off the original price

    d. Coats: 0.50 off the original price

    e. Shirts: $\frac{2}{6}$ off the original price

    f. Pants: $\frac{4}{17}$ off the original price

    g. Socks: 0.080 off the original price

    h. T-shirts: 0.0770 off the original price

All Three at Once

Applying Skills

Write each decimal as a fraction.

1. 0.6   **2.** 0.06   **3.** 0.98

4. 0.2   **5.** 0.17   **6.** 0.01

Copy the table. For items **7** and **8**, fill in the table as directed.

Decimal Name	Exact Fraction	Familiar Fraction
0.26		
0.44		
0.676		
0.6		
0.903		
0.4		
0.2		
0.334		
0.8		

7. For each decimal listed in the table, enter an exact fraction equivalent in the column "Exact Fraction."

8. Fill in the column "Familiar Fraction" with a familiar equivalent fraction or a more familiar fraction that is close to each decimal. Use the smallest denominator you can. Put a star beside each familiar fraction that is close but not exactly equivalent to the decimal.

9. Write the numbers below in order from smallest to largest.

$$\frac{652}{900}, 0.012, \frac{7}{10}, 32\%, \frac{1}{10}, 0.721, 65\%$$

10. Write the numbers below in order from smallest to largest.

$$63\%, \frac{2}{10}, 0.8, \frac{8}{29}, 85\%, 0.12, \frac{55}{90}, 89\%$$

Extending Concepts

11. How is place value in decimals related to the denominator in an equivalent fraction?

12. Find the decimal name for each fraction listed in the table. You may use your calculator if necessary.

Decimal Name	Exact Fraction	Familiar Fraction
	$\frac{12}{100}$	
	$\frac{2}{10}$	
	$\frac{34}{1,000}$	
	$\frac{2}{8}$	
	$\frac{88}{91}$	
	$\frac{3}{10}$	
	$\frac{4}{5}$	

13. Now, find a familiar equivalent fraction (smallest denominator) or a more familiar fraction that is close to each fraction. Put a star beside each familiar fraction that approximates but does not equal the exact fraction.

Going Beyond

Applying Skills

Rename each mixed number as an improper fraction and each improper fraction as a mixed number.

1. $2\frac{5}{8}$

2. $\frac{28}{9}$

3. $\frac{38}{10}$

4. $9\frac{2}{9}$

5. $\frac{6}{4}$

6. $8\frac{11}{20}$

7. $\frac{44}{8}$

8. $4\frac{4}{5}$

9. Sketch a number line from 0 to 10. Locate each of the numbers listed in items **1** through **8**. Write both the improper fraction and mixed number name for each.

10. Tell whether each inequality is true or false. Rewrite the false statements to make them true.

a. $-2 < -1$

b. $-10 < -5$

c. $-2 > -3$

d. $-17 > -16$

e. $-2\frac{1}{2} > -4$

f. $-3.3 < -3$

g. $-1 < -1\frac{3}{4}$

h. $-6 > 9$

Extending Concepts

11. Place the following numbers in order from smallest to largest.

$-1.2 \qquad 8 \qquad 9.1 \qquad 2\frac{2}{3} \qquad -6.7$

$-6\frac{4}{5} \qquad 2.3 \qquad 6.7 \qquad -0.021 \qquad -2\frac{2}{3}$

Making Connections

12. Shabnam recorded the temperature at her cabin in the Sierras for 10 days. The temperatures are shown in the table.

Day	Temperature (Celsius)
1	0.2
2	$2\frac{3}{4}$
3	-1.78
4	$-1\frac{1}{2}$
5	-8.75
6	$-6\frac{3}{5}$
7	-2.6
8	0
9	1.75
10	$4\frac{4}{5}$

Make a number line from -10 to 10 and label the temperatures. For each improper fraction, write the mixed number name. For each mixed number, write the improper fraction.

Root for Yourself

Homework 11

Applying Skills

For each number given, draw a square with sides of the given measure. Then give the area of each square. The first one is done for you.

1. 3 (**Answer:** Area is 9)

2. 5   **3.** 2   **4.** 4

5. 9   **6.** 6

7. Draw a square with an area of 49.

8. Draw a square with an area of 16.

9. Draw a square with an area of 36.

Find each value.

10. $\sqrt{25}$ **11.** $\sqrt{49}$

12. $\sqrt{16}$ **13.** $\sqrt{36}$

14. 5^2 **15.** 10^2

16. 3^2 **17.** 4^2

Extending Concepts

18. What is the relationship between the area of a square and square root?

19. Make a list of the first ten perfect squares. Explain any pattern you see in the numbers.

Making Connections

20. The formula $a^2 + b^2 = c^2$ is used to figure out the length of the sides in right triangles (see the diagram).

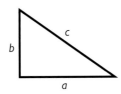

For example, if the length of Side $a = 4.47$ and the length of Side b is 2.24, you can use the formula to find the length of Side c.

$$a^2 + b^2 = c^2$$
$$4.47^2 + 2.24^2 = c^2$$
$$20 + 5 = c^2$$
$$25 = c^2$$
$$c = \sqrt{25} = 5$$

Use the formula to find the length of the slide shown.

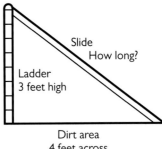

Slide
How long?

Ladder
3 feet high

Dirt area
4 feet across

Powering Up

Applying Skills

Find the following powers.

1. 2^2 **2.** 2^3

3. 2^4 **4.** 3^2

5. 4^3 **6.** 6^3

7. 8^2 **8.** 15^4

Write the expressions for the following:

9. thirteen squared   **10.** eight cubed

11. two cubed   **12.** four squared

In the expressions listed, what is the base? the exponent?

13. 4^3 **14.** 2^3

15. 4^4 **16.** 12^5

17. 3^2 **18.** 6^{10}

19. Make a number line that shows the numbers from -10 to 10. Then place each of the numbers on the line.

$$-6 \qquad \frac{3}{4} \qquad 0.80 \qquad 40\% \qquad -3.5 \qquad 1\frac{2}{3}$$

$$\frac{12}{10} \qquad 2^3 \qquad -2^2 \qquad \sqrt{49} \qquad 78\%$$

Extending Concepts

20. Make a number line that shows the numbers from -100 to 100. Place each of the following numbers in the correct position.

$$\frac{22}{8} \qquad -55 \qquad 0.69 \qquad 35\% \qquad 2^6 \qquad \sqrt{64}$$

$$32.75 \qquad -4\frac{1}{2} \qquad 3^3 \qquad 10^2 \qquad -60\frac{2}{5} \qquad 0.01$$

$$\frac{97}{20} \qquad \sqrt{169} \qquad 10\%$$

21. Make a number line that shows the numbers from 500 to 1,500. Label all the powers of 2 that fit between 500 and 1,500.

Writing

22. Answer the letter to Dr. Math.

> Dear Dr. Math,
> On my last math test, I figured out that $4^2 \times 4^2$ is 64. I was really proud of myself till the next day when I got the test back and the teacher said it was 256. I don't get it! What did I do wrong?
> Sincerely,
> Confused About Squares

STUDENT GALLERY

The Seeing and Thinking Mathematically project is based at Education Development Center, Inc. (EDC), Newton, MA, and was supported, in part, by the National Science Foundation Grant No. 9054677. Opinions expressed are those of the authors and not necessarily those of the National Science Foundation. ✸

CREDITS: Photography: Don Johnson • Beverley Harper (cover). Illustrations: Rod Vass: pp. 2, 6, 14, 17, 19, 27, 35 • Manfred Geier: pp. 7, 9, 15, 18, 22, 31, 39.

Creative Publications and MathScape are trademarks or registered trademarks of Creative Publications.

© 1998 Creative Publications
1300 Villa Street, Mountain View, California 94041

Printed in the United States of America.

0-7622-0207-6

1 2 3 4 5 6 7 8 9 10 . 02 01 00 99 98 97

DESIGNING SPACES

VISUALIZING, PLANNING, AND BUILDING

STUDENT GUIDE

DESIGNING SPACES

VISUALIZING, PLANNING, AND BUILDING

MathScape™
SEEING AND THINKING MATHEMATICALLY

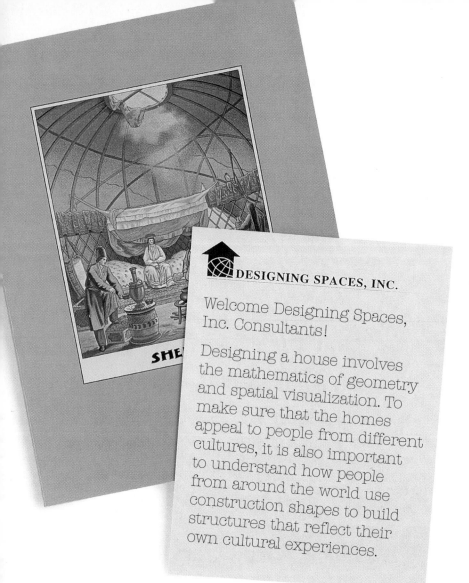

DESIGNING SPACES, INC.

Welcome Designing Spaces, Inc. Consultants!

Designing a house involves the mathematics of geometry and spatial visualization. To make sure that the homes appeal to people from different cultures, it is also important to understand how people from around the world use construction shapes to build structures that reflect their own cultural experiences.

SHE

How can you describe houses from around the world?

DESIGNING SPACES

PHASE**ONE**
Visualizing and Representing
Cube Structures

Your job as a consultant for
Designing Spaces, Inc. will
begin with exploring different
ways to represent three-
dimensional structures. In this
first phase, you will build
houses made from cubes. Then
you will create building plans of
a house. The true test of your
plans will be whether another
person can follow them to build
the house. The skills you
develop in this phase are an
important basis for
understanding geometry.

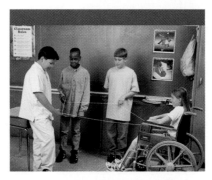

PHASE**TWO**
Functions and Properties
of Shapes

What shapes do you see in the
houses pictured on these
pages? In this phase, you will
explore the properties of two-
dimensional shapes. You will
apply what you learn to decode
the formulas for making the
construction shapes developed
by the Designing Spaces, Inc.
technical research group. At the
end of the phase, Designing
Spaces, Inc. will turn to you for
advice about the dimensions of
their construction shapes.

PHASE**THREE**
Visualizing and Representing
Polyhedrons

In Phase Three, you will explore
how you can use the building
shapes you helped design in
Phase Two to make a variety of
three-dimensional structures.
You'll learn names for the
structures you create and make
drawings of them. The phase
ends with a final project. You
will use the building shapes to
design a home for a cold and
snowy climate, or a warm and
rainy climate. Then you'll create
building plans for your design.

PHASE ONE

To: House Designers
From: General Manager
         Designing Spaces, Inc.

Welcome to Designing Spaces, Inc.! In your new job as a house designer, you will be asked to design different kinds of homes for our customers.
One kind of home our company designs is a low-cost modular home. These homes are made from cube-shaped rooms that are all the same size. We can make many different kinds of modular homes because the rooms fit together in so many different ways.

In Phase One, you will take on the special assignment of designing houses made of cube-shaped rooms. You will learn helpful ways to make building plans for your structures. Your plans must be clear. Someone else should be able to build your house from your plans.

Visualizing and Representing Cube Structures

WHAT'S THE MATH?

Investigations in this section focus on:

MULTIPLE REPRESENTATIONS

- Represent three-dimensional structures with isometric and orthogonal drawings.

PROPERTIES and COMPONENTS of SHAPES

- Identify two-dimensional shapes that make up three-dimensional structures.

- Describe properties of structures in writing so that someone else can build the structure.

VISUALIZATION

- Build three-dimensional structures from two-dimensional representations.

1 Planning and Building a Modular House

A modular house is made of parts that can be put together in different ways. You can use cubes to design a modular house model. Then you can record your design in a set of building plans. These plans are a way of communicating about your house design so that someone else could build it.

Use Cubes to Design a House

What kind of structure can you make from cubes that meets the design guidelines?

One kind of home that Designing Spaces, Inc. designs is a low-cost modular home made from cube-shaped rooms. For your first assignment, use eight to ten cubes to design a modular house model. Let each cube represent a room in the house. Follow the Design Guidelines for Modular Houses.

Cubes in the structure you design can be arranged like these.

Cubes cannot be arranged like these.

 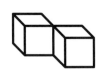

Design Guidelines for Modular Houses

- A face of one cube must line up exactly with a face of at least one other cube so that the rooms can be connected by stairways and doorways.

- No rooms can defy gravity. Each cube must rest on the desktop or directly on top of another cube.

Create Building Plans

Now that you have designed and built your modular house model, make a set of plans that someone else could use to build the same structure. Your plans should include the following:

- Create at least one drawing of the house.

- Write a description of the steps someone would follow to build the house.

How can you make two-dimensional drawings of three-dimensional structures?

Add to the Visual Glossary

In this unit, you will create your own Visual Glossary of geometric terms that describe shapes. These terms will help you to share your building plans with others. One example is the term *face*. The term is used in the Design Guidelines for Modular Houses.

- After your class discusses the meaning of the term *face*, add the class definition to your Visual Glossary.

- Include drawings to illustrate your definition.

hot **words** | face

Homework

page 34

2 Seeing Around the Corners

REPRESENTING
THREE DIMENSIONS
IN ISOMETRIC
DRAWINGS

How many different houses do you think you can make with three cubes? How many can you make with four cubes? As you explore the possibilities, you will find that a special type of drawing called *isometric drawing* can help you record the different structures you make.

Build and Represent Three-Room Houses

How many different structures is it possible to build with three cubes?

Design as many different modular houses as you can using three cubes.

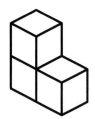 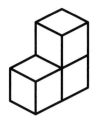

These two houses are the same. You can rotate one to be just like the other, without lifting it.

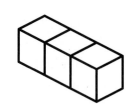 

These two houses are different. You have to lift one house to make it just like the other.

- Follow the Design Guidelines for Modular Houses presented on page 6.

- Make an isometric drawing to record each different structure you make.

Sample Isometric Drawings

Isometric drawings show three faces of a structure in one sketch.

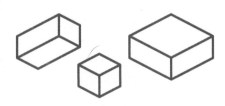

You can use isometric dot paper to help you in making isometric drawings.

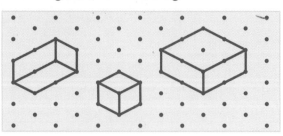

Build and Represent Four-Room Houses

You have explored the number of houses it is possible to build with three cubes. Now try using four cubes to design as many different houses as you can.

- Follow the Design Guidelines for Modular Houses presented on page 6.

- Record each different structure you make as an isometric drawing or another type of drawing.

Two houses are the same if they can be rotated either by turning or lifting them. How many different houses can you make with four cubes?

How many different structures is it possible to build with four cubes?

Add to the Visual Glossary

Think about the isometric drawings you made in this lesson. Look at the illustrations shown on this page. Then compare the lengths of the sides and the sizes of the angles in both kinds of drawings.

- After discussing with the class, add the class definition of the term *isometric drawing* to your Visual Glossary.

- Be sure to include drawings to illustrate the definition.

Isometric Drawings

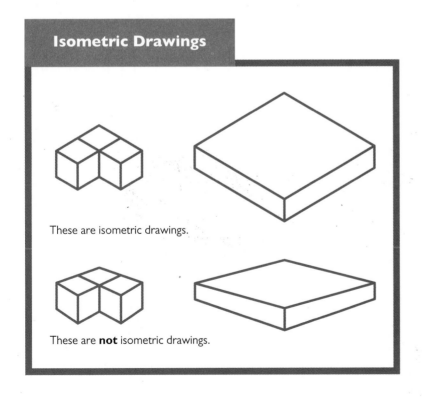

These are isometric drawings.

These are **not** isometric drawings.

hot **words** | isometric drawing

Homework

page 35

3 Seeing All Possibilities

You have explored using isometric drawings to show three-dimensional structures on paper. Here you will try another drawing method called *orthogonal drawing*. You need to understand both types of drawings, so you can read building plans and create plans of your own.

Construct Houses from Orthogonal Drawings

How can you use orthogonal drawings to build three-dimensional structures?

Four sets of building plans for modular houses are shown here. Each plan is represented with orthogonal drawings that show three views of the house. Your job is to build each house with cubes and record the least number of cubes you needed to build the house.

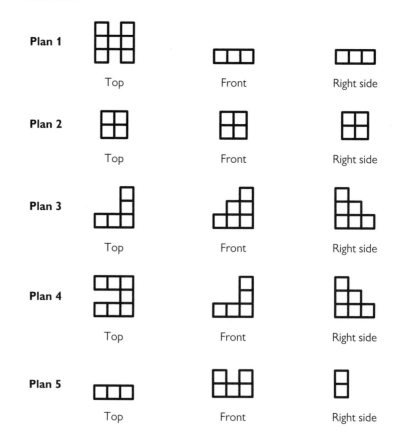

Plan 1 — Top, Front, Right side

Plan 2 — Top, Front, Right side

Plan 3 — Top, Front, Right side

Plan 4 — Top, Front, Right side

Plan 5 — Top, Front, Right side

Make Orthogonal Drawings

These plans are isometric drawings of several houses. Your job is to make orthogonal drawings showing the top, front, and right side of each house.

How can you make orthogonal drawings from an isometric drawing of a house?

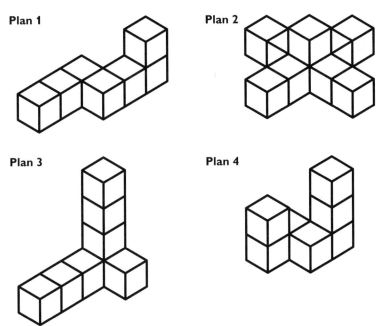

Plan 1

Plan 2

Plan 3

Plan 4

Add to the Visual Glossary

Think about the orthogonal drawings you made. Look at the illustrations showing drawings that are orthogonal and drawings that are not orthogonal.

- After class discussion, add the class definition of the term *orthogonal drawing* to your Visual Glossary.

- Be sure to include drawings to illustrate the definition.

Orthogonal Drawing

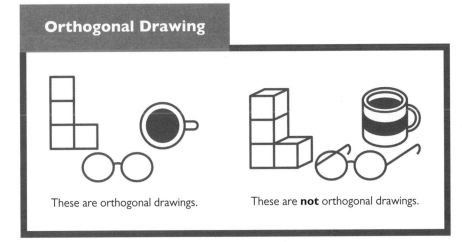

These are orthogonal drawings.   These are **not** orthogonal drawings.

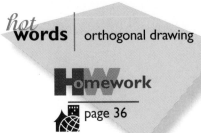

hot **words** | orthogonal drawing

Ho**mework**

page 36

4 Picture This

You have learned how to make isometric and orthogonal drawings. In this lesson, you will use what you have learned to improve the building plans you made for your first assignment. One way to check how well your plans communicate is to get someone else's comments on your plans.

How can you apply what you know to improve how well your plans communicate?

Evaluate and Improve Building Plans

1 Evaluate your building plans from Lesson 1. Think about these questions and make changes to improve your building plans.

a. Can you tell how many cubes were used in each structure? How do you know?

b. Can you tell how the cubes should be arranged? How would you make the drawings clearer?

c. Do the written plans include a step-by-step description of the building process? Are any steps missing?

d. What are one or two things that you think are done well in the plans? What are one or two things that you think need to be changed in the plans?

2 Exchange your plans with a partner. Carefully follow your partner's plans and build the structure. Write down any suggestions that you think would improve your partner's building plans.

a. Are the drawings clear? How could you make them clearer?

b. Are the step-by-step written instructions easy to follow? What suggestions can you give to improve the instructions?

c. What are one or two things that you think are done well in the plans?

Use Feedback to Revise Building Plans

Carefully review the feedback you received from your partner. Use it to make final changes to your plans.

- Keep in mind that feedback is suggestions and opinions that can help you improve your work.

- It is up to you to decide whether to use the feedback and how to use it.

How can you improve your plans so that they are easier for someone else to use?

Write About the Changes

When you finish changing your building plans, write a memo to the General Manager of Designing Spaces, Inc. The memo should summarize the revisions you made.

- Describe the changes you made in your drawings.

- Describe the steps it took to build your structure.

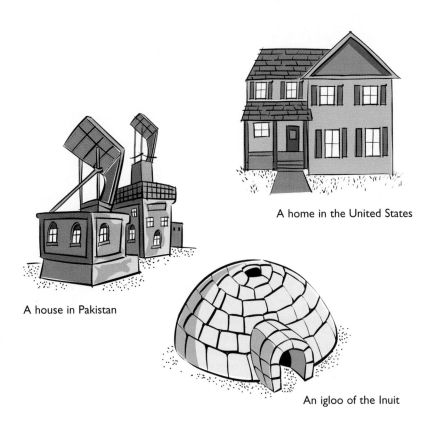

A home in the United States

A house in Pakistan

An igloo of the Inuit

hot words | three-dimensional
two-dimensional

Homework

page 37

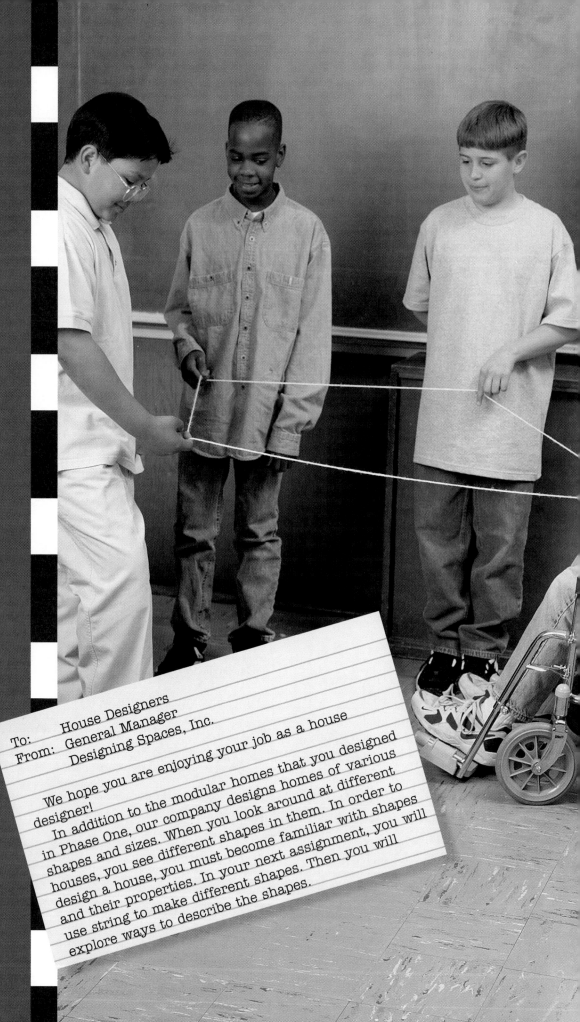

PHASE TWO

To: House Designers

From: General Manager
Designing Spaces, Inc.

We hope you are enjoying your job as a house
designer!

In addition to the modular homes that you designed
in Phase One, our company designs homes of various
shapes and sizes. When you look around at different
houses, you see different shapes in them. In order to
design a house, you must become familiar with shapes
and their properties. In your next assignment, you will
use string to make different shapes. Then you will
explore ways to describe the shapes.

In Phase Two, you will investigate various shapes that can be used to design and build houses. You will learn about the properties of shapes and how to measure angles with a protractor—ideas that are good to know when constructing a house.

Functions and Properties of Shapes

WHAT'S THE MATH?

Investigations in this section focus on:

PROPERTIES and COMPONENTS of SHAPES

- Identify two-dimensional shapes and their properties.

- Measure sides and angles of shapes.

- Estimate area and perimeter of shapes.

- Use geometric notation to indicate relationships between angles and sides in shapes.

- Describe properties of shapes in writing.

- Expand vocabulary for describing shapes.

VISUALIZATION

- Visualize shapes from clues about their sides and angles.

- Perform visual and mental experiments with shapes.

5 String Shapes

INVESTIGATING PROPERTIES OF SIDES

What shapes can you find in the houses in your neighborhood? Shapes that have three or more sides are called **polygons.** As you make shapes from string, you will learn some special properties of sides of polygons. You'll also learn mathematical names for the shapes you create.

Make Shapes from Clues

Can you find a shape that satisfies clues about parallel and equilateral sides?

Do the following for each shape clue given:

1 Try making a shape that fits the description in the clue.

2 If you can make the shape, record it. Then label the equal sides and the parallel sides. (The top of the handout Naming and Labeling Polygons will help you with this.) If you can't make the shape, write "Impossible."

3 Label the shape you draw with a mathematical name. If you don't know a name for the shape, make up a name that you think describes the properties of the shape. (The bottom of the handout Naming and Labeling Polygons will help you with this.)

Shape Clue 1: An equilateral shape with more than 3 sides and no parallel sides.	**Shape Clue 2:** A shape with 2 sides equal and 2 different sides parallel but not equal. (Hint: Your shape can have more than 4 sides.)
Shape Clue 3: A quadrilateral with 2 pairs of parallel sides and only 2 sides equal.	**Shape Clue 4:** A shape with at least 2 pairs of parallel sides that is not an equilateral shape. (Hint: Your shape can have more than 4 sides.)
Shape Clue 5: A quadrilateral that is equilateral and has no parallel sides.	**Shape Clue 6:** Make up a clue of your own and write it down. Test it to see if you can make the shape, and write a sentence telling why you can or cannot make it.

DESIGNING SPACES   LESSON 5

16   © Creative Publications • MathScape

Make Animated Shapes

Animated shapes are shapes that a group makes with string. The group starts with one shape, and then one member of the group changes positions to change the shape as the rest stand still. Make each of the animated shapes on the handout Animated Shapes.

1 Try to make the shape by moving the fewest people.

2 Record how you made the shape with drawings or words. Include your starting positions, who moved, and where.

Using string, how can you change a square into a triangle? a trapezoid into a square?

Add to the Visual Glossary

Think about how you used the terms *parallel* and *equilateral* to describe the sides of shapes. Then look at the illustrations showing lines and walls that are parallel and lines and walls that are not parallel.

■ After some class discussion, write the class's description of what is meant by the terms *parallel* and *equilateral* in your Visual Glossary.

■ Be sure to include drawings to illustrate your description.

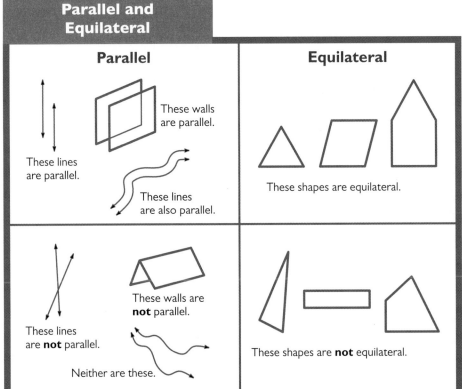

Parallel and Equilateral

Parallel

These lines are parallel.

These walls are parallel.

These lines are also parallel.

These lines are **not** parallel.

These walls are **not** parallel.

Neither are these.

Equilateral

These shapes are equilateral.

These shapes are **not** equilateral.

hot **words** | parallel
equilateral

Ho**m**e**w**ork

🏙 page 38

 **6 Polygon Paths**

Where the sides of a shape meet, they form angles.
Building plans for houses have to show the measures of angles and the lengths of sides. Here you will explore how measuring angles is different from measuring lengths. Then you will use what you have learned to describe polygons.

Measure Angles

How can you tell if two angles are equal?

Use a protractor to measure the angles in this polygon. Be sure to refer to the guidelines on How to Use a Protractor.

- Which is the smallest angle? How did you measure it?

- Which is the largest angle? How did you measure it?

- Are any of the angles equal?

How to Use a Protractor

To use a protractor to measure an angle:

- Place the 0° line along one side of the angle.

- Read the degree mark that is closest to where the other side of the angle crosses the protractor.

TIP: If the side of an angle doesn't cross the protractor, imagine where it would cross if the line was longer. Or copy the figure and extend the line.

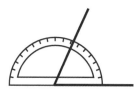

Write Polygon Path Instructions

Polygon path instructions describe the steps you take when drawing a polygon. Study the example shown. Then write polygon path instructions for the shapes on the handout.

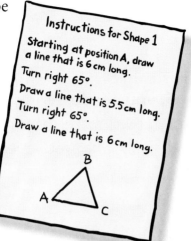

Instructions for Shape 1

Starting at position A, draw a line that is 6 cm long.

Turn right 65°.

Draw a line that is 5.5 cm long.

Turn right 65°.

Draw a line that is 6 cm long.

Add to the Visual Glossary

Think about how you have used the terms *equal angles* and *right angles* to describe angles in this lesson. Study the pictures of equal angles and right angles.

- After the class discussion, write in your Visual Glossary the meanings of *equal angles* and *right angles* that your class developed.

- Include drawings to illustrate the definitions.

Types of Angles

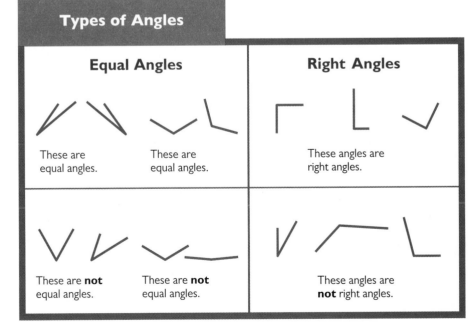

Equal Angles	Right Angles
These are equal angles. These are equal angles.	These angles are right angles.
These are **not** equal angles. These are **not** equal angles.	These angles are **not** right angles.

hot **words** | equal angles
right angles

Homework

page 39

7 Shaping Up

INVESTIGATING PROPERTIES OF SIDES AND ANGLES

In Lesson 5, you made string shapes from clues about sides. Here, you will make shapes from clues about angles. Then you will apply what you've learned so far in the Sides and Angles Game.

Make Shapes from Clues

How can you use what you know about the properties of sides and angles to make shapes?

Do the following for each shape clue given:

1. Try making a shape that fits the description in the clue.

2. If you can make the shape, record it. Then label the equal angles and the right angles. (The top of the handout Naming and Labeling Polygons will help you with this.) If you can't make the shape, write "Impossible."

3. Label the shape you draw with a mathematical name. If you don't know a name for the shape, make up a name that you think describes the properties of the shape. (The bottom of the handout Naming and Labeling Polygons will help you with this.)

Shape Clue 1
A quadrilateral with exactly 2 right angles.

Shape Clue 2
A quadrilateral with exactly 2 right angles that are also opposite angles.

Shape Clue 3
A shape with exactly 3 right angles.

Shape Clue 5
A shape with 5 equal angles.

Shape Clue 4
A quadrilateral with only 1 pair of opposite angles that are equal.

Shape Clue 6
A quadrilateral in which each pair of opposite angles are the same size and at least 1 pair are right angles.

Shape Clue 7
Make up a clue of your own and write it down. Test it to see if you can make the shape, and write a sentence telling why you can or cannot make it.

Play the Sides and Angles Game

In the Sides and Angles Game, you will try to make shapes that fit two different descriptions. One description is of the sides of the shape. The other is of the angles. Be sure to read the rules carefully before beginning.

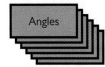
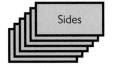

What shapes can you make from clues about sides and angles?

The Sides and Angles Game Rules

Before beginning the game, place the Sides cards face-down in one pile. Place the Angles cards face-down in another pile.

1. The first player takes one card from each pile.

2. The player tries to draw a shape that fits the descriptions on the two cards. Then the player marks the drawing to show any parallel sides, equal sides, equal angles, or right angles. The player should label the shape with a mathematical name or create a name that fits. If the player cannot make a shape, the player should describe why.

3. Players take turns trying to find another way to draw the shape, following the directions in Step 2. When the group draws four shapes or runs out of possible drawings, the next player picks two new cards. Play begins again.

Add to the Visual Glossary

Think how you have used the terms *regular shapes* and *opposite angles* to describe the shapes you made in this lesson.

- After class discussion, write the class definition for each term in your Visual Glossary.

- Include drawings to illustrate the definitions.

Shapes and Angles

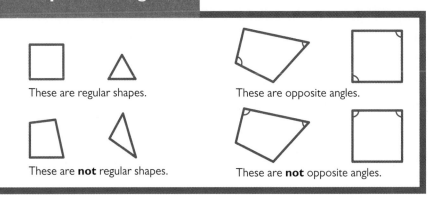

These are regular shapes.

These are opposite angles.

These are **not** regular shapes.

These are **not** opposite angles.

 regular shapes
opposite angles

 page 40

8 Assembling the Pieces

You've explored sides, angles, and shape names when describing two-dimensional shapes. In this lesson, you will investigate two more properties of shapes—perimeter and area. Then you will apply everything you've learned to describe six shapes. You will use the shapes in the next phase to build a model home.

Investigate Perimeter and Area

How many shapes can you draw with a perimeter of 10 cm? 15 cm?

Perimeter and *area* are properties of shapes. **Perimeter** is the distance around a shape. **Area** is the number of square units a shape contains. Follow the directions given to investigate these two properties. You'll need a ruler for this activity.

The area of this rectangle is 12 cm². The perimeter is 14 cm. Can you estimate the area and perimeter of this triangle?

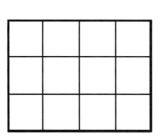 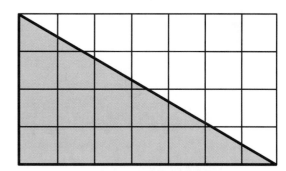

1 Choose a perimeter between 8 cm and 16 cm. Make at least four different shapes with that perimeter. Then record each shape you made and label the lengths of the sides.

2 Estimate the area in square centimeters of some of the shapes you recorded. You may find it helpful to trace the shapes on centimeter grid paper.

As you were drawing different shapes with the same perimeter, what did you notice about the area of the shapes? Why do you think this is true?

Describe Construction Shapes

Later in the unit, you will use six shapes to design and build a house. Your teacher will give you samples of these six shapes.

- Pretend that you are explaining to a manufacturer the shapes and the sizes you will be using.

- Describe each shape in as many ways as you can.

- Be sure to refer to the assessment criteria when writing your descriptions.

How can you use what you've learned to describe a shape so that someone else could draw it?

hot **words** | perimeter area

Homework

page 41

PHASE THREE

To: House Designers
From: General Manager
Designing Spaces, Inc.

Designing Spaces, Inc. has just been hired to create a new collection of house designs. Your work on the next few assignments leads up to designing one of these houses. Your house will be located in one of two climates: hot and rainy or cold and snowy. This project will give us a chance to see how much you've learned while working for Designing Spaces, Inc.

In Phase Two, you explored the properties of two-dimensional shapes that make up three-dimensional structures. In this phase, you will investigate the properties of the three-dimensional structures themselves. Using this information in the final project, you will design, build, and make plans for a model home!

Visualizing and Representing Polyhedrons

WHAT'S THE MATH?

Investigations in this section focus on:

MULTIPLE REPRESENTATIONS

- Use perspective drawing techniques to represent prisms and pyramids.
- Identify orthogonal views of a structure.

PROPERTIES and COMPONENTS of SHAPES

- Identify prisms and pyramids.
- Investigate the properties of edge, vertex, and face.
- Explore the relationships among the properties of two- and three-dimensional shapes.

VISUALIZATION

- Form visual images of structures in your mind from clues given about the structure.

© Creative Publications • MathScape

Beyond Boxes

In Phase One, you designed houses with cubes. If you look at houses around the world, however, you will see many different shapes. Here you will use the shapes you made in Lesson 8 to build three-dimensional structures.

Construct Closed Three-Dimensional Structures

What three-dimensional structures can you build by choosing from six different shapes?

A **polyhedron** is any solid shape whose surface is made up of polygons. Using the shapes from Lesson 8, you will build three-dimensional structures. The structures you build, however, are not solid.

1 Use the Shape Tracers to trace four of each of the following shapes on heavy paper: triangles, rectangles, squares, rhombi, trapezoids, and hexagons. Then carefully cut out the shapes.

2 Build at least two different structures from the shapes you cut out. Be sure to follow the Building Guidelines.

A thatched roof house in Central America

Building Guidelines

- Use 3–15 pieces for each structure that you build. If you need more pieces, cut them out.

- The base, or bottom, of the structure can be made of only **one** piece.

- The pieces must **not** overlap.

- The structure must be **closed.** No gaps are allowed. (Use tape to hold the shapes together.)

- No hidden pieces are allowed; you must be able to see them all.

Record and Describe Properties of Structures

In Phase Two, you used properties of sides and angles to describe polygons. You can use properties of faces, vertices, and edges to describe polyhedrons.

What are the properties of the three-dimensional structures you built?

1 For each structure you made, create a table of properties. Record the following numbers:

    a. faces   **b.** vertices   **c.** edges

    d. sets of parallel faces   **e.** sets of parallel edges

2 Write a description of one of the structures you built. Include enough information so that your classmates would be able to pick out your structure from all the others. You can include drawings. Think about the following when you write your description:

    a. What shapes did you use in the structure? What shape is the base?

    b. How many faces, vertices, and edges does the structure have?

    c. Are any edges parallel to each other?

    d. Are any faces parallel to each other?

Table of Properties

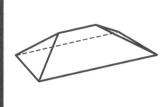

Shape of Base	Shapes Used	No. of Faces	No. of Vertices (Corners)	No. of Edges	Sets of Parallel Faces?	Sets of Parallel Edges?
Rectangle	1 rectangle 2 triangles 2 trapezoids	5	6	9	No (0)	Yes (2)

Add to the Visual Glossary

In this lesson, you used the terms *vertex* and *edge* to describe properties of polyhedrons. Write definitions for vertex and edge.

- After class discussion, add the class definitions of the terms *vertex* and *edge* to your Visual Glossary.

- Be sure to add drawings to illustrate your definitions.

hot **words** | vertex edge

Homework

page 42

10 Drawing Tricks

VISUALIZING AND
DRAWING PRISMS
AND PYRAMIDS

Architects draw many different views of their house designs. In Phase One, you learned to create isometric drawings of houses made of cubes. The methods you learn here for drawing prisms and pyramids will prepare you for drawing house plans that include other shapes.

Draw Prisms

How can you draw a prism in two dimensions?

A **prism** has two parallel faces that can be any shape. These are its **bases.** A prism gets its name from the shape of its bases. For example, if the base is a square, it is called a square prism. Read the tips on How to Draw a Prism.

- Draw some prisms on your own.
- Label each prism you draw with its name.

How to Draw a Prism

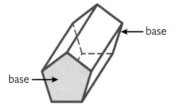
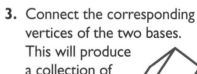
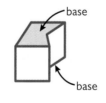

1. Draw the base of the prism. The example shown is the base for a pentagonal prism.

2. Draw the second base by making a copy of the first base. Keep corresponding sides parallel.

3. Connect the corresponding vertices of the two bases. This will produce a collection of parallel edges with the same length.

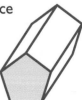

DESIGNING SPACES LESSON 10

Draw Pyramids

In a *pyramid*, the base can be any shape. All the other faces are triangles. A pyramid gets its name from the shape of its base. For example, if the base is a triangle, it is called a triangular pyramid. Read the tips for How to Draw a Pyramid.

How can you draw a pyramid in two dimensions?

- Draw some pyramids on your own. Try some with different shapes as their bases.

- Label each pyramid you draw with its name.

How to Draw a Pyramid

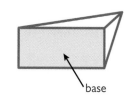
base

base

1. Draw the base. The example shown is the base for a pentagonal pyramid.

2. Mark any point outside the base.

3. Draw line segments from each vertex of the base to the point.

Add to the Visual Glossary

Think about the drawings you made of pyramids and prisms. What do pyramids have in common? What do prisms have in common?

- After class discussion, add the class definitions of the terms *prism* and *pyramid* to your Visual Glossary.

- Be sure to add drawings to illustrate your definitions.

hot **words** | prism
pyramid

Homework
page 43

11 Mystery Structures

Have you ever solved a puzzle from a set of clues? That's what you will do to build three-dimensional Mystery Structures. Then you will build your own Mystery Structure and write clues to go with it. To create an answer key for your clues, you will use the drawing skills you have learned.

Solve the Mystery Structures Game

How can you apply what you know about two-dimensional shapes to solve clues about three-dimensional structures?

The Mystery Structures Game pulls together all of the geometric concepts you have learned in this unit. Play the Mystery Structures Game with your group. You will need the following: Round 1 clues, a set of shapes (4 each of the triangle, rhombus, trapezoid, and hexagon; 6 each of the rectangle and square), and tape.

The Mystery Structures Game

How to play:

1. Each player reads, but does not show, one of the clues to the group. If your clue has a picture on it, describe the picture.

2. Discuss what the structure might look like.

3. Build a structure that matches all the clues. Recheck each clue to make sure the structure satisfies each one. You may need to revise the structure several times.

4. Make a drawing of the structure that shows depth.

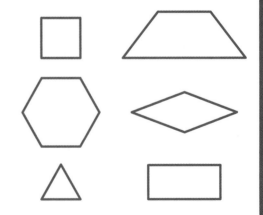

Create Clues

Now that you know how the Mystery Structures Game works, follow these steps to write your own set of clues for the game:

1 Build a closed, three-dimensional shape with up to 12 shape pieces. Make a structure that will be an interesting project for someone else to build.

2 Write a set of four clues about your structure. Write each clue on a separate sheet of paper. Use at least one orthogonal drawing. From your four clues, someone else should be able to build your structure.

3 Make a drawing of the structure showing depth to serve as an answer key for other students who try to follow your clues.

How can you use what you have learned about shapes to describe three-dimensional structures?

Give Feedback on Clues

Exchange clues with a partner. Then try to build your partner's structure. When you are done, compare your structure with the answer key. Write feedback on how your partner's clues might be improved.

- Are the drawings clear? How could you make them clearer?

- Are the clues easy to follow? What suggestions can you give to improve the clues?

- What are one or two things that you think are done well?

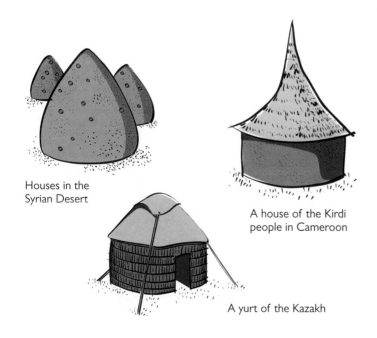

Houses in the Syrian Desert

A house of the Kirdi people in Cameroon

A yurt of the Kazakh

hot **words** | polygon
polyhedron

Homework
page 44

12 Putting the Pieces Together

The climate in which a house is built can influence the shape of the house and the materials used to build the house. For your final project, you will research houses in different climates around the world. Then you will apply what you have learned to design a house model for a specific climate.

Build a House

What kind of three-dimensional structure can you make that meets the building guidelines?

Before you start building your house, read about home designs in different climates. Choose the climate for your house model: a hot and rainy climate or a cold and snowy climate. Think about the design features that your house should have for that climate. Then build the house model.

1 Use the Shape Tracers to trace and cut out a set of building shapes.

2 Build a house using the shape pieces. Be sure to follow the Building Guidelines when constructing your house.

Building Guidelines

- The home must have a roof. The roof should be constructed carefully so that it will not leak.

- The home must be able to stand on its own.

- You must use 20–24 shape pieces. You do not need to use each type of shape.

- You may add one new type of shape.

Create a Set of Plans

After building your house, make a set of plans. Another person should be able to use the plans to build your house. Use the following guidelines to help you create your plans:

- Include both orthogonal and isometric drawings of your house. Be sure to label the drawings. The labels will make your plans easier to understand.

- Include a written, step-by-step description of the building process so that someone else could build your house. Use the names and properties of shapes to make your description clear and precise.

How can you represent your house in two dimensions?

Write Design Specifications

Write a memo to the Directors of Designing Spaces, Inc. describing your house. The specifications should explain the design clearly. The Marketing Department should be able to understand and sell the design. The designers should be able to make the shapes and calculate the approximate costs. The memo should answer the following questions:

- What does your home look like?

- How would you describe the shape of the entire house?

- How would you describe the shape of its base, its roof, and any special features?

- What climate is your house designed for?

- What features does your home have to make it well suited to the climate?

- Where in the world could your house be located?

- What shapes are used in your house?

- How many of each shape are there?

- How many edges and vertices does your house have?

- Does your house have any parallel faces? If so, how many?

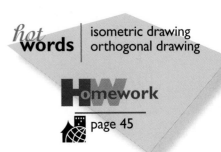

hot **words** | isometric drawing
orthogonal drawing

Homework
page 45

Planning and Building a Modular House

Applying Skills

How many faces does each structure have?

1.

2.

3.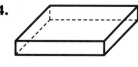

4.

How many cubes are in each model? Remember that each cube on an upper level must have a cube below to support it.

5.

6.

7.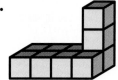

8.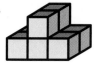

9. Of models 5–8, which ones have the same bottom layer?

Extending Concepts

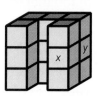

Look at this model house. Suppose you painted all the outside surfaces of the model, including the underside.

10. How many squares would you paint?

11. How many faces would be painted on the cube marked *x*? on the cube marked *y*?

12. Would any cube have 4 faces painted? 5 faces painted? Why or why not?

13. Draw a 6-face figure that is not a cube.

Writing

14. Look in the real estate section of a newspaper or in magazines about housing to find pictures that show houses or buildings in different ways. Find two or three examples of different ways to show structures. Tell why you think the artist chose each one.

Seeing Around the Corners

Applying Skills

Look at the first structure in each box. Tell which of the other structures are rotations of the sample. Answer *yes* or *no* for each structure.

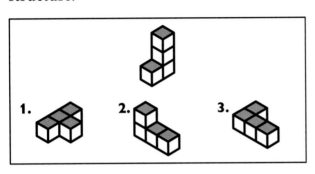

1. **2.** **3.**

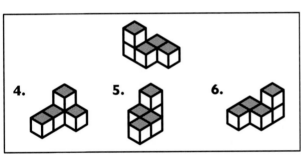

4. **5.** **6.**

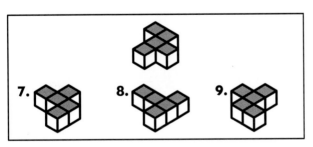

7. **8.** **9.**

Extending Concepts

10. Draw this structure in a different position. Show how it would look:

   a. rotated halfway around

   b. lifted up, standing on its side

Making Connections

11. Draw the next structure in this pattern.

12. Make an isometric drawing of your house, school, or other building as if you were looking at it from the front. Then, make an isometric drawing of the structure as if you were looking at it from the left side.

35

Seeing All Possibilities

Applying Skills

Look carefully at each isometric drawing. The top side is shaded. Write *front, back, top, side,* or *not possible* for each orthogonal view.

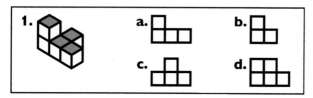

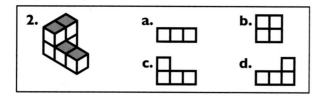

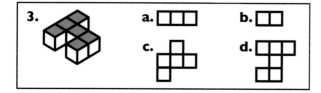

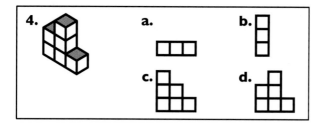

Extending Concepts

5. Make orthogonal drawings of this model that show these views:

   a. top view

   b. back view

   c. right side view

6. How would you tell a friend on the telephone how to build this structure?

Writing

7. This dwelling is located in the Southwest of the United States. Why do you think it is shaped this way? What materials do you think are used? Give your reasons.

Picture This

Applying Skills

Look carefully at each set of orthogonal drawings. Choose which isometric drawings could show the same structure. Answer *possible* or *not possible*. Some structures may be rotations.

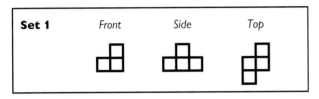

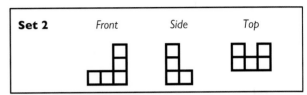

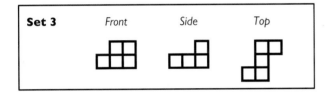

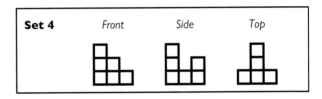

Extending Concepts

Front view   Side view

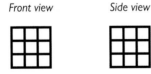

5. Draw at least three different top views of structures that all could have this front view and right side view.

Making Connections

6. Make orthogonal sketches of your school building. Show how you think it looks from the top, front, and right side.

String Shapes

Applying Skills

1. Which polygons have at least two parallel sides?

2. Which polygons have more than two pairs of parallel sides?

3. List all the equilateral polygons.

4. Which equilateral polygons have four sides?

5. List all the polygons with an odd number of sides.

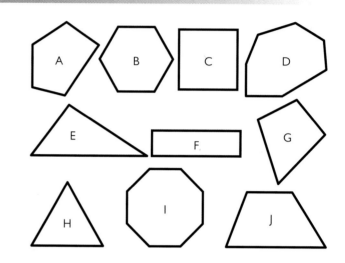

Extending Concepts

```
tri-
quad-
penta-
hexa-
hepta-
octo-
```

6. Choose a prefix for each of the polygons above that would help describe each figure.

7. Draw a different polygon to fit each prefix.

   a. Label the parallel and equal sides.

   b. Write clues to help someone identify each of your polygons.

Making Connections

8. Match the titles to the pictures. Tell why you made each choice.

The Pentagon

Tripod

Hexagram

Octopus

Quartet

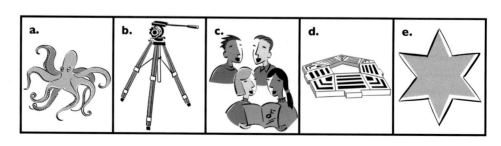

Polygon Paths

Applying Skills

For items 1 through 6, use a protractor and ruler.

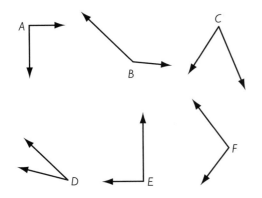

1. Which angles measure less than 90°?

2. Which angles measure greater than 90°?

3. Which angles measure exactly 90°?

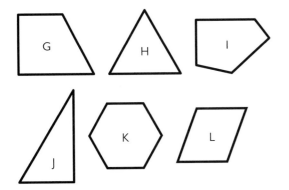

4. Which polygons have at least one right angle?

5. Which polygons have at least two equal angles?

6. Which polygons have all equal angles?

Extending Concepts

7. Use a protractor and ruler. Design and draw a path to create a polygon for each of the following specifications. What is the name of each polygon?

  a. four sides

   at least two sides parallel

   no 90° angles

  b. three sides

   one 90° angle

   two sides of equal length

Writing

8. Draw an imaginary neighborhood that includes a path made up of straight line segments (going from one end of the neighborhood to the other). Describe the path by giving the length of each line segment and the angle and direction of each turn that makes a path through the neighborhood.

Example:

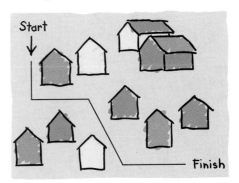

Shaping Up

Applying Skills

Tell whether each polygon is *regular* or *not regular*.

1.

2.

3.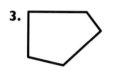

4.

5.

6.

7.

8.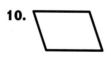

Copy each quadrilateral and mark one pair of opposite angles.

9.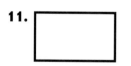

10.

11.

12.

Extending Concepts

String or rope can be used as a tool for making right angles.

Method: A twelve-foot length of rope is marked at every foot and staked into a triangle. The sides are adjusted until one side is 3 feet, one side is 4 feet, and the third side is 5 feet. When these sides are exact, the triangle will contain a right angle.

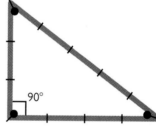

13. Find another trio of side lengths that will create a right triangle. Explain how you know you have a right angle. You can use string or rope to make a model. (An easy scale factor to use is 1 foot of rope in the problem equals 1 inch of string in your model.)

Making Connections

14. Find two other trios of side lengths that will create a right angle in a triangle. There are patterns to some of these trios of side lengths. If you see a pattern, describe it and make a prediction for how you would find other side lengths.

Assembling the Pieces

Applying Skills

1. Which of rectangles A–H have the same perimeter?

2. Which of rectangles A–H have the same area?

Use dot paper.

3. Draw a polygon that is not regular and has the same perimeter as rectangle B.

4. Draw a regular polygon that has the same perimeter as rectangle F.

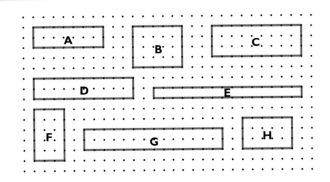

Extending Concepts

5. Use a piece of string about 20 cm long. Knot it into a loop. Use the loop as the perimeter of at least three different triangles. Sketch your triangles on dot paper or grid paper to compare them. Estimate the area of each triangle.

6. Look over these definitions. Do they exactly describe each polygon? Can you improve the lists of clues?

   a.

   It has equal sides.

   It has parallel sides.

   It has four sides.

   b.

   It is not regular.

   Its sides are not equal.

   It has no parallel sides.

Writing

7. Answer the letter to Dr. Math.

Dear Dr. Math:

I don't understand how two rectangles with exactly the same perimeter can enclose different areas. Can you explain that to me?

Perry Mitter

 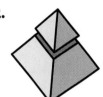

Beyond Boxes

Applying Skills

What two-dimensional shape will you see on the inside of each slice?

1.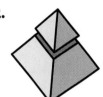

2.

3.

4.

Copy the chart and fill it in for each structure.

5. **6.** **7.**

Shape of base			
Shapes used			
Number of faces			
Number of vertices			
Number of edges			
Sets of parallel faces			
Sets of parallel edges			

Extending Concepts

8. Draw three more three-dimensional figures. Add them to the chart you made for items **5–7.** Can you find a pattern in the relationship between the numbers of edges, vertices, and faces in the shapes? Tell all the steps in your thinking.

9. Can you draw a figure that does not follow the pattern you described in item **8**?

Writing

10. Imagine a penny. Now imagine ten pennies stacked carefully so that all the edges line up evenly.

a. Describe the shape of the stack. What properties does it have?

b. Imagine slicing that stack of pennies down the middle and opening the two halves. What shape do you see now?

c. Think of another example of stacking a group of flat objects to form a new shape. Describe the new shape and how you would make it.

Drawing Tricks

Applying Skills

Is the figure a prism or a pyramid? Name the polygon forming the base.

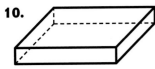

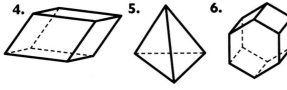

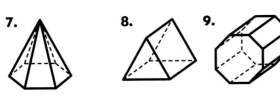

10.

Draw each polyhedron. Tell how many faces it has.

11. Pentagonal pyramid

12. Pentagonal prism

13. Triangular prism

14. Triangular pyramid

Extending Concepts

15. Imagine that you are walking around the group of buildings in the pictures. Choose one picture as a starting point. List the pictures in the order that shows what you would see as you circle the buildings.

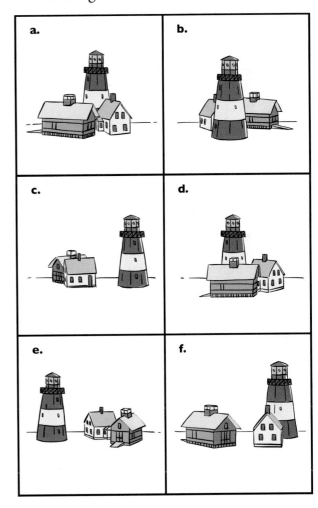

Writing

16. Tell how you visualized moving around the group of buildings.

Mystery Structures

Applying Skills

For items 1–8, give the letters of the polyhedrons that fit the clues.

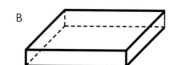
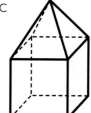

A   B

C   D

E   F

1. It has 7 vertices.

2. Its base is a square.

3. The structure is a prism.

4. It has exactly 3 sets of parallel faces.

5. All sides are equilateral.

6. It has 16 edges.

7. It has 4 sets of parallel faces.

8. It has no sets of parallel faces.

Extending Concepts

9. Draw two different polyhedrons with quadrilateral bases. Make a list of clues for each structure to help someone tell them apart.

Writing

My Mystery Structure
It has some edges.
All the edges are the same length.
It comes to a point on top.
Some of the pieces are triangles.
The base is a square.

10. Do you think this student wrote a good list of clues?

a. Draw a structure that fits the clues.

b. Could you draw a different structure that fits the same clues?

c. Rewrite this list of clues if you think it can be improved. Explain your changes.

Putting the Pieces Together

Applying Skills

Make a chart like the one shown. Fill in the chart to describe each shape or structure.

	1.	2.	3.	4.	5.	6.
Name of shape or structure						
Polygon or polyhedron						
Number of sides or faces						
Number of vertices						
Number of right angles						
Sets of parallel sides or edges						

Extending Concepts

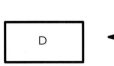

Using the pieces shown, tell how many of each piece you would need to make each polyhedron. (Assume that matching edges will fit.)

7. Hexagonal pyramid

8. Triangular prism

9. Cube

10. Pentagonal prism

Writing

11. Write a letter giving some good advice for next year's designers. Tell about some things that helped you with the investigations.

STUDENT
GALLERY

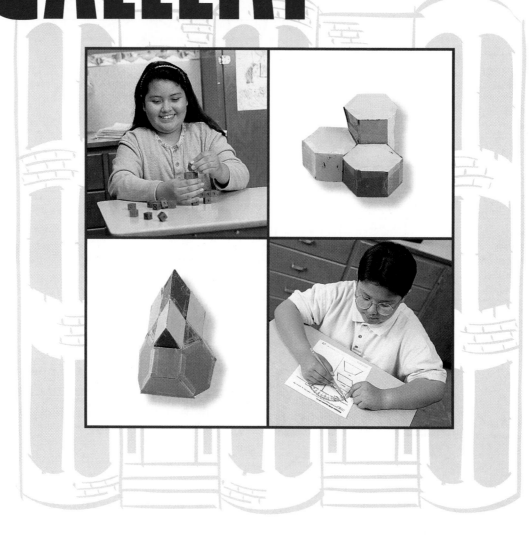

Australia

United States

Russia

Canada

Kenya

Indonesia

United States

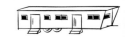

England

Canada

The Seeing and Thinking Mathematically project is based at Education Development Center, Inc. (EDC), Newton, MA, and was supported, in part, by the National Science Foundation (Grant No. 9054677). Opinions expressed are those of the authors and not necessarily those of the National Science Foundation.

CREDITS: Photographs: Chris Conroy Photography • Beverly Harper (cover) • © Norris Taylor/Photo Researchers: pp. 4-5T • © Sylvain Grandadam/Photo Researchers: p. 4TC • © Andrea Moore: pp. 3TL, 4-5C • Images pp. 2, 3TL/TR, 4C, 24bkgd; bar art pp. 17, 19, 21, 23, 27, 29, 31, 33) excerpted from *Shelter* © 1973 by Shelter Publications, Inc., P. O. Box 279, Bolinas, CA 94924; distributed in bookstores by Random House; reprinted by permission • Images © Photodisc, Inc. 1997: pp. 4, 14, 24 frgd. Illustrators: Gary Taxali • Manfred Geier • Mike Reed • Burton Morris • Susan Williams • Christine Benjamin.

Creative Publications and MathScape are trademarks or registered trademarks of Creative Publications.

© 1998 Creative Publications
1300 Villa Street
Mountain View, California 94041

Printed in the United States of America.

0-7622-0223-8

1 2 3 4 5 6 7 8 9 10 . 02 01 00 99 98 97

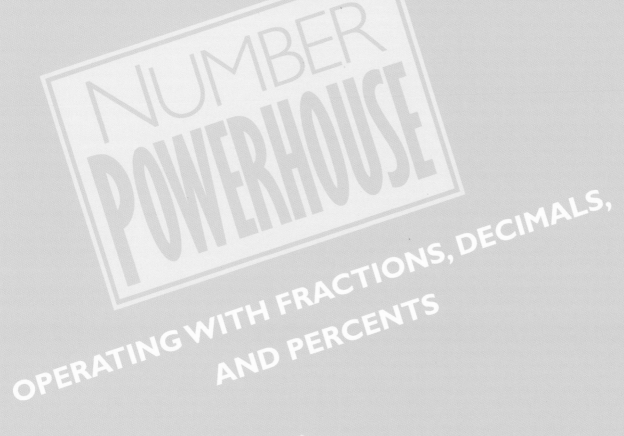

NUMBER POWERHOUSE

OPERATING WITH FRACTIONS, DECIMALS, AND PERCENTS

STUDENT GUIDE

NUMBER POWERHOUSE

OPERATING WITH FRACTIONS, DECIMALS, AND PERCENTS

$\dfrac{1}{10}$

0.1

10%

MathScape
SEEING AND THINKING
MATHEMATICALLY

How can you use your own number sense to solve problems involving integers, fractions, decimals, and percents?

NUMBER
POWERHOUSE

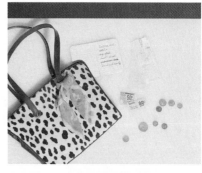

PHASE**ONE**
Integer Power

Your estimation skills and your ability to find the exact answers—using mental math, paper and pencil, or a calculator—are important in becoming a number powerhouse. In this phase, you will develop these skills with whole-number operations and use cubes to investigate rules for signed-number addition and subtraction.

PHASE**TWO**
Fraction Power

Many different strategies can be used to add, subtract, multiply, and divide fractions and mixed numbers. Solving these problems with paper and pencil using the rules you may have learned is one strategy. Other strategies are mental math and estimation, which you will explore in depth in this phase.

PHASE**THREE**
Decimal and Percent Power

In this phase, you will investigate decimals and percents. To help you figure out just where to place the decimal point when adding, subtracting, multiplying, and dividing decimals, you will use estimation and mental math. By using what you know about 50%, 10%, and 1%, you will be able to calculate the percents of any number.

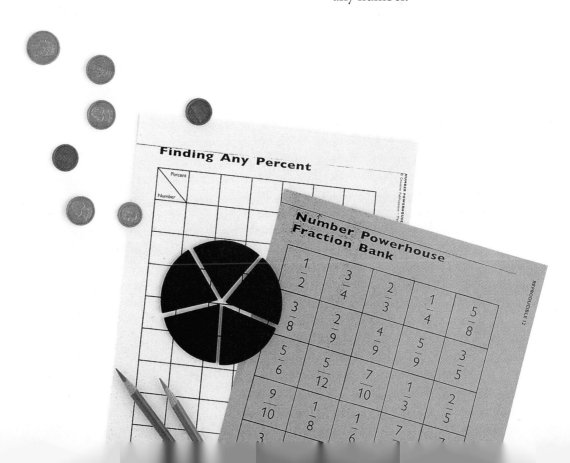

PHASE ONE

The mathematics that people need to use in everyday situations sometimes can be done with pencil and paper. But is that always the only and best way to go about adding, subtracting, multiplying, or dividing?

Estimation, mental arithmetic, and the calculator are also important tools for solving everyday problems. The most powerful method is the one that is most efficient and effective for the problem situation.

Integer Power

WHAT'S THE MATH?

Investigations in this section focus on:

COMPUTATION

- Understanding whole numbers and integers

- Adding, subtracting, multiplying, and dividing whole numbers

- Adding and subtracting integers

- Using paper and pencil, calculator, and mental math to get exact answers with whole numbers and integers

ESTIMATION

- Using estimation to check whether or not results are reasonable

- Understanding why an order of operations is necessary

1 Start with What You Know

You have known how to add, subtract, multiply, and divide whole numbers for a long time. But what do you *really* know about these operations? Here you will explore some useful ways to estimate and calculate answers to whole-number problems.

Play the "What MUST Be True?" Game

How much can you find out about an answer without doing calculations?

Sometimes it is more important to be able to give a quick estimate for an answer than to find the exact result. Try out your estimation skills as you play the "What MUST Be True?" Game.

1 Work with your group to write four problems that are difficult to solve quickly. Each problem should use a different operation: addition, subtraction, multiplication, or division. For each problem, write the following:

a. three statements that you know MUST be true about the answer to this problem

b. one statement about the answer that you know MUST be false

Scramble the true and false statements for a problem, so that the false one isn't always last. This will make your classmates work harder to find your false statement.

2 Exchange your group's problems and statements with another group. Figure out which statements for each problem MUST be true and which one MUST be false.

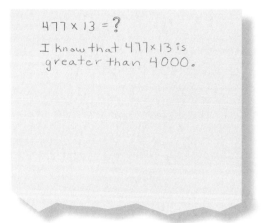

$477 \times 13 = ?$

I know that 477×13 is greater than 4000.

Use Different Methods to Solve Problems

Sometimes you need to know the exact answer to an arithmetic problem. However, there is more than one way to find a sum (or difference, product, or quotient)!

What are some different ways to calculate answers to arithmetic problems?

Calculate the answer to each problem in two different ways. Make notes about your two ways. If you use mental math to solve any of the problems without using pencil and paper, write down the thinking you used.

Problem 1	Problem 2	Problem 3	Problem 4
$6{,}413 + 9{,}892$	$12{,}348 - 4{,}837$	$147 \div 22$	713×19

Why do different methods produce the same answer?

Write About Estimation and Exact Answers

Write your own problems that can be solved by adding, subtracting, multiplying, or dividing.

- Write one problem for which it makes sense to estimate a solution.

- Write another problem for which it makes more sense to find an exact answer.

Solve each problem and describe how you found your answer.

hot **words** | whole numbers
estimate

Homework

page 34

2 Follow the Laws of Order

Order matters when you're putting on your shoes and socks, baking a cake, or setting a VCR to record your favorite program. You will see how the order in which you do addition, subtraction, multiplication, and division also makes a difference.

Evaluate an Expression in Different Ways

How does the order in which you perform operations affect the answer?

In the steps below, you will investigate different ways of evaluating the same expression. After you complete step 2, stop and participate in a class discussion before going on to step 3.

1 Use your calculator to evaluate the following expression: $14 \div 2 - 4 + 1 \times 6 \div 3 \times 2 + 10$. Enter the numbers and operation symbols from left to right. Press the $\boxed{=}$ key only after you enter the entire expression. Record your answer.

2 Try to figure out in what order the calculator evaluated the expression in step 1. Describe what you think is actually going on "inside" the calculator. Hint: One way to discover the order of operations a calculator uses is to record the number your calculator shows each time you press an operation sign.

3 Evaluate the expression in step 1 in a way that is different from the way you think your calculator did it. Explain your answer.

4 Exchange papers with a partner.

a. Try to figure out what was going on inside your partner's calculator.

b. Try to figure out how your partner evaluated the expression in a different way.

c. Do you agree with the two ways your partner evaluated the expression? Why?

Use the Order of Operations

What's the answer to a problem, such as $5 + 2 \times 3$, that has no parentheses to tell you which operation to do first? If you add first, then the answer you get is 21. If you multiply first, then the answer is 11. Mathematicians have developed a set of rules so that everyone will get the same answer. These rules are shown in the box below.

1 Use the order of operations to evaluate the expression shown below. Then use parentheses to get as many different answers as possible for the expression.

$22 + 8 \div 4 - 3 \times 7$

2 Write as many expressions as you can that give each of the following answers:

a. 18   **b.** 50   **c.** 36

How can you use the order of operations to evaluate expressions?

The Order of Operations

1. Evaluate expressions in parentheses.

2. Evaluate powers.

3. Do multiplication and division from left to right.

4. Do addition and subtraction from left to right.

For example, you would evaluate $32 - (5 + 3) \times 5 \div 2^2$ as follows:

$32 - (5 + 3) \times 5 \div 2^2$	Evaluate the expression in parentheses.
$32 - 8 \times 5 \div 2^2$	Evaluate the power.
$32 - 8 \times 5 \div 4$	Do the multiplication before the division, since it is further to the left.
$32 - 40 \div 4$	Do division before addition.
$32 - 10$	
22	

hot **words**   order of operations
powers

 Homework

 page 35

3 Know How to Read the Signs

You know how to add and subtract positive numbers. But what happens when negative numbers are mixed in? Here you will try showing numbers with "positive" and "negative" cubes to think about these problems.

Find Rules for Adding Integers

How can you develop rules for adding positive and negative numbers?

The handout Using Cubes to Add and Subtract Integers shows how you can use cubes to model adding with integers.

1 Write two example problems for each of these possible combinations:

   a. Positive + Positive   **b.** Positive + Negative

   c. Negative + Positive   **d.** Negative + Negative

2 Use cubes to experiment with the eight problems you have written. For each problem, sketch the cubes and write the equation.

3 Think about the equations you wrote and sketched. Write a set of rules that someone could follow when adding positive and negative numbers. Be sure your rules work for all problems with positive and negative numbers.

What Are Integers?

Integers are whole numbers (0, 1, 2, 3, 4, 5, ...) and their opposites. We call the whole numbers positive numbers. We call their opposites negative numbers. Zero is not positive and it is not negative. The figure below shows how integers appear on the number line.

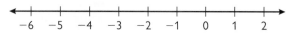

$$-6 \quad -5 \quad -4 \quad -3 \quad -2 \quad -1 \quad 0 \quad 1 \quad 2$$

Find Rules for Subtracting Integers

You have found some rules for adding positive and negative numbers. Now you will create a set of rules for subtracting integers. The handout Using Cubes to Add and Subtract Integers shows how you can use cubes to model subtracting with integers.

1 List all of the possible combinations to subtract positive and negative numbers.

2 Experiment with cubes until you can write a rule for each possible combination. Be sure each rule tells how to find both the number and the sign of the answer.

This is 4   minus -3.

There is +7 left!

3 Choose one especially tricky problem. Sketch the cubes and write about your solution.

How can you develop rules for subtracting positive and negative numbers?

Write About Addition and Subtraction Rules

Summarize the rules for adding and subtracting signed numbers. Make sure you include the following:

- Write the rules in your own words.

- Be sure you give rules for all positive and negative numbers.

hot **words** | positive integers
negative integers

Homework

 page 36

4 The Problems Are All Yours

Some game shows give you an answer and ask you to provide the question. But does every answer have just *one* question? You will be given some "answers," and you will write as many addition and subtraction equations as you can for each of them. Then you will write a test about everything you have learned in this unit so far.

If you are given an answer, can you write integer addition and subtraction equations with that result?

Represent Integers in Different Ways

Here are some equations for which the answer is positive 4:

$2 + 2 = 4$, and $6 - 2 = 4$, and $-6 + 10 = 4$

Can you come up with a list of equations for which the answer is positive 4?

1 First make a list of addition equations whose answer is positive 4. Then make a list of subtraction equations whose answer is positive 4.

  a. Use cubes to help you get started.

  b. Look for patterns that can help you write more equations.

$$3 + 1 = 4$$

$$-1 + 5 = 4$$

2 Make a list of addition equations and a list of subtraction equations for each of these answers.

  a. -5 **b.** 0 **c.** 13 **d.** -12

Write a Test About Operations

Here's your chance—now, *you* get to write a test! Your test shouldn't be so easy that everyone gets all the answers right away, but it shouldn't be so hard that no one can do it.

There are six types of problems that should be on your test. Include at least one of each of the following problems:

1 An integer addition problem.

2 An integer subtraction problem.

3 A problem that involves addition, subtraction, multiplication, or division of whole numbers. In this problem, ask for the exact answer. Don't make the numbers too easy! There should be at least two or three digits.

4 A true/false problem about a sum, difference, product, or quotient of whole numbers. This problem should involve estimation skills, so be sure the numbers have at least two or three digits.

5 A problem that uses the order of operations rule. It should involve parentheses, powers, addition, subtraction, multiplication, and division. This must be a multiple-choice problem with at least four answer choices.

6 A writing problem that asks students to tell about something they have learned.

Prepare an answer key for your test. This will help you make sure your test isn't too easy or too difficult!

How can you write good test questions?

hot words | whole numbers
integers

Ho**mework**

page 37

PHASE TWO

In this phase you will be exploring fractions and mixed numbers. Using estimation and mental math to help you make sense of adding, subtracting, multiplying, and dividing fractions and mixed numbers will help you develop your own "number powerhouse" strategies.

Tools such as Fraction Circles and sketches can help you think about fraction operations. Why do you think they might be useful?

Fraction Power

WHAT'S THE MATH?

Investigations in this section focus on:

COMPUTATION

- Understanding fractions and mixed numbers

- Adding, subtracting, multiplying, and dividing fractions and mixed numbers

- Using paper and pencil, calculator, and mental math to get exact answers with fractions and mixed numbers

ESTIMATION

- Using estimation to check whether or not the results make sense

5 Pluses and Minuses

Quick—what's $\frac{3}{8} + \frac{5}{12}$**?** Although you may have learned rules for adding and subtracting fractions, those rules can be hard to remember or use quickly. Do you think you could solve this problem mentally? In this lesson, you will use what makes sense to you to develop your own number powerhouse strategies.

Use Thinking Strategies to Add Fractions

How can you solve fraction addition problems by using logical thinking?

You should have a set of fractions the class has chosen from the handout Number Powerhouse Fraction Bank. Follow the steps below to create fraction addition problems and find strategies that make sense to you for solving the problems. Remember, there is not just one "right way" to solve problems like these.

1 From the set of fractions your class agreed on, choose pairs of fractions to write fraction addition problems with. Try to challenge yourself by writing some addition problems that you think might be hard to solve.

2 Set aside any rules you might have learned and look for other ways to think about these problems that make sense to you. Use what you know about fractions.

3 Record your thinking for each problem. You may want to draw sketches to explain your thinking. The Fraction Circles are available to use. You will need to be prepared to give a Powerhouse Presentation to your classmates about your way of solving these problems.

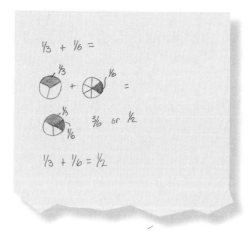

$$\frac{1}{3} + \frac{1}{6} =$$
$$\frac{1}{3} + \frac{1}{6} = \quad \frac{3}{6} \text{ or } \frac{1}{2}$$
$$\frac{1}{3} + \frac{1}{6} = \frac{1}{2}$$

Use Thinking Strategies to Subtract Fractions

Now that you have had some experience with new ways of thinking about addition problems, see what you can come up with for subtraction.

Can you solve fraction subtraction problems by using logical thinking?

1 From the set of fractions your class agreed on, choose pairs of fractions to write fraction subtraction problems with. What you know about comparing fractions will be important. The problems you write should involve subtracting a lesser fraction from a greater fraction.

2 Once again, set aside any rules you might have learned. Look for other ways to think about these problems that make sense to you and make it easier to solve the problems mentally.

3 Record your thinking for each problem. You may want to draw sketches to explain your thinking. The Fraction Circles are available to use. You will need to be prepared to give a Powerhouse Presentation on your way of solving these problems to your classmates.

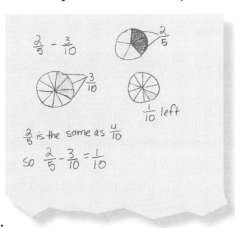

Write About Fraction Addition and Subtraction

Write about the strategies you used to add and subtract fractions mentally.

- Include an example of an addition problem and a subtraction problem you can solve mentally. Tell how you solved it.

- If you had different methods for different types of problems, explain how you decided which method to use.

hot **words** | fractions
equivalent fractions

HW**omework**

page 38

6 Multiplication Made Easy

MULTIPLYING FRACTIONS

If you understand the question behind a fraction problem, you can figure out the exact answer or make a mental estimate. With fraction multiplication, the key is thinking about groups. In this lesson, you will use this kind of thinking to get exact answers to easy fraction multiplication problems and estimates for more difficult ones.

Multiply Fractions by Thinking About the Question

How can you use what you know about the question asked by a fraction multiplication problem to solve the problem?

You will look for exact answers to fraction multiplication problems that can be solved mentally by just thinking about the question behind the problem. The secret is to read the multiplication symbol as "groups of." Follow these steps for each pair of fractions the class has chosen from the handout Number Powerhouse Fraction Bank.

1 Write out the question asked by the multiplication problem. The example in the box What's the Multiplication Question? can help you think about the question.

2 Use the question to find the exact answer to the problem mentally. You may find it helpful to use Fraction Circles or sketches to help with your thinking.

3 Use sketches and words to explain your thinking. Be prepared to share your results and your thinking with the class.

What's the Multiplication Question?

$3 \times 6 =$
What's 3 groups of 6?
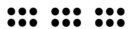

$3 \times \frac{1}{6} =$
What's 3 groups of $\frac{1}{6}$?

$\frac{1}{2} \times \frac{1}{6} =$
What's half of a group of $\frac{1}{6}$?

$\frac{1}{4} \times \frac{1}{3} =$
What's a fourth of a group of $\frac{1}{3}$?
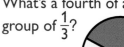

Estimate Answers to Multiplication Problems

For problems like $\frac{3}{4} \times \frac{7}{15}$ it would be difficult to find an exact answer mentally. But you can come up with an estimate by thinking about what you know for sure.

1 Choose pairs of fractions from the handout Number Powerhouse Fraction Bank.

2 For each pair of fractions, write a multiplication problem and list the things you know for sure.

3 Estimate the answer to the problem.

> what can you say for sure?
>
> Here are some "for sure" statements I can make about 3/4 × 7/15:
>
> • It asks the question "What's 3/4 of a group of 7/15?"
>
> • It's less than 7/15.
>
> • Half of 7/15 would be 3 and a half fifteenths, so it's more than that.

How can you estimate answers to problems that are not easy to solve mentally?

Write About How Estimates Compare to Exact Answers

For each fraction problem you answered with an estimation, calculate the exact answer by following the rules for multiplying fractions that you reviewed in class discussion. Write about how the estimate and the exact answer compare.

- How do the "for sure" statements you made compare to the exact answer?

- Can you think of situations in which it is useful to be able to estimate the answer to a fraction multiplication problem?

- When is it useful to be able to calculate an exact answer?

hot **words** | numerator denominator

Homework
page 39

7 The Great Fraction Divide

As with fraction multiplication, some problems that involve dividing fractions are easy to solve if you understand the question being asked. When you are a "number powerhouse," you can do more than just solve the problems. You can also explain what the answer means!

Divide Fractions by Thinking About the Question

How can you use what you know about multiplication to solve fraction division problems mentally?

In this investigation, you will look for exact answers to fraction division problems that can be solved mentally by just thinking about the question behind the problem. Follow these steps for each pair of fractions the class has chosen to work with from the handout Number Powerhouse Fraction Bank.

1 Write the question being asked by the division problem. The example in the box below can help you think about the question.

2 Use the question to find the exact answer to the problem mentally. You may find it helpful to use Fraction Circles or sketches to help with your thinking.

3 Use   sketches and words to explain your thinking. Be   prepared to share your results and your thinking with the class.

What's the Division Question?

$$\frac{1}{6} \div \frac{1}{2}$$

How many halves are there in $\frac{1}{6}$?

There is one-third of $\frac{1}{2}$ in $\frac{1}{6}$.

Estimate Answers to Fraction Division Problems

For problems like $\frac{3}{4} \div \frac{1}{7}$, it can be difficult to find an exact answer mentally. But you can come up with an estimate by thinking about what you know for sure.

1 Choose pairs of fractions from the Number Powerhouse Fraction Bank.

2 For each pair of fractions, write a division problem and list the things you know for sure.

3 Estimate the answer to the problem.

How can you estimate answers to fraction division problems that are not easy to solve mentally?

Write About Estimate and Exact Answer

For each fraction problem you answered with an estimation, calculate the exact answer by following the rules for dividing fractions that you reviewed in class discussion. Write about how the estimate and the exact answer compare.

- How do the "for sure" statements you made compare to the exact answer?

- Can you think of situations in which it is useful to be able to estimate the answer to a fraction division problem?

- When is it useful to be able to calculate an exact answer?

$$\frac{3}{4} \div \frac{1}{7}$$

How many $\frac{1}{7}$ths are there in $\frac{3}{4}$?

- There are less than 7, because there are 7 sevenths in 1.

- There are $3\frac{1}{2}$ sevenths in $\frac{1}{2}$ so it's more than that. Actually, it's halfway between $3\frac{1}{2}$ sevenths and 7 sevenths. Maybe about 5 sevenths.

hot **words** | inverse reciprocal

Homework
page 40

8 Powerhouse Show-Off

ADDING,
SUBTRACTING,
MULTIPLYING,
AND DIVIDING
FRACTIONS

What about adding, subtracting, multiplying, and dividing with mixed numbers? After you investigate problems involving mixed numbers, it will be your turn to be the teacher. You will write true and false statements about a set of fraction problems and summarize what you have learned by writing a Number Powerhouse Guide to fraction operations.

How can you use what you know about operating with fractions to solve problems involving mixed numbers?

Investigate Operations with Mixed Numbers

The problems in the box below involve mixed numbers. Use what you know about fraction operations to think about and solve the problems.

1 For each problem in the box, write at least one statement about the answer that you know must be true. Do this without solving the problem.

2 Which of the problems can you solve mentally? Choose at least two problems you think you can solve mentally. For each problem, write the answer and describe your thinking.

3 For the problems that you did not solve mentally, find solutions using pencil and paper. Record your work.

Mixed-Number Problems			
a. $1\frac{1}{2} + 1\frac{1}{3}$	b. $3\frac{1}{4} - 1\frac{1}{2}$	c. $2\frac{5}{8} + 3\frac{1}{4}$	d. $4\frac{3}{10} - 3\frac{3}{5}$
e. $2\frac{2}{3} \times 3\frac{1}{2}$	f. $1\frac{3}{4} \div 2\frac{1}{2}$	g. $3\frac{1}{2} \div \frac{1}{4}$	h. $\frac{1}{6} \div 2\frac{1}{3}$

Write True and False Statements

You will come up with true and false statements about fraction problems to be used for a class test. Think about what you know for sure about the answer to each fraction problem.

1 Choose a pair of fractions from the handout Number Powerhouse Fraction Bank. Use the pair of fractions to write an addition, subtraction, multiplication, and division problem. Be sure to choose a pair of fractions that will be challenging enough for your classmates.

2 Write three statements for each problem. Two of the statements should be true, and one should be false. Use the following words to start your three statements:
   a. The answer is greater than _____.
   b. The answer is less than _____.
   c. The answer is equal to _____.

3 Be prepared to present a problem to the class. Your classmates will try to pick out the false statement.

How can you use what you know about estimating answers to fraction problems to write true and false statements?

Write Your Own Number Powerhouse Guide

Think about what you've learned about adding, subtracting, multiplying, and dividing fractions. Write your own Number Powerhouse Guide to operating with fractions using these guidelines.

- Use a set of four problems as your examples.

- Describe ways to think about some of the problems to come up with an answer mentally.

- Describe ways to think about some of the problems to come up with an estimate.

- Show ways to solve some of the problems by following rules and using pencil and paper.

Can you find the False statement for each problem?

$1\frac{1}{3} + \frac{3}{4}$
a. The answer is greater than $1\frac{3}{4}$.
b. The answer is less than 2.
c. The answer is equal to $2\frac{1}{2}$.

$1\frac{1}{3} - \frac{3}{4}$
a. The answer is greater than $\frac{1}{3}$.
b. The answer is less than $\frac{1}{2}$.
c. The answer is equal to $\frac{1}{3} + \frac{1}{4}$.

$1\frac{1}{3} \times \frac{3}{4}$
a. The answer is greater than $\frac{3}{4}$.
b. The answer is less than 1.
c. The answer is equal to $\frac{9}{12} + \frac{3}{4}$.

$1\frac{1}{3} \div \frac{3}{4}$
a. The answer is greater than $1\frac{1}{3}$.
b. The answer is less than 2.
c. The answer is equal to 1.

hot words mixed number
improper fraction

Homework
_____
page 41

PHASE THREE

In this phase you will be making sense of decimal operations as you think about money and play a game. Figuring out where the decimal point goes when you are adding, subtracting, multipying, and dividing decimals is important. You will become an expert at figuring out the percent of any number, too!

Think about how decimals and percents are used in everyday experience. How can mental math and estimation help you come up with quick answers?

Decimal and Percent Power

WHAT'S THE MATH?

Investigations in this section focus on:

COMPUTATION

- Understanding decimals and percents

- Adding, subtracting, multiplying, and dividing decimals and understanding where the decimal point should be placed

- Using paper and pencil, calculator, and mental math to get exact answers with decimals and percents

ESTIMATION

- Using estimation to determine where the decimal point goes

- Using estimation to check whether or not the results make sense

Making Cents of Decimals

INVESTIGATING
DECIMAL ADDITION
AND SUBTRACTION

When you buy something and get change, how do you know the total was right and that you got the correct change? Thinking about money helps you make sense of adding and subtracting decimals. Then, by estimating and using mental math for adding and subtracting decimals, you can determine where to place the decimal point without a doubt!

Use Decimals to Make Change

How can you use decimal addition and subtraction to calculate change?

When you make change, you have to solve two problems: How much should the customer get back, and what's the best way to give the change? In this investigation, you will solve both of these problems.

1 For each receipt shown, find the amount of change you should give mentally (by doing the math in your head) and write it down.

2 For each receipt, use pencil and paper to solve the problem. Write the entire equations. Check this answer against your estimations.

3 No one wants a pocket full of pennies and nickels! Tell in writing how you would give the change to the customer using the *fewest* possible coins and/or dollar bills for each receipt.

4 Check your answers to item 3 by writing and solving an addition problem in which you add up the change for each receipt.

| apple | $0.50 |
| CASH GIVEN | $0.75 |

| small drink | $0.74 |
| CASH GIVEN | $0.80 |

| laundry detergent | $3.20 |
| CASH GIVEN | $5.00 |

| 15 lbs. dog food | $21.68 |
| CASH GIVEN | $22.00 |

| paperback book | $7.36 |
| CASH GIVEN | $12.41 |

Make Decimal Decisions

The placement of the decimal point can make a big difference, such as the difference between an answer of 140.57 and an answer of 14.057 or 1.4057. In this investigation you will use mental math and estimation skills to determine the placement of the decimal point and to identify errors in decimal addition and subtraction problems.

Without recalculating, how can you tell where the decimal point belongs in an answer, or whether an error was made in the calculation?

1 Copy items **a** through **d** shown below. Use your estimation skills to locate the decimal point in each answer. (You may need to add one or more zeros to the answer.) For each problem, write a short explanation telling how you decided where the decimal point should go.

a. $15 + 25 = 400$

$1.5 + 2.5 = 400$

$0.15 + 0.25 = 400$

b. $0.573 - 0.335 = 238$

$5.73 - 3.35 = 238$

$57.3 - 33.5 = 238$

c. $104.87 + 245.002 = 349872$ **d.** $14.4 - 33.81 = 1941$

2 Each problem below shows a correct solution and an incorrect solution that could result if someone wasn't careful about the decimal point when adding or subtracting. For each problem, use mental arithmetic or estimation to figure out which is the correct solution. Then write about the error someone might have made to arrive at the incorrect solution.

a. For the problem $0.412 + 0.3$, is the correct solution 0.712 or 0.415?

b. For the problem $0.5 - 0.01$, is the correct solution 0.4 or 0.49?

3 Make up two decimal addition problems and two decimal subtraction problems of your own. Use the calculator to find the answer to each problem. Check your answers to see that they are reasonable. Then write about some errors to watch out for when using a calculator to add or subtract decimals.

hot **words** | addition subtraction

HW**omework**

page 42

10 The Cost Is Correct

**INVESTIGATING
DECIMAL
MULTIPLICATION
AND DIVISION**

You have learned where the decimal point belongs in problems that involve adding and subtracting. Do you think it would be the same for multiplication and division problems? You will play a game that shows what you know about decimal multiplication and division, and then use your estimation skills to figure out where the decimal point goes.

Play "The Cost Is Correct" Game

How can you think out answers to decimal multiplication and division problems?

Your teacher will give you a handout with the rules for the Cost Is Correct game. In the handout Rules for the Cost Is Correct, there are two questions to answer: What's the cost? and What's the weight? This is a mental math game—no calculators today. First you will play some practice rounds. In your practice rounds, check your answers to make sure your strategies are working.

1 Play Practice Rounds 1, 2, and 3, using the information given below to answer the question, "What's the Cost?"

2 Play Practice Rounds 4, 5, and 6, using the information given below to answer the question, "What's the Weight?"

3 After your practice rounds, play the game using the numbers the teacher gives you. This time you will have to figure out which question to answer, as described in the handout Rules for the Cost Is Correct game.

What's the Cost and Weight?

What's the Cost?	What's the Weight?
Practice Round 1: 4 pounds of raisins	Practice Round 4: $2.80
Practice Round 2: 1.5 pounds of raisins	Practice Round 5: $3.50
Practice Round 3: 2.75 pounds of granola	Practice Round 6: $0.75

Locate the Decimal Point

If your calculator tells you that $14.27 \times 2.2 = 313.94$, did you press the right keys? Use the problems in the box below. Follow these steps to try to figure out where the decimal point goes when you multiply and divide decimals.

How can you tell where the decimal point belongs in an answer?

1 Copy the problems in Set 1. Use your estimation skills to locate the decimal point in each answer. (You may need to add one or more zeros to the answer.) Then solve the problems on the calculator to see how close your estimates were.

2 Calculate the answers to the problems shown in Set 2. For each problem, write a short explanation telling how you decided where the decimal point should go. Then check your answers on the calculator.

Write About Decimal Dilemmas

Now it's time to return to Decimal Dilemmas. Use the handout Decimal Dilemmas to explain your strategy for each question. Be ready to share your strategies.

Decimal Problems

Set 1	Set 2
a. $21 \times 11 = 231$	**a.** $6.2 \div 0.8 = $ _____
$2.1 \times 11 = 231$	**b.** $74.23 \times 10.877 = $ _____
$2.1 \times 1.1 = 231$	**c.** $89.4 \times 105.765 = $ _____
b. $870 \div 2.5 = 348$	**d.** $123.42 \div 0.217 = $ _____
$870 \div 25 = 348$	
$8.70 \div 2.5 = 348$	
$870 \div 0.25 = 348$	
c. $92 \times 1.5 = 1380$	
$0.92 \times 0.15 = 1380$	
d. $0.6 \div 0.3 = 2000$	
$0.06 \div 0.3 = 2000$	
$0.6 \div 0.03 = 2000$	

hot **words** | multiplication
division

omework

 page 43

11 Percent Powerhouse

FINDING A PERCENT OF A NUMBER

Amaze your friends! Impress your parents! By using simple percents like 50%, 10%, and 1%, you can calculate percents of any number!

Find Important Percents

How can you mentally find 50%, 10%, and 1% of a number?

Three of the most important percents are 50%, 10%, and 1%. Fortunately, these are percents that you can calculate quickly. As you work with the lists of numbers your class comes up with, you will discover strategies for finding 50%, 10%, and 1% of a number.

1 Work with List A.

a. Choose one number from List A. On your own, find 50%, 10%, and 1% of that number. Use any strategy that makes sense to you. Write down each answer and explain how you found it.

b. On your own, find 50%, 10%, and 1% of another number on List A. See if you can use a strategy that is different from the one you used to find percents of the first number. Look for patterns in your answers.

c. Share your answers and strategies with your partner. Discuss any patterns you see.

d. With your partner, find 50%, 10%, and 1% of any numbers on List A that you have not worked with. Remember to write down your answers and strategies.

2 Work with List B.

a. With your partner, choose at least three numbers in List B. Find 50%, 10%, and 1% of each number.

b. When you have finished, write a short paragraph on your own explaining how you can quickly find 50%, 10%, and 1% of *any* number.

Find 1% to 99% of Any Number

In this investigation, you will use your ability to find 50%, 10%, and 1% of a number to calculate other percents. Use the table in the handout Finding Any Percent and follow these steps with a partner.

1 Across the top row of the table, fill in any six percents. (Do not include 1%, 10%, or 50%.) In the left-hand column, fill in at least six whole numbers from 25 to 2,000. Include two-, three-, and four-digit numbers.

2 Complete the table. When you cannot find an exact answer, give a good estimate. Circle any answers that are not exact. (Do not use a calculator for this part of the investigation.)

3 Exchange your table with another pair of students. Use a calculator to check their answers. Keep track of any errors you find. If an answer is an estimate, think about whether it is "close enough" to the exact answer before you mark it as an error. Meet with the other pair and report any errors that you think you found. Then exchange tables again so that you have your original table.

4 Check any answers in your original table that may be errors. Remember that your original answer may be correct!

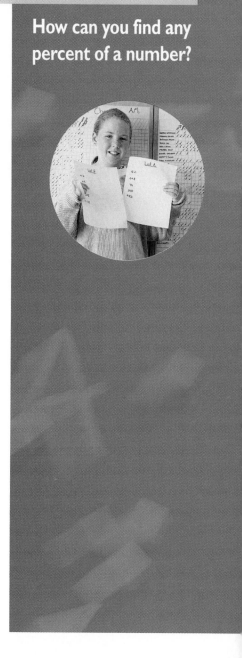

How can you find any percent of a number?

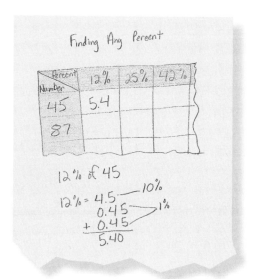

Finding Any Percent

Percent / Number	12%	25%	42%
45	5.4		
87			

12% of 45

12% = 4.5 — 10%
      0.45 ⟩ 1%
    + 0.45
    ———
      5.40

hot **words** | percent
multiplication

Homework

page 44

12 Powerhouse Challenge

You have investigated operations with whole numbers, integers, fractions, and decimals, and you have found ways to calculate a percent of a number. Now it's time to use all of the calculation and estimation skills you have learned.

Solve Percent Problems

How can you use percents to solve real-world problems?

Your strategies for finding the percent of a number can help you in real-world situations. For each situation, write down your answer and explain how you found it. If you cannot give an exact answer, make a good estimate.

1. Tips: An average tip for a waiter is 15% of the amount on the bill. Suppose your family's dinner bill comes to $48. How much would a 15% tip be?

2. Sale Price: CD Conspiracy is having a "25% off" sale. If a CD usually costs $12.00, how much would you save? What would the sale price be?

3. **BLOWOUT** Sale Price: CD Conspiracy decides to hold a "45% off" sale! During this sale, how much would you save on a $12.00 CD? What is the sale price?

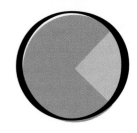

4. Income tax: In 1996, 28% of Selma's total salary went to federal and state income tax. If she earned $35,128.00, how much income tax did she pay?

5. Statistics: In 1990, 87% of the population of Utah lived in urban areas (cities and towns). If Utah's 1990 population was 1,461,037, how many people lived in urban areas?

Close In on the Targets

Copy each equation below. Using only the numerals 1 through 6, fill in the boxes to come as close as you can to each target number. Then write how far off you were from the target number. You may use each numeral only *once* in any equation. When you have finished, find your total score. Your score depends on how close you get!

Can you arrange digits in an equation to give an exact answer?

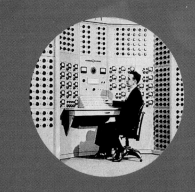

How Far Off?

a. $\square\square \times \square\square = 515$ _____

b. $\square\square - \square\square\square = -86$ _____

c. $\dfrac{\square}{\square} + \dfrac{\square}{\square} = 1$ _____

(Hint: Convert your answer to decimal form to make this calculation easier.)

d. $\dfrac{\square}{\square} \div \dfrac{\square}{\square} = 1$ _____

e. $\square\square.\square\square + \square.\square = 33$ _____

f. $\square\square \times \square.\square = 42$ _____

g. $\square\square\% \text{ of } \square\square\square = 62$ _____

Total difference from targets $\boxed{}$

Write About Operations

A student who is about to begin this unit has some questions for you. So that you don't give away too much, choose only *two* of the student's questions to answer.

- My teacher says that it is important to add, subtract, multiply, and divide in the right order. Is this true? Why does the order matter?

- What are the most important things to know about adding and subtracting signed numbers?

- I've heard that it is hard to add and subtract fractions. Is it? What did you learn that helped you?

- Someone told me that you can find percents in your head. How do you do it?

hot **words** | percent fractions

Homework

page 45

Start with What You Know

Applying Skills

For items **1–8,** write an estimate for each problem. Then calculate the answer for each problem and check to see how close your estimate is to the answer.

1. 128 + 54   **2.** 78 ÷ 3

3. 32 × 18   **4.** 564 − 208

5. 7,986 + 4,062   **6.** 6,761 − 4,308

7. 63 × 21   **8.** 8,964 ÷ 9

For items **9** and **10,** write down which statements are true for each problem without calculating the exact answer.

9. 3,862 ÷ 92

   a. The answer is 44.

   b. The answer is not less than 40.

   c. The answer is greater than 35.

   d. The answer is less than 50.

10. 452 × 162

   a. The answer is greater than 40,000.

   b. The answer is less than 100,000.

   c. The answer is not less than 50,000.

   d. The answer is 53,000.

For items **11–14,** find the exact answer for each problem using two different methods. Remember to show your work. If you use mental math or sketches, record the thinking and any sketches you used.

11. 156 added to 28   **12.** 47 times 22

13. 96 divided by 4   **14.** 451 minus 380

Extending Concepts

Use this information for items **15** and **16:** Beatrice is putting new carpet in her 1,692 square foot apartment. The cost is $23.00 for 3 square feet.

15. Estimate and calculate the cost of putting carpet in the entire apartment.

16. Explain how you estimated the cost. Did your method come close? Why or why not? If it did not, how could you improve your method?

Writing

Use the following to answer item **17:** Benji is planning a vacation to Mali in western Africa to visit the ancient salt center, Timbuktu. The table shows his estimates of expenses for the trip. He thinks he can pay for everything with $3,000.

Cost per Unit	Estimate
One-way airfare at $928	$1,000
Meals @ $5/meal (36 meals)	100
Hotel @ $35/night (12 nights)	600
Jeep rental @ $75/day (12 days)	1,000
Gas @ $30/tank (3 tanks)	100
Spending money	200
TOTAL	$3,000

17. Write a letter to Benji telling whether or not you agree that he can pay for everything with $3,000. Include your results from checking Benji's estimates and your calculations of the exact costs.

Following the Laws of Order

Applying Skills

Use the order of operations on page 9 to evaluate the expressions in items 1–14.

1. $(9 \div 3) \times 2^3 - (1 + 2)$

2. $(14 \div 2) + 3^2 \times (6 - 2)$

3. $3 + 6 - 2^2 \times (16 \div 8)$

4. $14 - (3 \times 2) \div 2 + 1$

5. $12 + 4^3 \div 2 \times 3$

6. $(12 + 4) \times (18 \div 3) + 2$

7. $(4{,}572 - 2{,}381) \times 2^8 - 681$

8. $3^9 - 6{,}072 + 43$

9. $64 \times (5^4 \div 5)$

10. $4 + 1{,}622 \times 12 + 178$

11. $179 + (6^4 \div 2) \div 6$

12. Eight times five plus twelve divided by three.

13. Sixteen divided by two plus sixty minus forty-two.

14. Forty-seven plus six divided by three plus four.

Extending Concepts

15. Explain why 30 divided by 5 can also be written as $\frac{30}{5}$. Illustrate your answer by drawing a picture of 30 divided by 5 and $\frac{30}{5}$.

16. Think about the order of operations. Give reasons why mathematicians have agreed to use this specific order. If you agree with this order, explain why it makes sense to you. If you believe another order would make more sense, write your revised order of operations and give reasons why this new method makes sense. Be sure to include pictures and/or examples.

For items **17–20,** put operations and grouping symbols into each number list to write an expression that results in the smallest whole number possible.

17. 5, 2, 4, 9, 1

18. 8, 6, 1, 7, 2

19. 3, 5, 7, 9, 2

20. 2, 4, 6, 8, 7

For items **21–24,** put operations and grouping symbols into each number list to write as many different expressions as you can that result in whole numbers.

21. 2, 3, 4, 5, 6

22. 8, 9, 5, 4, 3

23. 3, 5, 6, 2, 1

24. 7, 5, 6, 8, 9

Writing

25. Answer the letter to Dr. Math.

> Dear Dr. Math,
> I'm confused! I think that twenty-five divided by five plus two times five equals thirty-five, but my friend Cedric says it's fifteen. Now he's talking about expressions and parentheses. What is he talking about, and who is right?
> Confused Connie

Know How to Read the Signs

Applying Skills

For items **1–4,** look at the cubes shown. If pink is positive and green is negative, write a problem that the cubes show. Describe how you would solve the problem.

1.

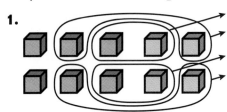

2.

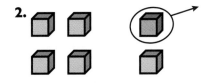

3.

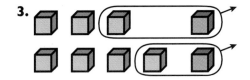

4.

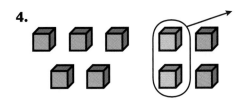

For items **5–12,** solve each problem.

5. 3 + 6   **6.** 3 + (−6)

7. (−9) + 6   **8.** 6 − (−3)

9. 4 − (−2)   **10.** (−8) − (−4)

11. 5 + 2   **12.** 10 + (−8)

Extending Concepts

13. Explain the difference between positive and negative numbers.

For items **14 and 15,** use the following: My friend Judy loves shopping at the mall. She spends an increasing amount of money each week. Three weeks ago she spent $3, two weeks ago she spent $9, and last week she spent $27. She charges everything, so she is going further into debt each time she shops.

14. Write an equation that shows how much money Judy has spent so far. Explain your thinking.

15. Today Judy decided to take a $25 sweater back to the store. Explain how this affects her debt situation.

Making Connections

Use the following information for item 16: The temperature on Monday was 40 degrees Fahrenheit. On Tuesday, the temperature went down 15 degrees. On Wednesday, the temperature fell another 35 degrees. Thursday, the temperature rose 8 degrees. Finally on Friday, the temperature increased by 16 degrees.

16. What was the temperature at the end of the week? You may want to draw a picture to show your answer.

The Problems Are All Yours

Applying Skills

1. Which of the following expressions equal 1? Explain why or why not.

   a. $3 - 2$ **b.** $1 - (-1)$

   c. $1 + 1$ **d.** $2 - (-1)$

2. Which of the following expressions equal 7? Explain why or why not.

   a. $3 + 4$ **b.** $(-2) + (-5)$

   c. $(-3) + 10$ **d.** $(-10) + 3$

3. Which of the following expressions equal 12? Explain why or why not.

   a. $(-17) + 5$ **b.** $(-8) + 20$

   c. $9 + 3$ **d.** $(-13) + 25$

For items **4–11,** write a list of at least three equations that will work for the answers given. Include addition and subtraction equations, and positive and negative numbers.

   4. 2   **5.** 3   **6.** 4

   7. 5   **8.** 11   **9.** 14

   10. 56   **11.** 37

Extending Concepts

12. Write one integer subtraction problem and calculate the answer for it. Give step-by-step instructions for solving the problem.

13. Write one problem that involves estimation and calculate the answer for it. Give step-by-step instructions for solving the problem.

14. Write one problem for which someone would have to use the order of operations. (Be sure to include parentheses, powers, addition, subtraction, multiplication, and division.) Calculate the answer for it. Give step-by-step instructions for solving the problem.

Writing

15. Answer the letter to Dr. Math.

> Dear Dr. Math,
>
> I know how to add two numbers when there are positive and negative signs, but what about adding three or more numbers? My older sister said $(-1) + 5 + 4 = 8$, but she couldn't tell me why. I'd like to know why. Can you explain this?
>
> Expressionless

Pluses and Minuses

Applying Skills

For items **1–4**, answer this question: If you combined the shaded portions of the two circles, what fraction of a circle would you have?

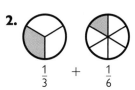

1. $\frac{1}{2} + \frac{1}{4}$ **2.** $\frac{1}{3} + \frac{1}{6}$

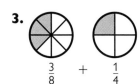

3. $\frac{3}{8} + \frac{1}{4}$ **4.** $\frac{2}{3} + \frac{1}{4}$

For items **5–8**, solve the addition problems mentally. Use sketches or words to help.

5. $\frac{1}{2} + \frac{2}{3}$ **6.** $\frac{4}{6} + \frac{3}{5}$

7. $\frac{1}{5} + \frac{1}{10}$ **8.** $\frac{1}{6} + \frac{7}{8}$

For items **9–12**, solve the subtraction problems mentally. Use sketches or words to help.

9. $\frac{5}{8} - \frac{1}{3}$ **10.** $\frac{3}{5} - \frac{1}{10}$

11. $\frac{1}{6} - \frac{1}{9}$ **12.** $\frac{2}{5} - \frac{1}{10}$

For items **13–16**, solve the problems mentally, or use paper and pencil.

13. $\frac{1}{2} - \frac{1}{4}$ **14.** $\frac{1}{12} + \frac{5}{6}$

15. $\frac{3}{10} + \frac{1}{2}$ **16.** $\frac{7}{15} - \frac{4}{15}$

Extending Concepts

17. Andrew is measuring the perimeter of a very small object. He found that it measured $\frac{1}{2}''$ on two sides and $\frac{1}{3}''$ on the other two sides. What is the perimeter of the object? Show how you solved the problem. What do you think the object might be?

18. Find two fractions whose sum is $\frac{5}{12}$ and whose difference is $\frac{1}{4}$. Explain how you figured it out.

Making Connections

For items **19–22**, use the information shown about musical notes. Draw one note that is equal to the sum of the notes in each item.

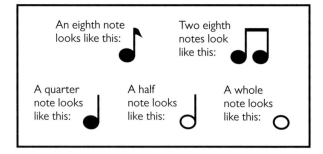

Notes in Music

An eighth note looks like this:

Two eighth notes look like this:

A quarter note looks like this:

A half note looks like this:

A whole note looks like this:

19. ♩ + ♩

20. ♩ + ♩ + ♩

21. ♫ + ♫

22. ♩ + ♩ + ♫

NUMBER POWERHOUSE HOMEWORK 5
© Creative Publications • MathScape

Multiplication Made Easy

Applying Skills

For the problems in items **1–6**, use words to write the multiplication question. Then find the exact answer using mental math. You may use sketches and words to help.

1. $\frac{1}{3} \times \frac{1}{6}$ **2.** $\frac{1}{6} \times \frac{7}{8}$ **3.** $\frac{1}{2} \times \frac{3}{8}$

4. $4 \times \frac{3}{4}$ **5.** $\frac{1}{4} \times \frac{1}{6}$ **6.** $\frac{1}{3} \times \frac{2}{3}$

For items **7–9**, estimate the answer for each problem and write about what you can say for sure.

7. $\frac{1}{4} \times \frac{9}{10}$ **8.** $\frac{2}{3} \times \frac{16}{17}$ **9.** $\frac{3}{4} \times \frac{6}{11}$

For items **10–12**, solve the problems by following the rules for multiplying fractions that you reviewed in class.

10. $\frac{2}{7} \times \frac{3}{5}$ **11.** $\frac{1}{12} \times \frac{9}{10}$ **12.** $\frac{4}{5} \times \frac{7}{15}$

13. Vince says he spends $\frac{1}{3}$ of his 24-hour day sleeping and another $\frac{1}{4}$ of his day in school. How much time does he have for other activities? Explain your answer.

Extending Concepts

15. Wendy's uncle has decided to help her pay for her guitar lessons for the next three years. The lessons cost $850 per year. Plans A–C show how much Wendy's uncle would pay. Choose the plan that is the best deal for Wendy. Explain your thinking.

Plan A: Year 1: $\frac{3}{5}$ of the tuition
Year 2: $\frac{11}{20}$ of the tuition
Year 3: $\frac{6}{15}$ of the tuition

Plan B: Year 1: all of the tuition
Year 2: $\frac{7}{10}$ of the tuition
Year 3: none of the tuition

Plan C: $\frac{8}{25}$ of the total tuition for all three years

Making Connections

Use the following for items **15–17**:
The table below shows the top ten favorite words to use and the probability of each word appearing in a Valentine. The probability for the word *cute* is $\frac{3}{11}$. Suppose you are sending 25 Valentines. Since $25 \times \frac{3}{11}$ is $\frac{75}{11}$, or $6\frac{9}{11}$, *cute* is likely to appear about 7 times among the cards you are sending.

15. How many times might the word *athletic* appear?

16. How many times might the word *happy* appear?

17. Choose a different word from the table. How many times might that word appear?

Valentine Trivia

Word	Probability
funny	$\frac{3}{7}$
smart	$\frac{7}{18}$
kind	$\frac{11}{27}$
cute	$\frac{3}{11}$
happy	$\frac{2}{5}$
friendly	$\frac{5}{12}$
loyal	$\frac{3}{10}$
pretty	$\frac{2}{9}$
athletic	$\frac{1}{6}$
interesting	$\frac{2}{7}$

The Great Fraction Divide

Applying Skills

For the problems in items **1–6,** use words to write the division question. Then find the exact answer using mental math. You may use sketches and words to help.

1. $\dfrac{1}{8} \div \dfrac{1}{4}$ **2.** $\dfrac{1}{3} \div \dfrac{1}{2}$ **3.** $\dfrac{1}{6} \div \dfrac{2}{3}$

4. $\dfrac{1}{3} \div \dfrac{3}{4}$ **5.** $\dfrac{7}{8} \div \dfrac{2}{3}$ **6.** $\dfrac{7}{9} \div \dfrac{1}{5}$

For items **7–12,** estimate the answer for each problem and write about what you can say for sure.

7. $\dfrac{2}{3} \div \dfrac{11}{12}$ **8.** $\dfrac{1}{9} \div \dfrac{5}{6}$ **9.** $\dfrac{7}{8} \div \dfrac{2}{15}$

10. $\dfrac{7}{12} \div \dfrac{5}{8}$ **11.** $\dfrac{13}{15} \div \dfrac{4}{9}$ **12.** $\dfrac{3}{14} \div \dfrac{3}{24}$

For items **13–18,** solve the problems by following the rules for dividing fractions that you reviewed in class discussion.

13. $\dfrac{2}{3} \div \dfrac{1}{4}$ **14.** $\dfrac{3}{8} \div \dfrac{2}{9}$ **15.** $\dfrac{5}{6} \div \dfrac{3}{4}$

16. $\dfrac{12}{16} \div \dfrac{2}{5}$ **17.** $\dfrac{15}{16} \div \dfrac{4}{5}$ **18.** $\dfrac{4}{5} \div \dfrac{3}{4}$

19. An inch is $\frac{1}{12}$ of a foot long. How many inches are there in $\frac{5}{6}$ of a foot? Show your thinking.

20. Rachel has a science project to do. She figures she can get $\frac{1}{4}$ of it done in $\frac{3}{4}$ of an hour. How long will it take her to complete the project? Explain your answer.

Extending Concepts

For items **21–22,** use the order of operations to solve the problems.

21. $\left(\dfrac{1}{8} + \dfrac{1}{4} \right) \div \dfrac{2}{3}$

22. $\left(\dfrac{1}{8} + \dfrac{3}{4} \right) \div \left(\dfrac{2}{3} - \dfrac{1}{6} \right)$

23. Joshua is confused about how to divide fractions. Write a set of rules for dividing fractions that he can follow. Be sure to explain why each step works and include sample problems.

Making Connections

24. On a recent dig near Brea, California, the archeologist X. K. Vator unearthed a mysterious clay tablet with strange symbols. The English translation is shown below. To celebrate this discovery, Dr. Vator asks her chef to make Woolly Mammoth Stew for 18 people. Use fraction division equations to figure out how much of each ingredient the chef will need.

Woolly Mammoth Stew (Serves 8)
3 Pleistocine onions, chopped
28 lbs Woolly Mammoth meat, cubed
8 edible tubers, sliced
$\frac{1}{2}$ cup hot tar or molasses
$\frac{2}{3}$ tbsp salt

Powerhouse Show-Off

Applying Skills

For items **1–6,** solve the problems mentally, or use paper and pencil.

1. $1\frac{1}{2} - \frac{2}{3}$ **2.** $3\frac{4}{5} \times 1\frac{5}{6}$ **3.** $1\frac{2}{7} \times 1\frac{3}{5}$

4. $\frac{1}{3} + 2\frac{8}{9}$ **5.** $1\frac{6}{7} - 1\frac{4}{5}$ **6.** $3\frac{2}{3} \div \frac{6}{9}$

7. Choose four of the problems in items **1–6.** Write three statements for each problem. Two of the statements should be true. One of the statements should be false. Circle the one that is false.

For items **8 and 9,** write an equation to solve the problem. Write a sentence explaining why the equation solves the problem.

8. Keisha and eleven prospecting partners were looking for gold. They discovered $\frac{5}{6}$ pound of gold. If each partner received $\frac{1}{12}$ of the gold, how much did each one get?

9. Keisha then found another $\frac{1}{12}$ of a pound. How much gold was discovered altogether?

Extending Concepts

For items **10–15,** decide which of the statements should be rules. A rule is a statement that is always true. If you believe that a statement is a rule, write a short explanation telling why it works. If a statement is not a rule, show a counterexample. A counterexample is an example that makes the statement false.

Hint: An easy way to begin testing a statement is to think of an example and see if it works. For item **10,** you could start by testing whether or not $\frac{1}{3} + \frac{1}{2} = \frac{2}{5}$.

10. When you add two fractions, the numerator of the answer is the sum of their numerators, and the denominator of the answer is the sum of their denominators.

11. To subtract fractions with different denominators, first write them with the same denominator.

12. You can only add two fractions when one of the denominators divides evenly into the other.

13. You can always find a common denominator for two fractions by multiplying their original denominators.

14. When you subtract fractions with the same numerator, keep the numerator the same and subtract the denominators.

15. To add fractions with different denominators, first write them with the same denominator.

Writing

16. Write a letter to a fifth-grade student explaining how to add, subtract, multiply, and divide fractions. Include example problems and drawings where appropriate.

Making Cents of Decimals

Applying Skills

For items **1** and **2**, copy the equation and put the decimal point in the correct place.

1. $0.007 + 23.6 = 23607$

2. $34.079 - 13.24 = 20839$

For items **3–6**, copy and solve the equation.

3. $1.25 + $0.68   **4.** $13.82 - $6.91

5. $15.3 + 0.062   **6.** $16.923 + 2.3

7. Which is greater, 0.3 or 0.08? Why?

8. Asako and her family are planning a camping trip with a budget of $500.00. They would like to buy these items: sleeping bag ($108.35), gas stove ($31.78), tent ($359.20), cook set ($39.42), first-aid kit ($21.89), Global Positioning System ($199.99), compass ($26.14), binoculars ($109.76), knife ($19.56), and lantern ($20.88). What different combinations of camping equipment could Asako's family afford with the money they have? Name as many as you can. Show your work.

Extending Concepts

9. When Miguel adds numbers in his head, he likes to use expanded notation. For example, $1.32 + 0.276$ can be interpreted as $1 + 0 = 1$, and $0.3 + 0.2 = 0.5$, and $0.02 + 0.07 = 0.09$, and $0.000 + 0.006 = 0.006$. The total is added up to make 1.596. Explain what Miguel has done and why it works.

For items **10** and **11**, tell what the next two numbers are in each sequence. Explain how you found out.

10. 10, 10.4, 10.8, 11.2, 11.6, 12.0, …

11. 2, 1.25, 0.5, −0.25, −1, −1.75, …

Making Connections

For items **12–14**, use the following information from *The World Almanac* about platform diving at the Olympic Games.

Year	Name/Country	Points
1948	Victoria M. Draves/U.S.	68.87
1952	Patricia McCormick/U.S.	79.37
1956	Patricia McCormick/U.S.	84.85
1960	Ingrid Kramer/Germany	91.28
1964	Lesley Bush/U.S.	99.80
1968	Milena Duchkova/Czechoslovakia	109.59
1972	Ulrika Knape/Sweden	390.00
1976	Elena Vaytsekhouskaya/USSR	406.59

12. Which two consecutive Olympic years had the greatest difference in points scored? What was the difference?

13. What is the total number of points scored by someone from the United States?

14. What is the difference between points scored in 1948 and 1976?

The Cost Is Correct

Applying Skills

For items 1–4, copy the equation and put the decimal point in the correct place.

1. $18.15 \div 5.5 = 33$

2. $38.2 \times 0.032 = 12224$

3. $16.8 \div 0.8 = 21$

4. $6.2 \times 0.876 = 54312$

For items 5–10, write and solve the equation.

5. 3.722×0.68

6. $\$15.61 \times 3$

7. $\$15.50 \div \$0.25$

8. $82.26 \div 0.004$

9. $\$27.32 \div 4$

10. $\$4.56 \times 5$

11. Choose one multiplication equation and one division equation from items 5–10. Explain how you decided where the decimal point should be placed in the answer.

12. Vladik's dad filled up the gas tank in his car. The gasoline cost $1.47 per gallon. The total cost of the gasoline was $23.48. Estimate how many gallons of gasoline Vladik's dad put in the tank. Show your thinking.

13. Miwa and her mom went grocery shopping. Her mom bought 2 dozen oranges for $2.69 per dozen. Estimate the cost of each orange. Explain how you got your estimate.

14. Alex and Sanjeevi are buying their first home. During the first year, they figure their total mortgage payments will be $12,159.36. How much will their monthly mortage payment be? Show your work.

Extending Concepts

15. Lex wants to invite as many friends as he can to go to the movies with him. He has $20.00. The cost of each ticket is $4.50. Estimate how many friends he can take. A bag of popcorn costs $1.75. Estimate how many friends he can take if he is going to buy everyone, including himself, a bag of popcorn.

For items 16–18, give the next two numbers in each sequence. Explain how you found out. You might want to use a calculator.

16. 5, 6.5, 8.45, 10.985, 14.2805, 18.56465, …

17. 15.8, 31.6, 63.2, 126.4, 252.8, 505.6, …

18. 4, 10, 25, 62.5, 156.25, 390.625, …

19. Write an addition or subtraction sequence of your own. Include at least six numbers.

20. Write a multiplication sequence of your own. Include at least six numbers.

Writing

21. Answer the letter to Dr. Math.

> Dear Dr. Math,
> What is all the hoopla about the decimal point? I mean, is it really all that important and if it is, why?
> Dec-Inez

Percent Powerhouse

Applying Skills

For items **1–6,** find 50%, 10%, and 1% of each number. Write your strategies.

1. 58   **2.** 116   **3.** 293

4. 41   **5.** 1,080   **6.** 1,593

For items **7–13,** find the percent of each number without using a calculator. Circle the answers that are estimates.

7. 32% of 68   **8.** 7% of 92

9. 66% of 43   **10.** 100% of 1,062

11. 62.5% of 51   **12.** 1.3% of 100

13. 156% of 22

14. Choose two problems that you solved in items **7–13.** Explain how you solved each one.

For items **15–18,** change the percents to decimals.

15. 62%   **16.** 83%   **17.** 4%   **18.** 157%

Extending Concepts

19. Ask five people which of the following colors is their favorite: blue, green, red, or yellow. Show the results in percents. Make a graph to illustrate your findings.

20. Now ask ten people a question of your own. Be sure to ask a question that has between two and five possible answers. Do not use a question that has a yes/no answer. Show your findings with percents and a graph.

21. One day a gardener picked about 20% of all the strawberries in his garden. Later that day, his wife picked about 25% of the remaining strawberries. Still later, the son of the gardener picked about 33% of the strawberries that were left. Even later, the daughter picked about 50% of the remaining strawberries in the garden. Finally, there were only 3 strawberries left. About how many strawberries were originally in the garden? Explain.

Making Connections

For a healthy diet, the total calories a person consumes should be no more than 30% fat. Tell whether the foods in items **22–25** meet these recommendations. Show how you found your answer.

22. "Reduced-fat" chips
Calories per serving: 140
Calories from fat: 70

23. "Low-fat" snack bar
Calories per serving: 150
Calories from fat: 25

24. "Light" popcorn
Calories per serving: 20
Calories from fat: 5

25. "Healthy" soup
Calories per serving: 110
Calories from fat: 25

Powerhouse Challenge

Applying Skills

For items **1–11**, solve and show your work. Round your answer to the nearest hundredth.

1. Find 8.5% of $32.16.

2. Find 15% of $87.17.

3. Find 25% of 1,061.

4. Find 2.5% of 587.

5. Find the total cost of a $25.50 meal after a tax of 8.5% and a tip of 15% is added.

6. A shirt that sold for $49.99 has been marked down 30%. Find the sale price.

7. In 1996, 27% of Camille's income went to state and federal taxes. If she earned $35,672.00, how much did she actually keep?

8. Jared's uncle bought 100 shares of stock for $37.25 a share. In 6 months the stock went up 30%. How much were the 100 shares of stock worth in 6 months?

9. Emily went to the doctor for an annual physical. The nurse measured her height and weight. She said that Emily's height had increased by 10% and her weight had increased by 5% since her physical last year. Emily weighs 95 pounds and is 5 feet tall this year. What were her height and weight at last year's physical?

10. Kyal's family bought a treadmill on sale. It was 25% off the original price of $1,399.95. They paid $\frac{1}{2}$ of the sales price as a down payment. What was the down payment?

11. Zachary and his family went on a vacation to San Francisco last summer. On the first day, they gave the taxi driver a 15% tip and the hotel bell boy $2.00 for taking the luggage to the room. The taxi fare was $15.75. How much did they spend in all?

Extending Concepts

12. Explain the connection between fractions, decimals, and percents. Show examples to illustrate your thinking.

13. Which concept is easier for you to understand—fractions, decimals, or percents? Why?

14. Describe a real-world problem or situation in which you would use fractions, decimals, or percents. Tell how you would solve the problem.

15. Make at least four equations similar to the one shown. Make sure you have fractions, decimals, and percents in your equations. Ask someone in your family to try to get as close as they can to the target number by filling in the boxes, using only the numerals 1 through 6.

$$\square\,\square \times \square\,.\,\square = 42 \qquad \text{How far off?}$$

Writing

16. What is the most important concept you have learned in *Number Powerhouse*? Tell how the concept works and why it is important.

STUDENT GALLERY

CREDITS: Photography: Chris Conroy • Beverley Harper (cover) • © SuperStock: pp. 2TR, 3TM, 6L, 14, 16L, 28TR. Illustrations: © Petrified Collection/The Image Bank: pp. 11B, 19BM • © Rob Blackard: pp. 26, 32, 40.

Creative Publications and MathScape are trademarks or registered trademarks of Creative Publications.

© 1998 Creative Publications
1300 Villa Street, Mountain View, California 94041

Printed in the United States of America.

0-7622-0211-4

1 2 3 4 5 6 7 8 9 10 . 02 01 00 99 98 97

MEASURING AND SCALING

STUDENT GUIDE

GULLIVER'S WORLDS

MEASURING AND SCALING

MathScape
SEEING AND THINKING
MATHEMATICALLY

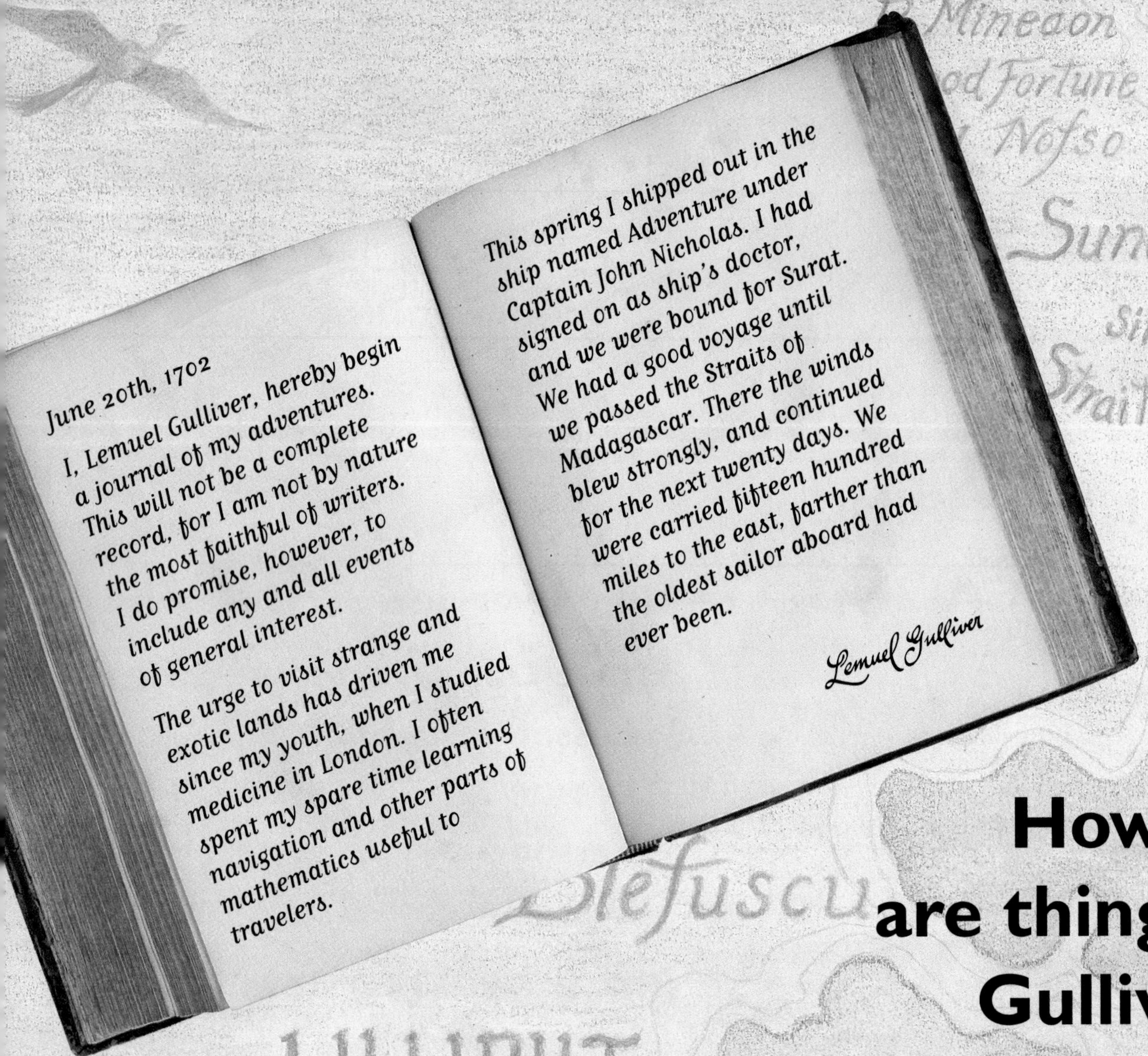

June 20th, 1702

I, Lemuel Gulliver, hereby begin a journal of my adventures. This will not be a complete record, for I am not by nature the most faithful of writers. I do promise, however, to include any and all events of general interest.

The urge to visit strange and exotic lands has driven me since my youth, when I studied medicine in London. I often spent my spare time learning navigation and other parts of mathematics useful to travelers.

This spring I shipped out in the ship named Adventure under Captain John Nicholas. I had signed on as ship's doctor, and we were bound for Surat. We had a good voyage until we passed the Straits of Madagascar. There the winds blew strongly, and continued for the next twenty days. We were carried fifteen hundred miles to the east, farther than the oldest sailor aboard had ever been.

Lemuel Gulliver

How big are things in Gulliver's Worlds?

LILLIPUT
Discovered
A.D. 169[...]

GULLIVER'S WORLDS

PHASE**ONE**
Brobdingnag

Gulliver's journal holds clues to sizes of things in Brobdingnag, a land of giants. Using these clues, you will find ways to predict the sizes of other things. Then you will use math to create a life-size drawing of a giant object. You will also compare sizes in the two lands. Finally, you will use what you know about scale to write a story set in Brobdingnag.

PHASE**TWO**
Lilliput

Lilliput is a land of tiny people. Gulliver's journal and drawings will help you find out about the sizes of things in Lilliput. You will compare the measurement system in Lilliput to ours. Then you will explore area and volume as you figure out how many Lilliputian objects are needed to feed and house Gulliver. Finally, you will write a story set in Lilliput.

PHASE**THREE**
Lands of the Large and Lands of the Little

Clues from pictures will help you write a scale factor that relates the sizes of things in different lands to the sizes of things in Ourland. You will continue to explore length, area, and volume, and see how these measures change as the scale changes. Finally, you will put together all you have learned to create a museum exhibit about one of these lands.

PHASE ONE

August 29, 1702

We finally sighted land again today. We went ashore near a small creek. I was gone only a short time. Yet when I headed back toward the landing site, the sailors were already rowing frantically out to sea. I could see a huge creature chasing them through the water. It stopped, though, at a sharp reef, and so the sailors escaped.

This was, I admit, of small comfort to me, because I was now alone. Fearing for my safety, I scampered inland. Beyond a steep hill, I discovered tall stalks, about eighteen feet high. They appeared to be wheat. I reached a stone stairway, but finding each step to rise six feet, I was unable to climb it. The trees along its edge were so tall I could not guess their height.

Lemuel Gulliver

Imagine a world in which everything is so large that you would be as small as a mouse. How can you predict how large things will be in this land?

In this phase you will learn to figure out a scale factor that describes how sizes of things are related. You will use the scale factor to create life-size drawings, solve problems, and write stories.

Brobdingnag

WHAT'S THE MATH?

Investigations in this section focus on:

DATA COLLECTION

- Gathering information from a story
- Organizing data to find patterns

MEASUREMENT and ESTIMATION

- Measuring with inches, feet, and fractions of inches
- Estimating the sizes of large objects

SCALE and PROPORTION

- Finding the scale factor that describes the relationship between sizes
- Applying the scale factor to predict sizes of objects
- Creating scale drawings
- Exploring the effect of rescaling on area and volume

1 The Sizes of Things in Brobdingnag

DETERMINING THE SCALE FACTOR

How well can you picture in your mind the events described in Gulliver's journal entry? Here you will gather clues from the journal entry about the sizes of things in Brobdingnag. As you compare sizes of things in Brobdingnag to sizes in Ourland, you will learn about scale.

August 29, 1702

I had not a moment to rest, as another monster was approaching. I now saw that in form he resembled a human being. It was his size—as tall as a ship's mast—that made him appear to be a monster. Scared and confused, I backed away, tripping over an apple core that lay like a log behind me. As I stood up again, the giant began cutting wheat with a great scythe. With every stride he traveled about ten yards closer to me, and I was faced with either being trampled on or cut in two. Therefore, I gave up my hiding place and shouted for his attention.

Compare Sizes to Determine a Scale Factor

A scale factor is a ratio that tells how the sizes of things are related. For example, some model trains use a 20:1 scale factor. This means that each part on the real train is 20 times as large as the same part on the model train. Follow these steps to find the scale factor that relates sizes in Brobdingnag to sizes in Ourland.

How are sizes of things in Brobdingnag related to sizes in Ourland?

1 Make a chart with three columns. Column 1 is for the name of each object. Column 2 is for the size of the object in Brobdingnag. Column 3 is for the size of the corresponding object in Ourland.

2 Fill out column 1 and column 2 with clues you found in the story about the sizes of objects in Brobdingnag. Measure or estimate how big each of the objects would be in Ourland. Enter that information in column 3.

3 Use the information in your chart to figure out a scale factor that tells how sizes of things in Brobdingnag are related to sizes in Ourland.

Object	Brobdingnag	Ourland
Stalk of wheat	About 18 feet	

How big would an Ourland object be in Brobdingnag?

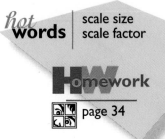

hot **words** | scale size
scale factor

Homework

 page 34

2 A Life-Size Object in Brobdingnag

The story continues as Gulliver describes more events from his life in Brobdingnag. In the last lesson, you figured out how sizes in Brobdingnag relate to sizes in Ourland. In this lesson you will use what you know to create a life-size drawing of a Brobdingnag object.

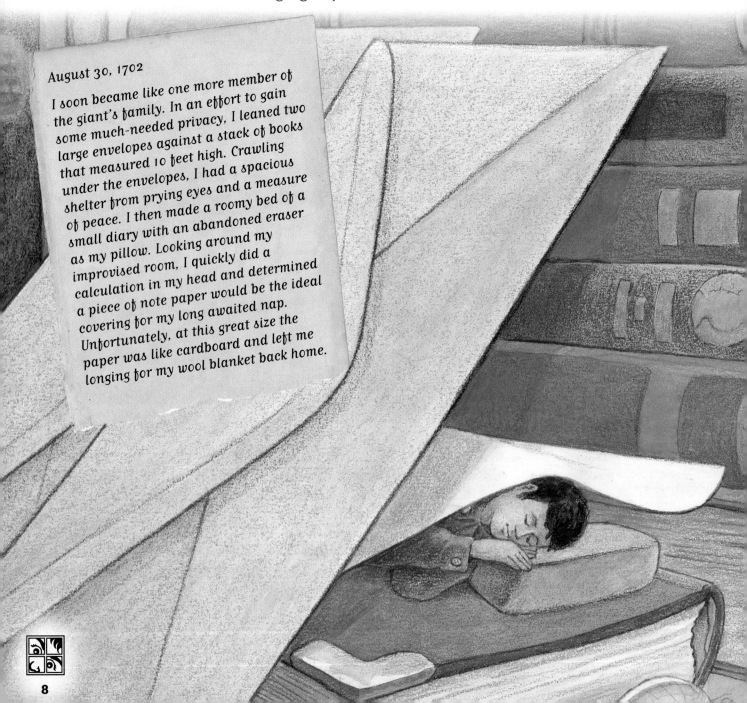

August 30, 1702

I soon became like one more member of the giant's family. In an effort to gain some much-needed privacy, I leaned two large envelopes against a stack of books that measured 10 feet high. Crawling under the envelopes, I had a spacious shelter from prying eyes and a measure of peace. I then made a roomy bed of a small diary with an abandoned eraser as my pillow. Looking around my improvised room, I quickly did a calculation in my head and determined a piece of note paper would be the ideal covering for my long awaited nap. Unfortunately, at this great size the paper was like cardboard and left me longing for my wool blanket back home.

Make a Life-Size Drawing

Choose an object from Ourland that is small enough to fit in your pocket or in your hand. What would be the size of your object in Brobdingnag? Make a life-size drawing of the Brobdingnag object.

1 Make the size of your drawing as accurate as possible. Label the measurements.

2 After you finish your drawing, figure out a way to check that your drawing and measurements are accurate.

3 Write a short description about how you determined the size of your drawing and how you checked that the drawing was accurate.

How can you figure out the size of a Brobdingnag object?

Investigate the Effect of Rescaling on Area

How many of the Ourland objects does it take to cover all of the Brobdingnag object? Use your drawing and the original Ourland object to investigate this question. Write about how you figured out how many Ourland objects it took to cover the Brodingnag object.

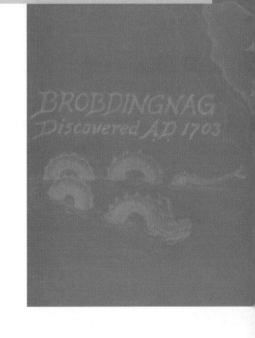

hot **words** | actual size
perimeter
ratio

Homework

page 35

3 How Big Is "Little" Glumdalclitch?

ESTIMATING
LENGTHS, AREAS,
AND VOLUMES

What if Glumdalclitch visited Ourland? Would she fit in your classroom? Drawing a picture of "little" Glumdalclitch in actual Ourland measurements would take a great deal of paper. To get a sense of the size of a very large object, it is sometimes easier to use estimation.

November 25, 1702

My first impression of the girl in the family proved to be correct. She was very good-natured, kind in spirit, and patient in teaching me her language. She was considered small for her age, being just under forty feet tall. Therefore I called her Glumdalclitch, which I learned means "Little Nurse" in her language. She called me Grildrig, meaning "Little Puppet."

Use Estimation to Solve Problems

Estimate the size of each Brobdingnag object. Answer the questions about how the size of the Brobdingnag object compares to size of the same Ourland object and explain how you found each answer.

1 Could a mattress that would fit Glumdalclitch fit in the classroom? How much of the floor would it cover? How many Ourland mattresses would it take to cover the same amount of floor?

2 How big would Glumdalclitch's notebook be? How many sheets of our notebook paper would we need to tape together to make one sheet for her notebook?

3 How big a shoe box do you think Glumdalclitch might have? How many of our shoe boxes would fit inside hers?

4 How many slices of our bread would it take to make one slice of bread big enough for Glumdalclitch to eat?

Why are so many Ourland objects needed to cover or to fill a Brobdingnag object?

How do objects from Ourland and Brobdingnag compare in length, area, and volume?

BROBDINGNAG
Discovered AD 1703

hot **words** | area rescaling

Homework

page 36

4 Telling Tales in Brobdingnag

Imagine how it would be for you to visit Brobdingnag. By now you have a good understanding of the scale factor in Brobdingnag. You can use what you know to write your own story. You will see that good mathematical thinking is important in writing a believable story.

June 12, 1704

My size led to some frightening situations. One morning, I was sitting by the window when twenty giant wasps came flying into the room. Some of them carried off the sweet cake I was about to eat for breakfast. Others flew around my head, confusing me with the noise and threatening me with their stings. I killed four of them with my sword and drove the rest off. In other situations, my small size proved very useful. For example, I was once lowered in a bucket down the well to retrieve a ring that the princess had dropped accidentally. She was so happy when they pulled me back up and she saw her prized ring, which I had placed over my head and around my neck for safekeeping.

Write a Story Using Accurate Dimensions

How can you use rescaling to write a story about Brobdingnag?

Choose one place in Brobdingnag. Imagine what it would be like to visit that place. Describe in detail the place and at least one adventure that happened to you there.

1 Write a story about Brobdingnag. Make the story believable by using accurate measurements for the objects you describe.

2 Include a size description of at least three objects found in that place.

3 Write a believable title. The title should include at least one size comparison between Brobdingnag and Ourland.

4 Record and check all of your measurements.

Summarize the Math Used in the Story

After you write your story, summarize how you used math to figure out the sizes of things in the story. Include the following in your summary:

- Make a table, list, or drawing showing the sizes of the three objects in both Ourland and Brobdingnag.

- Explain how you used scale, estimation, and measurement to figure out the sizes of these objects.

hot **words** | linear measures
scale drawing

Homework
page 37

PHASE TWO

August 5, 1706

Having been condemned by nature and fortune to a restless life, I took a post on the Antelope, a trading ship.

I had been spending much time on deck, until a storm suddenly came upon us. The storm grew steadily worse. The ship sank on a reef, and I became separated from my crew. Pushed toward shore by the tide, I fell exhausted upon the softest and shortest grass I had ever seen. But before I could examine it further, I fell into a deep sleep.

When I awoke, I found my arms and legs strongly fastened to the ground. Even my hair was tied down. My frustration gave way to surprise as I saw who had done this. Hundreds of them were scattered on the ground around me. They looked like men in every way but one—they were a mere six inches tall.

Lemuel Gulliver

Suddenly you are in a world in which everything is tiny. You have to be careful where you step, so that you don't harm people or destroy houses. The name of this land is Lilliput.

In Phase Two, you will use a scale factor that makes things smaller. You will compare the different ways of measuring things using inches and feet, centimeters and meters and the measurement units used in Lilliput.

Lilliput

WHAT'S THE MATH?

Investigations in this section focus on:

DATA COLLECTION

- Gathering information from a story and pictures
- Organizing data to find patterns

MEASUREMENT and ESTIMATION

- Measuring accurately using fractions
- Comparing the U.S. customary and metric systems of measurement
- Estimating the sizes of objects
- Exploring area and volume measurements

SCALE and PROPORTION

- Working with a scale factor that reduces the sizes of objects
- Applying the scale factor to predict sizes of objects and to create a three-dimensional scale model
- Exploring the effect of rescaling on area and volume

5 Sizing Up the Lilliputians

DETERMINING
A SCALE FACTOR
LESS THAN ONE

Gulliver is swept overboard in a storm at sea and wakes up in a new land. He is the captive of tiny people in the land of Lilliput. How are the sizes of things in Lilliput related to sizes in Ourland? Clues in the journal will help you find out how small things are in Lilliput.

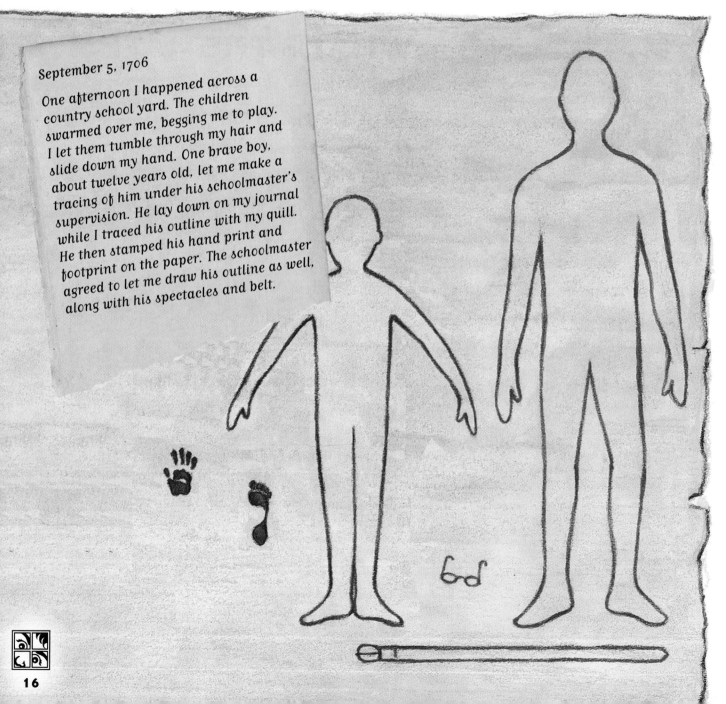

September 5, 1706

One afternoon I happened across a country school yard. The children swarmed over me, begging me to play. I let them tumble through my hair and slide down my hand. One brave boy, about twelve years old, let me make a tracing of him under his schoolmaster's supervision. He lay down on my journal while I traced his outline with my quill. He then stamped his hand print and footprint on the paper. The schoolmaster agreed to let me draw his outline as well, along with his spectacles and belt.

Create a Chart to Compare Sizes

How are sizes of things in Lilliput related to sizes in Ourland?

Make a scale chart with three columns. Column 1 is for the name of an object. Column 2 is for the size of the object in Lilliput. Column 3 is for the size in Ourland. Use a ruler to measure the tracings.

1 Use the words and tracings in the story to record the name of the object and its Lilliputian measurements on the chart. Measure or estimate the size of the same object in Ourland.

2 Use the information in your scale chart to find a scale factor that shows how sizes in Lilliput are related to sizes in Ourland.

3 Estimate or measure the sizes of some more objects in Ourland. Add these objects and their Ourland measurements to the chart. Find the size each object would be in Lilliput and add that information to the chart.

Do you think the Lilliputian student in the tracing is tall, short, or average-size in a Lilliputian sixth-grade class?

Write About Estimation Strategies

Write about what you did and learned as you investigated sizes of things in Lilliput.

- Describe the measurement and estimation strategies you used to find the sizes of things in Ourland and Lilliput. Show how you used the scale factor to complete your chart.

- What did you discover about finding the average size of an object?

hot
words | mean
median
mode

Homework
page 38

6 Glum-gluffs and Mum-gluffs

The same object can be measured in different units of measurement. Inches and feet are units in the U.S. customary system of measurement. Centimeters and meters are units in the metric system. How do these units compare to the units used in Lillilput?

October 5, 1706

During dinner, the King and Queen told stories about their country and people, and I told stories of mine. The King found it especially hard to believe that he, one of the tallest men in his land, would be no bigger than a child's doll in mine. He informed me that he was 8½ glum-gluffs tall, and that the Queen was 6 glum-gluffs tall. When I inquired what a glum-gluff was, he replied that it was $\frac{1}{20}$ of a mum-gluff. He then kindly agreed to have his steward mark the length of 1 glum-gluff in my journal.

———— 1 glum-gluff

Measure an Object in Different Systems

Choose an object that you added to the Lilliput scale chart you made in Lesson 5.

1 Use the measurements recorded in the chart to make an accurate, life-size drawing of the object in Lilliput.

2 Use a metric ruler to measure the drawing in metric units (centimeters). Write the metric measurements on the drawing.

3 Calculate what the measurements of the drawing would be in the Lilliputian units of glum-gluffs. Write the Lilliputian measurements on the drawing.

4 Compare the object in the drawing to any object in Ourland that would be about the same size. Write the name of the Ourland object on the drawing.

How do the units used in different measurement systems compare?

Compare Measurement Systems

Write a letter to the King and Queen of Lilliput. Compare the measurement systems of Ourland and Lilliput. Make sure your letter answers the following questions:

- When would you prefer to use the U.S. customary system of measurement? When would you prefer to use the metric system?

- Would you ever prefer to use glum-gluffs and mum-gluffs? Why?

- Suppose the people in Lilliput were going to adopt one of our measurement systems. Which one would you recommend to them? Why or why not?

hot **words** | standard measurement
measurement units

page 39

7 Housing and Feeding Gulliver

SOLVING PROBLEMS
INVOLVING AREA
AND VOLUME

Gulliver's needs for food and shelter in Lilliput present some interesting problems. These problems involve area and volume. In the last phase, you solved problems in one dimension. Now you will extend your work with the Lilliputian scale factor to solve problems in two and three dimensions.

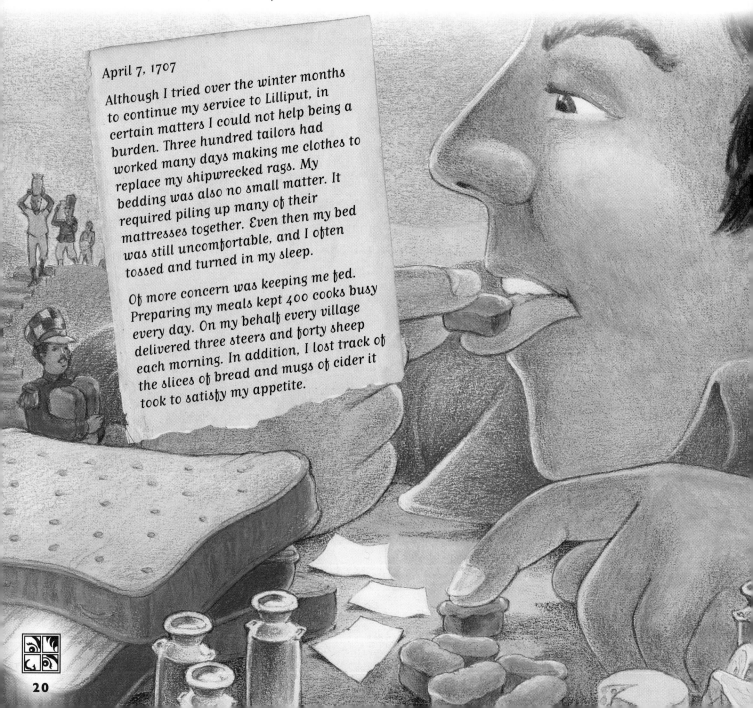

April 7, 1707

Although I tried over the winter months to continue my service to Lilliput, in certain matters I could not help being a burden. Three hundred tailors had worked many days making me clothes to replace my shipwrecked rags. My bedding was also no small matter. It required piling up many of their mattresses together. Even then my bed was still uncomfortable, and I often tossed and turned in my sleep.

Of more concern was keeping me fed. Preparing my meals kept 400 cooks busy every day. On my behalf every village delivered three steers and forty sheep each morning. In addition, I lost track of the slices of bread and mugs of cider it took to satisfy my appetite.

Estimate to Solve Area and Volume Problems

How can you use estimation to solve problems in two and three dimensions?

Estimate how many of the Lilliputian objects Gulliver needs. Then make a Lilliputian-size model of one of the four objects.

1 How many Lilliputian-size mattresses would Gulliver need to make a bed? How should Gulliver arrange those mattresses to make a comfortable-size bed?

2 How many sheets of Lilliputian paper would need to be taped together to made one sheet of writing paper for Gulliver?

3 At home, Gulliver would eat two loaves of bread each week. How many Lilliputian loaves of bread would Gulliver need each week?

4 At home, Gulliver drank 3 cups of milk each day. How many Lilliputian-size quarts of milk would Gulliver need each day?

Use a Model to Check an Estimate

Describe in writing how you can use your Lilliputian-size model to check your estimate. Include a sketch with measurements to show your thinking.

hot **words** | volume

Homework
page 40

8 Seeing Through Lilliputian Eyes

Imagine yourself in Lilliput. What objects would you bring with you? How would the Lilliputians describe these objects? You will use what you have learned about scale in one, two, and three dimensions when you write a story describing your own adventures in Lilliput.

Gulliver's Pocket Contents:

1. One great piece of coarse cloth, large enough to be a carpet for your Majesty's chief Room of State
2. A great bundle of white thin substances, folded one over another, about the thickness of three men, tied with a strong cable and marked with black figures, with every letter almost half as large as the palm of our hands
3. A long pole from the back of which extended 20 shorter poles, resembling the palace railings
4. Several round flat pieces of yellow and silver metal, of different bulk, some so large and heavy that my comrade and I could hardly lift them
5. Some wonderful kind of globe-like engine, part silver and part transparent metal, with a loud noise like the sound of a water-mill, attached by a great silver chain

Write a Story Using 3-D Measurements

How can you describe a three-dimensional Lilliputian world?

Write a believable story using three-dimensional measurements. You will need to figure out the correct length, width, and height of the objects you describe.

1 Imagine a place in Lilliput. Describe at least one adventure that could happen to you there.

2 Describe the measurements of at least three objects found in the place. You could include an Ourland object in your story for comparison.

3 Include a conversation with a Lilliputian that compares the sizes of the objects in the story to the same objects in Ourland.

4 Record and check all of your measurements.

Describe Rescaling Strategies

Summarize how you determined the length, width, and height of the three objects described in your story.

- Make a table, list, or drawing showing the length, width, and height of each object in both Ourland and Lilliput.

- Explain the methods you used to estimate or measure each object. Show how you rescaled it using the scale factor.

hot **words** | scale
metric system

Homework
page 41

September 13, 1708

It has now been some months since my journal was published. News of my travels has prompted a greater response than I expected. I must confess, too, a certain pleasure at the attentions I have received from my publisher. He has pronounced himself well-pleased with the sales figures, and credits both my nature and my writing for this success.

Although I did not anticipate it, I have recently received much correspondence from my readers. Pictures and letters have come from nearby countries— France, Spain and Holland—as well as more distant lands. It is my dream that someday all my treasures and adventures may be shared with the public as part of a glorious exhibit, but, alas, I fear it will not happen in my lifetime.

Your friend,

Lemuel Gulliver

Welcome to our BIGVILLE dinner party

Imagine you are in charge of a special exhibit about *Gulliver's Worlds*. How would you show the sizes of the different lands he visited? In this final phase, you will explore size relationships in different lands, both big and small. You will find ways to show how the sizes compare in length, area, and volume. Finally, your class will create displays of life-size objects from one of *Gulliver's Worlds*.

Lands of the Large and Lands of the Little

WHAT'S THE MATH?

Investigations in this section focus on:

DATA COLLECTION

- Gathering information from pictures
- Creating displays to show size relationships

MEASUREMENT and ESTIMATION

- Measuring accurately using fractions
- Exploring area and volume measurements

SCALE and PROPORTION

- Finding scale factors that describe relationships among sizes
- Enlarging and reducing the sizes of objects according to scale factors
- Creating 2-D scale drawings
- Creating a 3-D scale model
- Exploring the effects of rescaling on area and volume

© Creative Publications • MathScape

9 Lands of the Large

Ourland Museum needs a display that compares the sizes of objects from Lands of the Large to Ourland.
Can you figure out the scale factor for each of the Lands of the Large? Can you find a way to show the size relationships among the different lands?

Investigate Proportions of Faces

How large is a life-size face in each of the Lands of the Large?

Compare the objects in the photos to find the scale factor. The smaller object is always from Ourland. When you are finished, check to make sure your scale factor is correct before you do the following group investigation.

1 As a group, select one of the Lands of the Large for this investigation. Have each member of your group draw a different feature of a face from your group's land.

2 As a group, arrange the features to form a realistic face. Check to see if your measurements are correct and the features are in proportion. Work together to draw the outline of the face.

How tall would a person in your group's Land of the Large be?

Gargantua

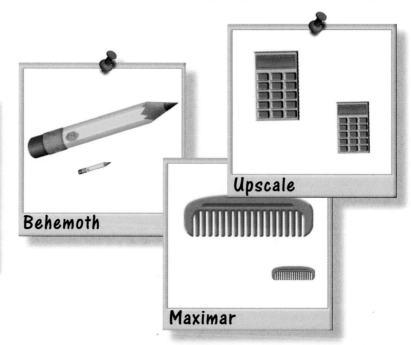

Behemoth

Upscale

Maximar

Represent Size Relationships

Use the scale drawing of an Ourland face on this page to make a simple scale drawing of a face from each of the Lands of the Large. Organize your drawings into a visual display to show size relationships.

How do things in the Lands of the Large compare in size to things in Ourland?

1 Measure the scale drawing of the Ourland face.

2 Use the scale factors from the Lands of the Large to make a scale drawing of a face from each land. You do not need to draw in the features.

3 Write the name of the land and the scale factor compared to Ourland next to each drawing.

4 Organize your drawings into a display of size relationships that compares the sizes of faces from different lands and shows how they are related.

Describe a Scale Factor for Brobdingnag

Compare the sizes of things in each of the Lands of the Large to the sizes of things in Brobdingnag. Use this to explain how the scale factor describes size relationships.

- Figure out the scale factor for each land compared to Brobdingnag. Write it next to the scale drawing from that land.

- Describe in writing how you figured out the scale factor. Tell why it is different from the Ourland scale factor.

hot **words** | like units
picture graph

Homework

page 42

10 Lands of the Little

Can you find the mistakes in the Lands of the Little display? Here you will correct the scale drawings and create a chart that you can use to find the size of any object in a Land of the Little.

Compare Objects in the Lands of the Little

How do things in the Lands of the Little compare in size to things in Ourland?

Measure each pair of scale drawings on this page. The larger object is always from Ourland. Does the size relationship for each Land of the Little object match the scale factor below it?

1 As a group, choose an Ourland object from your classroom. Draw your object on a piece of paper.

2 Use each of the four scale factors below to draw a new picture of your object. Now, which scale drawings below do you think are incorrect?

Quarterville 1:4 (.25:1)

Micropolus 3:8 (.375:1)

Small Town 2:3 (.67:1)

Dimutia 1:6 (.167:1)

Create a Table to Show Size Relationships

Make a table that shows how objects in the Lands of the Little compare in size to objects in Ourland. Record the size an object would be in other lands if you knew its size in Ourland.

How could you show the size relationships of things in different lands?

1 Fill in the names of the Lands of the Little at the top of each column. Mark the Ourland measurements (100 inches, 75 inches, 50 inches, 25 inches, 10 inches) in the Ourland column.

2 Figure out how big an object would be in the Lands of the Little for each of the Ourland measurements. Mark the Lands of the Little measurements in the appropriate columns.

3 Find a way to use your group's scale drawings to check that your table is correct.

Ourland	Lilliput	Dimutia	Quarterville	Micropolus	Small Town
100 inches					
75 inches					
50 inches					
25 inches					
10 inches					

Write a Guide for Using the Table

Explain how you can use your table to answer each question.

- If an object is 80 inches long in Ourland, how long would it be in each of the other lands?

- If an object is 5 inches long in Lilliput, how long would it be in Ourland?

- If an object is 25 inches long in Small Town, how long would it be in the other lands?

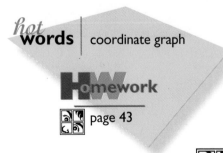

hot **words** | coordinate graph

Homework

page 43

11 Gulliver's Worlds Cubed

RESCALING IN ONE, TWO, AND THREE DIMENSIONS

The *Gulliver's Worlds* group exhibit needs a finishing touch. The exhibit needs to show how rescaling affects area and volume. How do length, area, and volume change when the scale of something changes? Can you create a display that will help visitors understand this?

How does a change in scale affect measurements of length, area, and volume?

Investigate Cube Sizes in Different Lands

Use the information on this page to figure out a way to use Ourland cubes to build a large cube at each of the following scale factors: 2:1, 3:1, 4:1.

1 Record how many Ourland cubes make up each large cube.

2 Estimate how many cubes it would take to make a Brobdingnag cube (scale factor = 12:1)

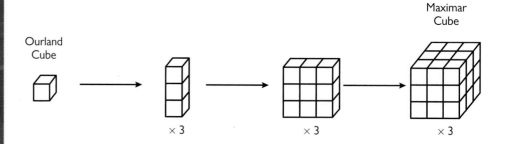

Ourland Cube   × 3   × 3   Maximar Cube   × 3

Comment Card

If Maximar is 3 times bigger than Ourland, why does it take more than 3 cubes from Ourland to make a cube in Maximar?

Collect Data for Two and Three Dimensions

Use your cubes to collect size information.

1 Organize the information into a table that answers the following questions:

   a. What is the scale factor of the cube?

   b. How many Ourland cubes high is one edge of this cube?

   c. How many Ourland cubes are needed to cover one face of this cube completely?

   d. How many Ourland cubes are needed to fill this cube completely?

Scale Factor	How Many Cubes Long Is an Edge? (length)	How Many Cubes Cover a Face? (area)	How Many Cubes Fill the Cube? (volume)
2:1			
3:1			
4:1			
5:1			
10:1			
25:1			

2 Find a rule that can predict how big a cube would be for each of the following scales. Then add the information to your table:

   2.5:1   6:1   20:1   100:1

Write About Scale, Area, and Volume

Write down the set of rules you used to complete your table. Make sure that someone else could apply your rules to any scale factor.

1 Explain how your rules work.

2 Make a diagram showing how to use the rules to predict the following:

   a. The length of one edge of a cube

   b. The area of one face of a cube

   c. The volume of a cube

hot **words** | exponents cubic centimeter

Homework

page 44

12 Stepping into Gulliver's Worlds

FINAL PROJECT

A life-size display in the correct scale and proportion can make you feel like you have stepped into another world. You will help the Ourland Museum create a life-size display of one of the lands in *Gulliver's Worlds*. The goal is for museum visitors to get involved with your display.

Create a Display Using Accurate Dimensions

What would it look like if you stepped into one of the lands in *Gulliver's Worlds*?

Choose one of the lands in *Gulliver's Worlds*. Create a display and tour that compares the sizes of things in that land to those in Ourland.

1. Create at least three objects in one, two, or three dimensions to use in the display.

2. Write a short tour that describes the measurements of the objects in the display and compares them to sizes in Ourland. Describe and label the areas and volumes of the objects.

3. Find a way for visitors to get involved with the display.

4. Include your writing from previous lessons and charts to help museum visitors understand the scale of the land.

Gulliver Show Opens At The Ourland Living Museum

by Jonathan Swift
Ourland News Correspondent

The *Gulliver's Worlds* exhibit at the Ourland Living Museum is an exciting journey to new lands. From my entrance, where I was met by a huge smile from a life-size Brobdingnag face, to the carefully crafted scale drawings of the Lands of the Little gallery, the exhibit showed this reporter what it would be like to actually live in the worlds that Gulliver explored hundreds of years ago in his famous journal.

Review a Display

You will be reviewing a classmate's display and presentation. As you review the exhibit, write down the scale factor and as many measurements as you can. Use the following questions to help write your review:

1 What parts of the display look life-size?

2 How did you check that the sizes of the objects in the display were correct?

3 How does the presentation describe linear, area, and volume measurements?

4 How does the presentation compare sizes to those in Ourland?

5 Would you add or change anything to make the display more believable?

How would you evaluate your own display?

hot **words** | two-dimensional
three-dimensional

H **W** omework

page 45

The Sizes of Things in Brobdingnag

Applying Skills

Fill in the missing height conversions to complete the chart.

	Name	Height (in.)	Height (ft and in.)	Height (ft)
	Marla	49″	4′1″	$4\frac{1}{12}′$
1.	Scott	56″		
2.	Jessica		4′7″	
3.	Shoshana	63″		
4.	Jamal	54″		
5.	Louise		4′11″	
6.	Kelvin	58″		
7.	Keisha		5′2″	
8.	Jeffrey		4′2″	

9. List the names in height order from tallest to shortest.

10. The scale factor of Giantland to Ourland is 11:1. That means that objects in Giantland are 11 times the size of the same objects in Ourland. Figure out how large the following Ourland objects would be in Giantland:

a. a tree that is 9 ft tall

b. a man that is 6 ft tall

c. a photo that is 7 in. wide and 5 in. high

11. The scale factor of Big City to Ourland is 5:1. That means that objects in Big City are 5 times the size of the same objects in Ourland. How large would each of the Ourland objects from item **10** be in Big City?

Extending Concepts

12. Duane made an amazing run at the football game Friday night.

Examine the diagram below and give the distance of the play in:

a. yards **b.** feet **c.** inches

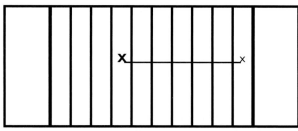

HINT: From goal line to goal line in a football field is 100 yards.

Making Connections

13. Answer this Dr. Math letter:

> Dear Dr. Math,
> Today in science class we were using microscopes. The lenses were 10×, 50×, and 100×. I think there is a way scale factor applies to what I see and what the actual size is. Is that true? If so, could you please explain?
> William Neye

A Life-Size Object in Brobdingnag

Applying Skills

Reduce these fractions to lowest terms.

1. $\dfrac{21}{49}$

2. $\dfrac{33}{126}$

3. $\dfrac{54}{81}$

4. $\dfrac{28}{48}$

5. $\dfrac{15}{75}$

6. $\dfrac{10}{18}$

7. $\dfrac{126}{252}$

8. $\dfrac{8}{24}$

9. $\dfrac{16}{12}$

10. $\dfrac{64}{6}$

Follow the instructions to describe each relationship in a different way.

11. Write $\dfrac{10}{1}$ as a ratio.

12. Write $4:1$ as a fraction.

13. Write "2 to 1" as a fraction.

14. Write out $6:1$ in words.

15. Write $\dfrac{8}{1}$ as a ratio.

Extending Concepts

16. The height of a blade of grass in a giant-size display is $4\frac{2}{3}$ ft. The blade of grass in your yard is 4 in. high. What is the scale factor?

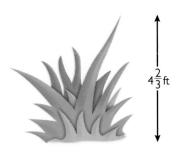

$4\frac{2}{3}$ ft

17. The scale factor of Vastland to Ourland is $20:1$. That means that objects in Vastland are 20 times the size of the same objects in Ourland. Figure out how large the following Ourland objects would be in Vastland:

   a. a car that is $4\frac{1}{2}$ ft high and 8 ft long

   b. a building that is 23 yd high and 40 ft long

   c. a piece of paper that is $8\frac{1}{2}$ in. wide and 11 in. long

Making Connections

18. The science class is creating insects that are larger than life. First they will study the ant. The queen ant that they have to observe is $\frac{1}{2}$ in. long. The large model they create will be 5 ft long. Mr. Estes wants to have a ladybug model created too. Tasha found a ladybug and measured it at $\frac{1}{8}$ in. long.

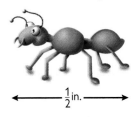

$\frac{1}{2}$ in.

   a. What is the scale factor for the ant model?

   b. How big will the ladybug model be if the same scale factor is used?

How Big Is "Little" Glumdalclitch?

Applying Skills

Reduce these fractions to the lowest terms.

1. $\dfrac{25}{75}$ **2.** $\dfrac{69}{23}$ **3.** $\dfrac{1,176}{21}$

4. $\dfrac{16}{4}$ **5.** $\dfrac{36}{30}$ **6.** $\dfrac{49}{14}$

7. $\dfrac{24}{3}$ **8.** $\dfrac{54}{18}$ **9.** $\dfrac{8}{12}$

Convert these fractions to like measurement units and then reduce each fraction to show a size relationship. See if you can make each fraction into a scale factor.

10. $\dfrac{3 \text{ in.}}{4 \text{ ft}}$ **11.** $\dfrac{8 \text{ in.}}{2 \text{ yd}}$ **12.** $\dfrac{440 \text{ yd}}{\frac{1}{2} \text{ mi}}$

13. $\dfrac{18 \text{ in.}}{1 \text{ yd}}$ **14.** $\dfrac{2 \text{ yd}}{12 \text{ ft}}$

Extending Concepts

15. Ali is writing a script for a new movie in which aliens that are 3 times the size of humans (3:1) take the game of football back to their home planet. HINT: U.S. regulation football fields measure 100 yards from goal line to goal line.

    a. How long is the aliens' field in yards?

    b. How long is the aliens' field in inches?

    c. How long is the aliens' field in feet?

16. The scale factor of Jumbolia to Ourland is 17:1. That means that objects in Jumbolia are 17 times the size of the same objects in Ourland. Figure out how large the following Ourland objects would be in Jumbolia:

    a. a radio that is $4\frac{1}{2}$ in. high, 8 in. long, and $3\frac{1}{2}$ in. wide

    b. a rug that is $6\frac{1}{2}$ ft wide and $9\frac{3}{4}$ ft long

    c. a desk that is $2\frac{1}{3}$ ft high, 3 ft long, and $2\frac{1}{2}$ ft wide

Making Connections

17. Provide the scale factor for the following map by measuring the distance with a ruler. The distance from the library to the school is $2\frac{1}{2}$ miles.

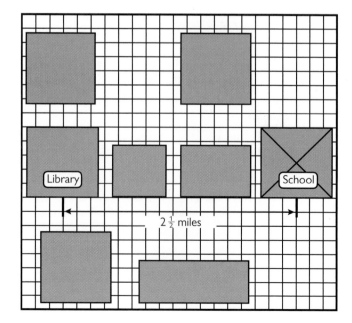

Telling Tales in Brobdingnag

Applying Skills

Convert these ratios to like measurement units and then reduce the fraction to create a scale factor.

Example $\frac{1}{2}$ yd: 6 in. $= \dfrac{\frac{1}{2}\text{ yd}}{6\text{ in.}} = \dfrac{18\text{ in.}}{6\text{ in.}} =$

$\dfrac{3\text{ in.}}{1\text{ in.}} =$ scale factor 3:1

1. $\frac{3}{4}$ ft: 3 in.

2. 6 ft: $\frac{1}{3}$ yd

3. $\frac{1}{2}$ mi: 528 ft

4. $2\frac{1}{2}$ yd: $\frac{1}{4}$ ft

5. 14 in: $\frac{7}{12}$ ft

6. $\frac{1}{6}$ yd: 2 in.

7. $\frac{1}{15}$ mi: 16 ft

8. $4\frac{1}{12}$ ft: 7 in.

9. 4 mi: 1,760 yd

10. 4,392 in: 6 ft

Extending Concepts

11. The scale factor of Mammothville to Ourland is 1 yd:1 in. That means if an object in Mammothville is one yard long, then the same object in Ourland would be only one inch long. Figure out how large the following Ourland objects would be in Mammothville:

   a. a soda can that is 5 in. tall and $2\frac{1}{2}$ in. wide

   b. a football field that is 100 yd long

   c. a table that is $3\frac{1}{2}$ ft high, 4 ft wide, and 2 yd long

12. The scale factor of Colossus to Ourland is $\frac{1}{4}$ yd: 3 in. That means if an object in Colossus is $\frac{1}{4}$ of a yard long, then the same object in Ourland would be only 3 inches long. How large would each of the Ourland objects from item **11** be in Colossus?

13. Match the following scale factors to the correct measurement units:

   a. 3:1

   b. 5,280:1

   c. 12:1

   d. 1,760:1

   i. 1 ft:1 in.

   ii. 1 mi:1 yd

   iii. 1 yd:1 ft

   iv. 1 mi:1 ft

Making Connections

14. In Humungoville the scale factor to Ourland is 4:1. Use the postage stamp from Ourland pictured below to draw a postage stamp for Humungoville. Make sure the length and width are at a scale factor of 4:1. You can be creative with the picture inside.

Sizing Up the Lilliputians

Applying Skills

Write each of the following decimals as a fraction.

Example $0.302 = \dfrac{302}{1,000}$

1. 0.2   **2.** 0.435

3. 0.1056   **4.** 0.78

5. 0.44   **6.** 0.025

7. 0.9   **8.** 0.5002

9. 0.001   **10.** 0.67

Write each decimal in words.

Example 0.5 = five tenths

11. 0.007   **12.** 0.25

13. 0.3892   **14.** 0.6

15. 0.04

16. The scale factor of Pint-Size Place to Ourland is 1:11. That means that objects in Ourland are 11 times the size of the same objects in Pint-Size Place. Figure out about how large the following Ourland objects would be in Pint-Size Place:

  a. a house that is 15 ft high, 33 ft wide, and 60 ft long

  b. a train that is 363 ft long and 20 ft high

  c. a woman who is 5 ft 6 in. tall

Extending Concepts

17. Measure the height of each picture. Compare the sizes of the pictures and determine the scale factor. What is the scale factor when:

  a. the larger picture is 1?

  b. the smaller picture is 1?

Making Connections

18. The regulation size of a soccer field varies from the largest size, 119 m × 91 m, to the smallest size allowed, 91 m × 46 m. What is the difference in the perimeters of the two field sizes? How do you think the difference in perimeters affects the game?

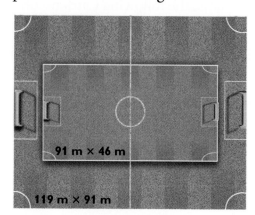

91 m × 46 m

119 m × 91 m

Glum-gluffs and Mum-gluffs

Applying Skills

Complete the following table showing equivalencies in the metric system.

	mm	cm	dm	m	km
1.				1,000	1
2.	1,000	100	10	1	
3.			1		
4.		1			
5.	1				

Supply the missing equivalent.

6. 42 dm = _____ m

7. 5 cm = _____ m

8. 0.5 m = _____ cm

9. 0.25 cm = _____ mm

10. 0.45 km = _____ m

11. 1.27 m = _____ dm

12. 24.5 dm = _____ cm

13. 38.69 cm = _____ m

14. 0.2 mm = _____ cm

15. 369,782 mm = _____ m

16. 0.128 cm = _____ mm

17. 7.3 m = _____ dm

Extending Concepts

18. Place the following measurements in height order from shortest to tallest.

- 1967 mm
- 0.0073 km
- 43.5 cm
- 0.5 m
- 7 dm

Making Connections

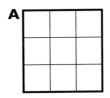
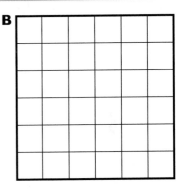

19. Count the smaller squares to figure out the sizes of squares A and B in square units.

a. What are the perimeter and the area of square A?

b. What are the perimeter and the area of square B?

20. Compare the two perimeters and the two areas. Describe each size relationship using a scale factor.

Housing and Feeding Gulliver

Applying Skills

Convert these fractions to like measurement units.

Example $\dfrac{4 \text{ m}}{4 \text{ cm}} = \dfrac{400 \text{ cm}}{4 \text{ cm}}$

1. $\dfrac{43 \text{ cm}}{43 \text{ mm}}$ **2.** $\dfrac{5 \text{ m}}{5 \text{ cm}}$ **3.** $\dfrac{6 \text{ km}}{6 \text{ m}}$

Use your answers from items 1–3 to show a scale factor that is less than one.
HINT: Reduce the larger number to one.

Example $\dfrac{400 \text{ cm} \div 400}{4 \text{ cm} \div 400} = \dfrac{1}{0.01} = 1{:}0.01$

4. $\dfrac{43 \text{ cm}}{43 \text{ mm}}$ **5.** $\dfrac{5 \text{ m}}{5 \text{ cm}}$ **6.** $\dfrac{6 \text{ km}}{6 \text{ m}}$

7. The scale factor of Teeny Town to Ourland is 1:6. That means that objects in Ourland are 6 times the size of the same objects in Teeny Town. Figure out how large the following Ourland objects would be in Teeny Town:

a. a book 30 cm high and 24 cm wide

b. a girl 156 cm tall

c. a table 1 m high, 150 cm wide, and 2 m long

Extending Concepts

8. Albert is using a scale factor of 3:1 for his school project. The height of the walls he measured are 3 m and the walls in the model he made are 1 m high. A 3-ft-high chair became a 1-ft-high chair in his project. Can he use both metric and U.S. customary measurement units in the same project? Why or why not?

9. The scale factor of Itty-Bittyville to Ourland is 1:4. That means that objects in Ourland are 4 times the size of the same objects in Itty-Bittyville. Estimate the sizes of each of the following Itty-Bittyville objects and find an object in Ourland that is about the same size:

a. an Itty-Bittyville textbook

b. an Itty-Bittyville double bed

c. an Itty-Bittyville two-story building

d. an Itty-Bittyville car

10. Estimate the scale factor of Peeweeopolis to Ourland if the area of an Ourland postage stamp is equal to the area of a Peeweeopolis sheet of paper.

Making Connections

For items 11–13 use the figure below.

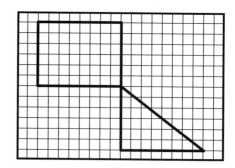

11. What is the area in square units of:

a. the rectangle?   **b.** the triangle?

12. Enlarge each shape using a scale factor of 3:1. What is the area in square units of:

a. the rectangle?   **b.** the triangle?

13. How did you figure out the area of each shape for items 11 and 12?

Seeing Through Lilliputian Eyes

Applying Skills

Reduce the following fractions to the lowest terms.

Example $\frac{36}{42} = \frac{6}{7}$

1. $\frac{81}{63}$ 2. $\frac{4}{24}$ 3. $\frac{16}{20}$

4. $\frac{5}{50}$ 5. $\frac{27}{36}$ 6. $\frac{36}{48}$

7. $\frac{90}{120}$ 8. $\frac{12}{10}$ 9. $\frac{75}{100}$

10. $\frac{11}{33}$ 11. $\frac{14}{21}$ 12. $\frac{80}{25}$

13. $\frac{9}{18}$ 14. $\frac{4}{12}$

Making Connections

17. In science-fiction movies, miniatures and scale-factor models are used to create many of the special effects. In one case, the special effects team created several different scale models of the hero's spaceship. The life-size ship that was built to use for the filming was 60 ft long. One scale model was 122 cm long by 173 cm wide by 61 cm high.

    a. What was the scale factor?

    b. What were the width and height of the life-size ship?

Extending Concepts

15. Measure the length and width of each of the following shapes. Which measurement system, metric or U.S. customary, would be the easiest to use to enlarge each object using a scale factor of 2:1? Why?

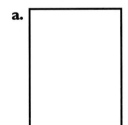

16. The scale factor of Miniopolis to Ourland is 1:7. That means that objects in Miniopolis are $\frac{1}{7}$ the size of the same objects in Ourland. Figure out how large the following Ourland objects would be in Miniopolis:

    a. a building that is 147 ft high, 77 ft wide, and 84 ft long

    b. a road that is 2 miles long

    c. a piece of paper that is $8\frac{1}{2}$ in. by 11 in.

Lands of the Large

Applying Skills

In the following exercises provide equivalent decimals.

Example $\frac{1}{2} = 0.5$

1. $\frac{1}{20}$ **2.** $\frac{1}{3}$ **3.** $\frac{1}{4}$

4. $\frac{1}{5}$ **5.** $\frac{1}{10}$ **6.** $\frac{1}{8}$

7. $\frac{3}{4}$ **8.** $\frac{1}{7}$

9. The scale factor of Big City to Ourland is 6.5:1. That means that objects in Big City are 6.5 times the size of the same objects in Ourland. Figure out how large the following Ourland objects would be in Big City:

   a. a tree that is 9 ft tall

   b. a man that is 6 ft tall

   c. a photo that is 7 in. wide and 5 in. long

Extending Concepts

10. Complete the following table by figuring out equivalent scale factors for each row.

	Decimals	Fractions	Whole Numbers
	1.5:1	$1\frac{1}{2}$:1	3:2
a.	6.5:1		
b.		$8\frac{1}{4}$:1	
c.			5:3

11. The scale factor of Big City to Hugeville is 3:2. That means that objects in Big City are 1.5, or $1\frac{1}{2}$, times the size of the same objects in Hugeville. How large would each of the Big City objects from item **9** be in Hugeville?

Making Connections

12. The scale factor is 5:1 for a giant ice cube in comparison to the school cafeteria's ice cubes.

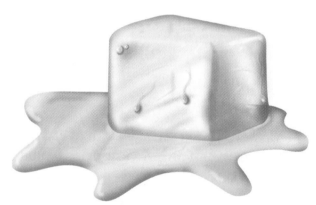

   a. Draw a picture that shows how many cafeteria ice cubes you would have to stack high, wide, and deep to build a giant ice cube.

   b. What is the total number of cafeteria ice cubes it would take to fill one giant ice cube?

Lands of the Little

Applying Skills

Complete the following chart by supplying the missing equivalents as decimals or fractions.

	Fractions	Decimals
1.	$\frac{1}{2}$	
2.		0.25
3.	$\frac{2}{3}$	
4.		0.7
5.	$\frac{3}{4}$	
6.		0.05
7.	$\frac{3}{8}$	
8.		0.125

Reduce the scale factor to a fraction. HINT: Divide each number by the largest number.

Example $10:7 = \frac{10}{10}:\frac{7}{10} = 1:\frac{7}{10}$

9. 3:2 **10.** 4:3 **11.** 5:3

Extending Concepts

12. The scale factor for Giantland to Ourland is 10:1. What is the scale factor from Ourland to Giantland? Write the scale factor using a decimal or fraction for Ourland to Giantland.

13. The scale factor of Wee World to Ourland is 0.5:1. That means that objects in Wee World are 0.5 the size of the same objects in Ourland. What is another way to write this scale factor without using a decimal?

14. Using the scale factor from item **13**, figure out how large the following Ourland objects would be in Wee World:

a. a house that is 15 ft high, 35 ft wide, and 60 ft long

b. a train that is 360 ft long and 20 ft high

c. a woman who is 5 ft 4 in. tall

Making Connections

15. Answer this Dr. Math letter:

> Dr. Math,
>
> When I was doing problems 9–11 in today's homework, my friend said there was a pattern between the whole-number scale factor and the fraction scale factor. I don't see it. Can you please explain it to me? Could I use this pattern to rescale objects more efficiently?
>
> D.S. Mall

Homework 11

Gulliver's Worlds Cubed

Applying Skills

Complete the following chart with equivalent expressions.

	Exponent	Arithmetic Expression	Value
	3^3	$3 \times 3 \times 3$	27
1.	2^2		
2.		$4 \times 4 \times 4$	
3.			25
4.	6^2		
5.			49
6.	8^3		
7.			81
8.	10^2		
9.	5^3		
10.		$6 \times 6 \times 6$	

Tell whether each unit of measurement would be used for area or volume.

11. yd^2 (square yard)

12. cm^3 (cubic centimeter)

13. m^2 (square meter)

14. in^2 (square inch)

15. ft^3 (cubic feet)

16. mm^3 (cubic millimeter)

Extending Concepts

17. Concrete To Go is going to pour a patio 4 yd long, 4 yd wide, and $\frac{1}{12}$ yd deep. Do they need to know the area or the volume to know how much concrete is needed? Come up with a strategy to figure out how much concrete they should pour.

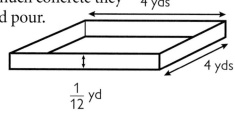

Making Connections

18. Imagine you have been hired by a famous clothing designer. It is your job to purchase the fabric for the upcoming designs. Your boss asks you to draw a smaller version of the designer's most successful scarf using a scale factor of 1:3. The original scarf is one yard long and one yard wide.

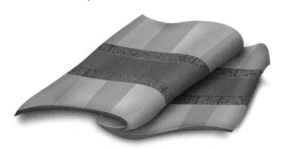

a. Draw a pattern with measurements for the new smaller scarf.

b. The company will make one hundred smaller scarves using your new pattern. How much fabric should you purchase?

Stepping into Gulliver's Worlds

Applying Skills

Complete the following chart by supplying the missing equivalents as decimals or fractions.

	Decimal	Fraction
1.	0.125	
2.		$\frac{3}{8}$
3.	0.75	
4.	0.67	
5.		$\frac{1}{2}$
6.	0.2	
7.		$\frac{1}{10}$
8.		$\frac{1}{20}$

9. Measure the sides of the square in inches. What is the:

   a. perimeter?   **b.** area?

10. Use the metric system to measure the height, width, and length of the cube below.

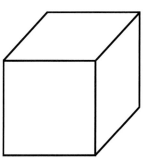

Extending Concepts

11. Shelley wants to cover a box with contact paper. The box is 1 ft high, 1 ft wide, and 1 ft deep.

   a. Draw the box and show the measurements.

   b. How many square feet of paper will she need to cover one face of the box?

   c. How many square feet will she need to cover all sides of the box?

Making Connections

12. The creator of a famous theme park wanted children to feel bigger than life. The scale factor of objects in real life to objects in the park is 1:0.75.

   a. Height of a street light?

     Real life: 12 ft

     Theme park:

   b. Length and width of a door?

     Real life: $32'' \times 80''$

     Theme park:

   c. Height, width, and depth of a box?

     Real life: 4 ft $\times$ 4 ft $\times$ 8 ft

     Theme park:

12 feet

STUDENT GALLERY

volume

Proportion

vatio

The Seeing and Thinking Mathematically project is based at Education Development Center, Inc. (EDC), Newton, MA, and was supported, in part, by the National Science Foundation Grant No. 9054677. Opinions expressed are those of the authors and not necessarily those of the National Science Foundation.

CREDITS: Photographs: Chris Conroy Photography • Beverley Harper (cover) • Duane Bibby: pp. 2–6, 8, 10, 12, 14–16, 18, 20, 22 • Saul Rosenbaum: pp. 26–28, 30, 32, 35–38, 42, 44–45.

© 1998 Creative Publications
1300 Villa Street
Mountain View, California 94041

Printed in the United States of America

0-7622-0213-0

2 3 4 5 6 7 8 9 10 . 02 01 00 99 98 97

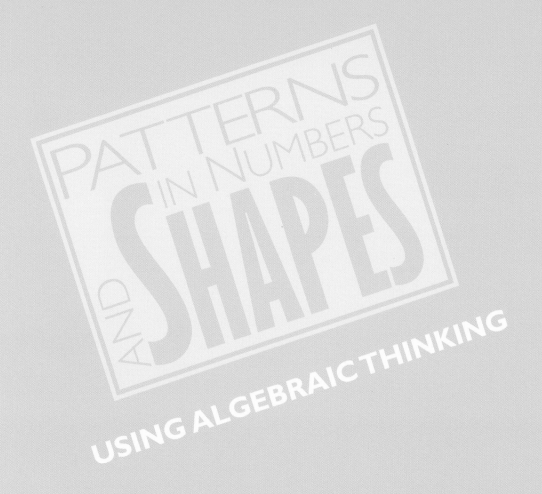

PATTERNS IN NUMBERS AND SHAPES

USING ALGEBRAIC THINKING

STUDENT GUIDE

PATTERNS IN NUMBERS AND SHAPES

USING ALGEBRAIC THINKING

MathScape™

SEEING AND THINKING MATHEMATICALLY

You will practice looking for
patterns in different places—
in drawings and numbers,
sometimes in a story. You will
even make up some patterns
of your own. By making
tables of the data you find, you
will discover ways to extend the
patterns to very large sizes.

How does math relate to patterns?

PATTERNS
IN NUMBERS
AND
SHAPES

PHASE**TWO**
Describing Patterns Using
Variables and Expressions

In this phase you look for
patterns in letters that grow and
chocolates in a box. You will
begin to use the language of
algebra by giving the rules for
these patterns using variables
and expressions. You will
practice using expressions to
compare different ways of
describing a pattern to see if
they give the same result.

PHASE**THREE**
Describing Patterns Using
Graphs

In this phase you will plot
points in all parts of the
coordinate grid to make a
mystery drawing for your
partner. You will turn number
rules into graphs and look at
the patterns they make. By
comparing graphs of some
teenagers' wages for summer
jobs, you will decide who has
the better pay rate.

PHASE**FOUR**
Finding and Extending Patterns

After you have learned some
ways to describe the rules for
patterns, this phase gives you a
chance to try out your skills in
new situations. You look for
patterns in a story about a
sneaky sheep and in animal
pictures that grow. You analyze
three different patterns for
inheriting some money in order
to give some good advice.

PHASE ONE

In this phase you will look for patterns in three different situations. By making tables of the data, you can see how the patterns develop and discover how to extend them to greater size. Working with patterns in numbers, shapes, and a story helps you to develop math skills that carry over into algebra problems. You will begin to be able to work out a rule that will apply to all cases of a situation, and use your rule to solve problems.

Describing Patterns Using Tables

WHAT'S THE MATH?

Investigations in this section focus on:

PATTERN SEEKING

- Developing skills in looking for patterns in new situations
- Writing rules for patterns
- Extending pattern rules to apply to all cases

RECORDING DATA

- Making tables of data to describe patterns

NUMBER

- Exploring number relationships to look for patterns

Calendar Tricks

Finding a pattern can help you solve problems in surprising ways. In this activity, you will think about patterns as you test whether tricks using the numbers on a calendar will always be true. Then you will invent and test your own tricks.

Look for a Pattern

How can you know whether number patterns on a grid will always be true?

Paul invented three tricks for a block of four numbers. Find which of Paul's tricks are true for every possible two-by-two block of numbers on the calendar.

- Which tricks always worked? Which did not? How did you find out?

- For any tricks that did not always work, how can you revise them so that they do always work?

Paul's Box of Tricks

Sun	Mon	Tue	Wed	Thurs	Fri	Sat
1	2	3	4	5	6	7
8	9	10	11	12	13	14
15	16	17	18	19	20	21
22	23	24	25	26	27	28
29	30	31				

Trick One: The sums of opposite pairs of numbers will be equal. For example: $2 + 10 = 3 + 9$.

Trick Two: If you add all four numbers, the sum will always be evenly divisible by 8. For example:
$2 + 3 + 9 + 10 = 24; 24 \div 8 = 3$.

Trick Three: If you multiply opposite pairs of numbers, the two answers will always differ by 7. For example:
$2 \times 10 = 20; 3 \times 9 = 27; 27 - 20 = 7$.

Invent Your Own Tricks

The calendar on this page shows sequences of three numbers going diagonally to the right, shaded blue, and to the left, outlined in red. Can you make up tricks about diagonals of three numbers like these?

Make up at least two tricks for diagonals of three numbers like the numbers shaded blue in the example.

- Will your tricks be true for every diagonal of three numbers? How do you know?

- Which of your tricks will still be true if the diagonal goes in the opposite direction like the numbers in the red outline?

Make up at least two more tricks using your own shapes. Your shapes should be different from the ones shown so far.

- Are your tricks always true, no matter where on the calendar you put your shape?

- How do you know your tricks will always be true?

How can you use patterns to invent tricks that will always work?

Write About Finding Patterns

Think about the patterns you explored and the tricks you invented in this lesson.

- How did you check whether your tricks will work everywhere on the calendar?

- What suggestions would you give to help another student find patterns?

Patterns on a Slant

Sun	Mon	Tue	Wed	Thurs	Fri	Sat
1	2	3	4	5	6	7
8	9	10	11	12	13	14
15	16	17	18	19	20	21
22	23	24	25	26	27	28
29	30	31				

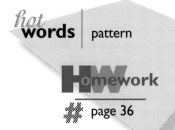

hot **words** | pattern

Homework

page 36

2 Painting Faces

Here is a problem about painting all sides of a three-dimensional shape. Sometimes using objects is helpful in solving problems like this. You can record the data you get when you solve for shorter lengths and organize it into a table to help you find a rule for any length.

Make a Table of the Data

How can you set up a table to record data about a pattern?

A company that makes colored rods uses a paint stamping machine to color the rods. The stamp paints exactly one square of area at a time. Every face of each rod has to be painted, so this length 2 rod would need 10 stamps of paint.

How many stamps would you need to paint rods from lengths 1 to 10? Record your answers in a table and look for a pattern.

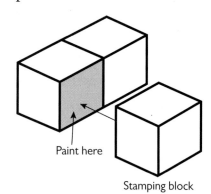

Length 2 rod;
each end equals 1 square.

Paint here

Stamping block

How to Organize Your Data in a Table

1. Use the first column to show the data you begin with. Write the numbers in order from least to greatest. In this example, the lengths of the rods go in the first column.

2. Use the second column to show numbers that give information about the first sequence. Here, the numbers of stamps needed to paint each length of rod go in the second column.

Length of Rod	Stamps Needed
1	
2	
3	

Extend the Pattern

Look at the table you made. Do you see a pattern in the data in the table?

1 Use what you learned from the table. Find the number of paint stamps you need to paint rods of lengths 25 and 66.

2 Write a rule you could use to extend the pattern to any length of rod.

Now look again at your table and your rule. Decide how you could use the number of stamps to find the size of the rod. Think about the operations you used in your rule.

3 What if it takes 86 stamps to paint the rod? How long is the rod?

4 If it takes 286 stamps to paint the rod, how long is the rod?

5 Write a rule you could use to find the length of any rod if you know the number of stamps needed to paint it.

Can you write a rule you could use to extend the pattern?

Write About Making a Table

Think about how you used the table you made to solve problems about painting the rods.

- How did making a table help you to find the pattern?

- Describe how far you think you would need to extend a table to be sure of a pattern.

hot **words** | pattern
table

Homework

page 37

3 Crossing the River

Examining a pattern can help you develop a general rule that applies to any stage of the pattern. In this investigation you will look for a pattern to solve the problem of getting a group of hikers across a river using one small boat.

Find a Rule for Any Number

How can finding a pattern help solve for all cases?

Think carefully about how the hikers could cross the river using just one boat. It may be helpful to act it out or use a diagram to solve the problem. As you work, make a table showing how many trips it takes for 1 to 5 adults and 2 children to cross. Look for the pattern, then use it to find how many trips are required for the other groups to cross to the other side.

1 How many one-way trips does it take for the entire group of 8 adults and 2 children to cross the river? Tell how you found your answer.

2 How many trips in all for 6 adults and 2 children?

3 15 adults and 2 children?

4 23 adults and 2 children?

5 100 adults and 2 children?

Tell how you would find the number of one-way trips needed for any number of adults and two children to cross the river. (Everyone can row the boat.)

Ten Hikers—One Boat

A group of 8 adults and 2 children needs to cross a river. They have a small boat that can hold either:

   or      or   

1 adult   1 child   2 children

Use Your Method in Another Way

Use the pattern to find the number of adults who need to cross
the river for each case.

**How can you work
backward from what
you know?**

1 It takes 13 trips to get all of the adults and the 2 children
across the river.

2 It takes 41 trips to get all of the adults and the 2 children
across the river.

3 It takes 57 trips to get all of the adults and the 2 children
across the river.

Tell How You Look for Patterns

Write a friend a letter telling how you look for patterns. Give
examples from the patterns you have investigated so far. Answers
to the following questions will help you write your letter.

- How can a table help you discover and describe a pattern?

- What other tools are helpful?

- How does finding a pattern help you solve problems?

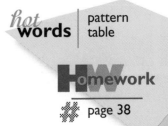

hot words | pattern
table

Homework

page 38

As you look for patterns in this phase, you will think about how you can describe their rules in a way that applies to all situations. You will begin to use the language of algebra by writing rules using variables and expressions. You will compare your rules to those of other students to see if they give the same result. Some of the patterns change in more than one way and you will need to find a way to express that in your rule.

Describing Patterns Using Variables and Expressions

WHAT'S THE MATH?

Investigations in this section focus on:

PATTERN SEEKING

- Looking for patterns in numbers and shapes
- Examining patterns with two variables

ALGEBRA

- Using variables and expressions

EQUIVALENCE

- Exploring equivalence of expressions

 **Letter Perfect**

Using variables and expressions gives you a shorthand way to describe a pattern. These tile letters grow according to different patterns. You will explore how to write a rule to predict the number of tiles needed to make letters of any size.

Find a Rule That Fits Every Case

How can a pattern help you predict the number of tiles used for any size?

Find a rule that will tell how many tiles it takes to build any size of the letter *I*.

Size 1   Size 2   Size 3

1 Look for a pattern. Describe it clearly with words.

2 Describe the pattern using variables and expressions. This rule tells how the letter grows.

3 Use the rule to predict the number of tiles needed for each *I*:

   a. size 12   **b.** size 15   **c.** size 22   **d.** size 100

Suppose you had 39 tiles. What is the largest size of *I* that you could make?

Using Variables and Expressions to Describe Patterns

These are the first three sizes of the letter *O*.

Size 1   Size 2   Size 3

How many tiles are needed to make each size? The pattern that tells how many can be described in words: The number of tiles needed is four times the size.

You can write this as 4 × *size*.

A shorter way to write the same thing is 4 × *s* or 4*s*.

In this example, the letter *s* is called a **variable** because it can take on many values.

4*s* is an **expression.** An expression is a combination of variables, numbers, and operations.

Relate the Rule to the Pattern

For one letter in the chart See How They Grow, the number of tiles is always $4s + 1$. The variable s stands for the size number. Decide how many tiles are added at each step. Look for the pattern.

1 Which letter do you think fits the pattern, *L*, *T*, or *X*? How many tiles are needed for size 16 of the letter?

2 For each of the other letters, give a rule that tells the number of tiles in any size.

Write About Your Own Letter Pattern

Make up your own letter shape with tiles. Figure out how you can make the letter grow into larger sizes.

- Draw your letter and tell how it grows.

- Give the rule for your letter using variables and expressions.

- Show how you can use the rule to predict the number of tiles that it would take to build size 100 of your letter.

How can variables and expressions describe a pattern?

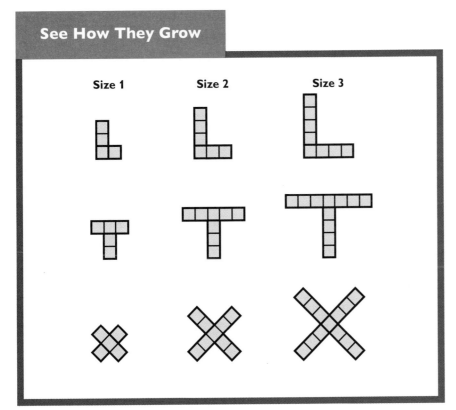

See How They Grow

Size 1   Size 2   Size 3

hot words   expression   variable

Homework

❋ page 39

5 Tiling Garden Beds

You have used tables and variables to describe different kinds of patterns. Here you will apply what you have learned to a new situation. You will show how each part of your solution relates to the situation. Then you can compare different ways of expressing the same idea.

What different rules or expressions can you write to describe a pattern?

Find the Number of Tiles

Here are three sizes of gardens framed with a single row of tiles:

Length 1   Length 2   Length 3

1. Begin a table that shows the number of tiles for each length. Use the table to write an expression that describes the number of tiles needed for a garden of any length.

Length of Garden	Number of Tiles
1	8
2	
3	

2. Use your expression to find how many tiles you would need to make a border around gardens of each of these lengths.

   a. 20 squares   **b.** 30 squares   **c.** 100 squares

3. Tell how you would find the length of the garden if you knew only the number of tiles in the border.

   Test your method. How long is the garden if the following numbers of tiles are used for the border?

   a. 68 tiles   **b.** 152 tiles   **c.** 512 tiles

4. Relate each part of your expression to the garden and the tiles.

Extend the Rule

Some gardens are two squares wide, and vary in length.
For example:

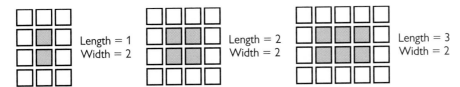

Length = 1
Width = 2

Length = 2
Width = 2

Length = 3
Width = 2

Can you write a rule for tiling a garden of any length and any width?

Can you figure out the number of tiles needed for gardens of any length and a width of 2? Use an expression that describes your method. Use the method to solve these problems.

How many tiles do you need to make a border around each of the following gardens?

1 $l = 5, w = 2$ **2** $l = 10, w = 2$

3 $l = 20, w = 2$ **4** $l = 100, w = 2$

Write About Equivalent Expressions

You and your classmates may use different expressions to describe these patterns. Compare your ideas with others.

- What equivalent expressions did you and your classmates write?

- How do you know they are equivalent?

Conventions for Algebraic Notation

Writing variables and expressions in standard ways avoids confusion. The numeral is placed before the letter representing a variable:

$$2l \text{ not } l2$$

The numeral 1 is not required before a variable:

$$\text{Use } l \text{ instead of } 1l$$

"Two times the length" can be stated several ways:

$$2l \quad 2 \cdot l \quad 2 \times l$$

Place parentheses carefully.

$$l + 3 \times 2 \text{ does not equal } (l + 3) \times 2.$$

hot**words** | equivalent expression

Homework

page 40

6 Chocolates by the Box

EXPLORING PATTERNS WITH TWO VARIABLES

Some patterns can be described using more than one variable. The boxes of chocolates in this lesson are an example of this type of pattern. You will look for a way to write a rule that will apply to all sizes of chocolate boxes.

Find the Contents for Each Size

How can you use variables to describe the pattern?

Buy a Box of Chocolates—Get a Bonus

2 by 2 size

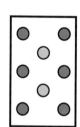

2 by 3 size

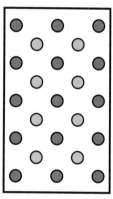

3 by 5 size

When you buy a box of Choco Chocolates, you get a bonus light chocolate between every group of four dark chocolates, as the diagrams show. The size of the box tells you how many columns and how many rows of dark chocolates come in the box.

1 How many *dark* chocolates will you get in each size of box?

    a. 4 by 4   **b.** 4 by 8   **c.** 6 by 7

    d. 12 by 25   **e.** 20 by 20   **f.** 100 by 100

2 How can you figure out the number of dark chocolates in any size box? Explain your method using words, diagrams, or expressions.

Rewrite Your Rule

Now that you have developed a rule for finding the number of dark chocolates, how can you figure out the number of light chocolates in any size box?

How can you use your method to write another rule?

1 Explain your method using words, diagrams, or expressions.

2 Test your method. How many *light* chocolates will you get in each box of these sizes?

a. 4 by 4   **b.** 4 by 8   **c.** 6 by 7

d. 12 by 25   **e.** 20 by 20   **f.** 100 by 100

3 Use variables and expressions to describe the total number of all chocolates in any box.

Write About Using Variables

Think about how you have used variables and expressions to describe patterns. Write a note to one of next year's students telling how you use these tools to solve problems.

- Give some examples of using expressions to describe patterns.

- Tell how you decide whether two expressions are equivalent.

A Pattern of Js with Two Variables

Choco Company uses chocolate squares to make letters you can eat. They make the letter J in different heights and widths.

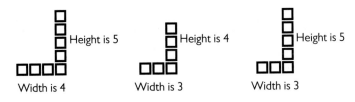

To find the total number of squares needed to make a letter J, you can add the height and width and subtract 1.

You can write this with words and symbols:
height + width − 1

Or you can use two variables (one for height and one for width) and say it this way: $h + w - 1$

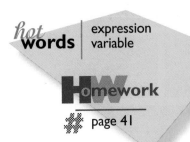

hot **words** | expression variable

Homework
page 41

PHASE THREE

In this phase, you will move around the coordinate plane to identify points and to graph data that you develop when you are looking for patterns. As you work with number rules for patterns, you begin to see the relationship of a list of ordered pairs to the line they form when they are graphed. You will use the information you find in the graphs to solve problems about some real-life situations involving summer jobs for two teenagers.

Describing Patterns Using Graphs

WHAT'S THE MATH?

Investigations in this section focus on:

PATTERN SEEKING

- Relating a pattern rule to a graphed line and the line to the rule

ALGEBRA

- Identifying points on the coordinate plane
- Making tables of ordered pairs
- Graphing ordered pairs on the coordinate plane

PROBLEM SOLVING

- Interpreting data from a graph
- Using patterns on a graph to solve problems

Gridpoint Pictures

USING A
COORDINATE PLANE

So far, you've described patterns using words, pictures, tables, variables, and expressions. Now you will look at another tool: the coordinate grid or plane. Before using this tool, review some of the basic definitions in "Finding Your Way Around the Coordinate Plane."

Describe a Picture on the Coordinate Plane

How can you make and describe a picture on a coordinate plane?

Draw a simple picture on a coordinate plane. You may want to write your initials in block letters or draw a house or other simple object. Be sure your picture has parts in all four quadrants.

Using coordinates, write a description of how to make your picture. You can also include other directions, but you may not use pictures.

Finding Your Way Around the Coordinate Plane

The coordinate plane is divided into four quadrants by the horizontal x-axis and the vertical y-axis. The axes intersect at the origin. You can locate any point on the plane if you know the coordinates for x and y. The x-coordinate is always stated first.

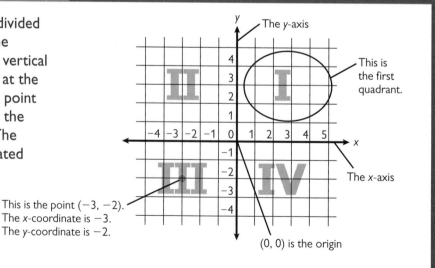

The y-axis

This is the first quadrant.

The x-axis

This is the point $(-3, -2)$.
The x-coordinate is -3.
The y-coordinate is -2.

$(0, 0)$ is the origin

PATTERNS IN NUMBERS AND SHAPES   LESSON 7

© Creative Publications • MathScape

Decode a Gridpoint Picture

When your picture and list are finished, trade descriptions with a partner. Do not show your pictures until later.

1 Draw the picture your partner has described. Keep notes on anything that is not clear.

2 Return the description and your picture to your partner. Check the picture your partner drew from your description to see if it matches your original drawing. If there are differences, what caused them? If necessary, revise your description.

How can coordinates help you draw a gridpoint picture?

Write About What You See

Suppose you are given the coordinates for a set of points. How could you tell if the points are all on a straight vertical line? a straight horizontal line? Explain.

hot **words** | coordinate graph
point

page 42

8 Points, Plots, and Patterns

When you used points on a coordinate plane to describe a picture, you followed a visual pattern. Now you will see what happens when the points all spring from a number rule. Keep an eye out for patterns!

What patterns in the points on the coordinate grid fit a number rule?

Find Some Patterns in the Plots

You may think of a number rule as being expressed only in words and numerals. Some surprising things develop when you plot a graph using ordered pairs that follow a rule.

1 Make up a number rule of your own.

2 Make a table of points that fit the rule.

3 Plot the points on the coordinate plane.

4 What patterns do you notice on the coordinate plane? Can you find points that fit the rule but do not fit the pattern?

Repeat the process with other number rules. Keep a record of your results.

Ordered Pairs and Number Rules

In the ordered pair (4, 8), 4 is the *x*-coordinate and 8 is the *y*-coordinate.

A number rule tells how the two numbers in an ordered pair are related. Here are some examples:

- The *x*-coordinate is half the *y*-coordinate.
- The *y*-coordinate is 6 more than the *x*-coordinate.
- The *x*-coordinate and the *y*-coordinate are the same.

Find the Rule for the Pattern

How does a line show a relationship between coordinates on a grid?

Think about the patterns that you have been plotting on the grid. Do you think you can find the rule for a line passing through two points?

Try this. Mark the two endpoints that are given. Carefully draw a line between the points. What is the pattern or rule for all the points falling exactly on the line?

1 $(6, 4)$ and $(-6, -8)$

2 $(3, 12)$ and $(-1, -4)$

Write About Graphing Number Rules

What do you notice about the graphs from your number rules and those of your classmates? Write a summary of as many generalizations as possible. Here are some possibilities that you might want to include:

- What can you say about any multiplication or division rule?

- What can you say about addition rules?

- What happens to the graph when you multiply by larger numbers in your number rule?

hot **words**   coordinate graph
ordered pair

Homework
page 43

Payday at Planet Adventure

Rachel and Enrico have summer jobs at Planet Adventure, a local amusement park. Since Rachel gets bonus pay, it's not easy to make a quick comparison of their wages. You will use a graph to compare how much they earn for different lengths of time.

Make a Graph of Earnings

What can a graph tell about wages?

Rachel works in the Hall of Mirrors. Her rate of pay each day is $5 per hour. She also gets a daily $9 bonus for wearing a strange costume.

- Make a table to show what pay she should receive for different numbers of hours worked each day.

- Next, draw a graph of the data for Rachel's pay. Label the axes and choose an appropriate scale for the graph.

How would you find the amount of money Rachel earns for any number of hours worked? Use words, diagrams, or equations to explain your method.

Compare Earning Rates

Enrico works at the Space Shot roller coaster. His rate of pay is $6.50 an hour.

- Make a table to show what pay he receives for different numbers of hours worked each day.

- On the same grid you used for Rachel's pay, draw a graph of the data for Enrico's pay.

- How would you find the amount of pay Enrico earns for any number of hours worked? Is the method different from the one you used for Rachel?

How can a graph help compare wages?

Write About the Graphs

Compare the graphs of Rachel's pay and Enrico's pay. Which job pays better? How did you decide?

- Tell how the graphs are the same and how they are different.

- In which hours does Rachel earn more than Enrico? Enrico more than Rachel?

- Do Rachel and Enrico ever earn the same amount for the same number of hours worked? How did you find out?

hot words | coordinate graph
words | table

page 44

PHASEFOUR

This phase gives you a chance to try out all the tools you have learned to use in describing patterns. You will examine the situations, decide how you will explain the pattern, and then write a rule to extend the pattern to any size. You will show what you know about how ordered pairs and graphs are related and how to use variables and expressions to describe patterns. You will soon see how much you have learned about looking for patterns.

Finding and Extending Patterns

WHAT'S THE MATH?

Investigations in this this section focus on:

PATTERN SEEKING

- Identifying, describing, and generalizing patterns
- Choosing appropriate tools to describe patterns

NUMBER and OPERATIONS

- Using inverse operations with pattern rules

ALGEBRA

- Using variables and expressions to describe patterns
- Making lists of ordered pairs to describe patterns
- Graphing ordered pairs

PROBLEM SOLVING

- Using patterns in problem situations

10

Sneaking Up the Line

SOLVING A SIMPLER PROBLEM TO FIND A PATTERN

Finding a pattern in a simpler problem can help you understand a problem with greater values. Careful reasoning in a sample problem will help you make a rule about this sneaky situation.

Solve a Simpler Problem

How can you identify a pattern by solving a simpler problem first?

After you read "A Woolly Tale" and make your prediction, try some small problems to help look for a pattern.

1. Can you find how many sheep would be shorn before Eric if there are 6 sheep ahead of him? Use counters, diagrams, or any other method to solve the problem.

   What if there are 11 sheep ahead of him? What if the number in front of Eric is 4 to 10? 11 to 13? It may help to make a table, then graph the data.

Use what you learned in the simpler problems.

2. Find how many sheep would be shorn before Eric if there were 49 sheep in front of him. Does the answer match the prediction you made at first?

3. Describe a rule or expression you would use to find the number shorn before Eric for any number of sheep in front of him.

A Woolly Tale

Eric the Sheep is at the end of a line of sheep waiting to be shorn. But being an impatient sort of a sheep, every time the shearer takes a sheep from the front to be shorn, Eric sneaks up the line two places.

Think about how long it will take Eric to reach the head of the line. Before you begin to work, make a prediction. If there are 49 sheep ahead of him, how many of the sheep will be shorn before Eric?

Test Your Rule

In each case, find how many sheep are shorn before Eric.

1 There were 37 sheep in front of Eric.

2 There were 296 sheep in front of him.

3 There were 1,000 sheep in front of him.

4 There were 7,695 sheep in front of the sneaky sheep.

Now try using your rule to find how many sheep were lined up in front of Eric if:

5 13 sheep were shorn before him.

6 21 sheep were shorn before Eric.

Will your rule work for any number?

Write About Your Sneaky Rule

Eric's pattern of sneaking up the line follows a rule with some new things to think about.

- How do situations 5 and 6 above differ from 1–4?

- Describe how you used your rule to find how many sheep were ahead of Eric.

hot **words** | coordinate graph
table

Homework

✳ page 45

11 Something Fishy

You have learned to identify the rule for many patterns from simple to complex. Here you find how to describe the pattern as an animal drawing changes in more than one way. Then you get to grow your own animals and describe their patterns.

Go Fishing for Some New Patterns of Growth

How can you describe the growth of some geometric patterns?

The fish in Patternville grow in a particular way. The diagram on dot paper shows the first four stages of this growth.

1 For fish in growth stages 1–6, figure out how many line segments and spots they would have in each stage. Show your answers using expressions, tables, and graphs.

2 Use what you observed about the growth in the number of *line segments* to answer these questions:

   a. How many line segments would a fish in stage 20 have?

   b. How many line segments would a fish in stage 101 have?

   c. In what stage of growth has the fish 98 line segments?

   d. In what stage of growth has the fish 399 line segments?

Something Fishy in Patternville

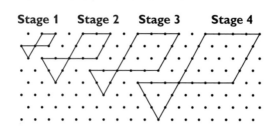

Stage 1   Stage 2   Stage 3   Stage 4

There are two ways to measure the growth of the fish: line segments and spots.

Line Segments
Count the line segments between dots needed to make the fish. It takes seven line segments to make the fish in stage 1.

Spots
Count the number of spots inside the fish's body (not including the tail). A fish in stage 1 has no spots and a fish in stage 2 has one spot.

3 Use what you observed about the growth in the number of *spots* to answer these questions:

   a. How many spots would a fish have in stage 20?

   b. How many spots would a fish have in stage 101?

How can you figure out how many line segments and spots a fish would have at any stage? Use words, diagrams, or equations to explain your method. Look for a short way to state it clearly.

Create Your Own Growing Patterns

Look at the examples from the Patternville Zoo. Then use graph paper, dot paper, or toothpicks to create your own "animal" and show how it grows in stages. Make sure you have a clear rule for the way it grows.

Draw your animal and write the rule for its growth at any stage on the back of the drawing. Create a table and a graph to show stages 1–5 of your animal's growth.

Write an explanation of why your rule will predict the number of dots or line segments for any size of your animal.

What are some different patterns that describe how a drawing can grow?

Examples from the Patternville Zoo

Stage	1	2	3
Dots	14	16	18
Area	6	7	8

Stage	1	2	3
Dots	14	16	18
Area	6	7	8

Stage	1	2	3
Dots	14	16	18
Area	6	7	8

hot **words** | expression variable

page 46

12 The Will

The results of a growth pattern are not always obvious at first. In this situation you will project the patterns into the future in order to make a good recommendation for Harriet. You may choose any tools you wish to describe the patterns.

Make a Prediction

Which payment plan looks like the best choice?

Harriet's uncle has just died. He has left her some money in his will, but she must decide how it is paid. Read about the three plans in the will. You can help her choose which plan would be the best for her.

Before doing any calculations, predict which plan would give Harriet the greatest amount of money at the end of year 25. Give your reasons for your choice.

From Harriet's Uncle's Will

... and to my niece Harriet, I give a cash amount of money to spend as she pleases at the end of each year for 25 years. Knowing how much she likes a bit of mathematics, I give her a choice of three payment plans.

Plan A:

$100	at the end of year 1
$300	at the end of year 2
$500	at the end of year 3
$700	at the end of year 4
$900	at the end of year 5
(and so on)	

Plan B:

$10	at the end of year 1
$40	at the end of year 2
$90	at the end of year 3
$160	at the end of year 4
$250	at the end of year 5
(and so on)	

Plan C:

1 cent	at the end of year 1
2 cents	at the end of year 2
4 cents	at the end of year 3
8 cents	at the end of year 4
16 cents	at the end of year 5
(and so on)	

Compare the Plans

Each plan pays a greater amount of money each year, but the amounts increase in different ways. In order to compare the plans, you will need to find the amount Harriet would receive for each plan in each year.

How can you describe the patterns and extend them into the future?

1 For each plan, what patterns did you see in the amount Harriet would receive each year? Use words, diagrams, or expressions to explain the patterns.

2 Make tables and graphs to show the amount she would receive for each plan in each year. What amount of money will Harriet receive at the end of the tenth year? the twentieth year? the twenty-fifth year?

3 Describe a method you could use to find the amount Harriet would get at the end of any year for each plan.

Give Some Good Advice

Write a letter to Harriet advising her as to which plan she should choose and why. Make sure to compare the three plans. You can choose words, diagrams, tables, graphs, and expressions to support your recommendation.

hot **words** | coordinate graph expression

page 47

Calendar Tricks

Applying Skills

Read the four statements A–D. Then tell which are true for each two-by-two block of four numbers.

A. The sum of the four numbers is divisible by 4.

B. The sum of the four numbers is divisible by 8.

C. The sum of the bottom two numbers differs from the sum of the top two numbers by 14.

D. The number in the bottom right corner is three times as big as the number in the top left corner.

Sun	Mon	Tue	Wed	Thurs	Fri	Sat
1	2	3	4	5	6	7
8	9	10	11	12	13	14
15	16	17	18	19	20	21
22	23	24	25	26	27	28
29	30	31				

1. Which statements are true for the shaded block on the calendar?

2. Which statements are true for the block formed by numbers 6, 7, 13, and 14?

3. Which statements are true for the block formed by numbers 19, 20, 26, and 27?

4. Which statements do you think are true for every possible two-by-two block of four numbers on the calendar?

Extending Concepts

5. Choose two different blocks of nine numbers arranged 3 across and 3 down on a calendar, and check that this rule holds: For any block of nine numbers the average of the four corner numbers is equal to the middle number. Show your work and explain why the rule works.

6. Make up your own trick which works for any three-by-three block of nine numbers. Explain why your trick works.

Making Connections

7. It is said that the seven-day week was based originally on the idea of the influence of the planets. For a long time people believed that seven celestial bodies revolved around the earth. The early Romans observed an eight-day week based on the recurrence of market days.

a. What pattern or trick do you notice about numbers on a diagonal of a calendar such as 2, 10, 18,…? Why does this trick work? Revise the rule for the pattern so that it would work for a calendar with 8 days in each row.

b. Would the rule in item 5 work for a calendar with 8 days in each row? Why or why not?

Painting Faces

Applying Skills

A company that makes colored rods uses a paint stamping block to paint only the front and one end of each rod like this:

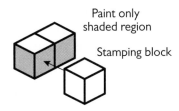

Paint only
shaded region

Stamping block

1. Copy and complete the table to show how many stamps would be needed to paint rods with lengths 1 to 10.

Length of Rod	Stamps Needed
1	2
2	3
3	
4	
5	
6	
7	
8	
9	
10	

2. What rule could you use to find the number of stamps needed for a rod of any length?

3. How many paint stamps are needed to paint a rod of length 23? 36? 64?

4. How long is the rod if the number of stamps needed is 23? 55? 217?

Extending Concepts

Suppose the company also makes cubes of different sizes and uses the stamping block to paint only the front face of each cube as shown.

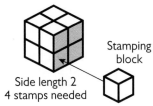

Side length 1

Side length 2
4 stamps needed

Stamping block

5. Make a table to show the number of paint stamps needed for cubes with side lengths 1 to 6. What pattern do you notice? Write a general rule for finding the number of paint stamps needed for any cube.

6. Use your rule from item **5** to find how many stamps you would need for a cube with side length 43.

Writing

7. Answer the letter to Dr. Math.

> Dear Dr. Math,
>
> I decided I didn't need to figure out the number of stamps for every different size rod. Instead, I just tested some sample lengths and made a table like this:
>
> | Length of Rod | Stamps Needed |
> |:---:|:---:|
> | 1 | 6 |
> | 3 | 14 |
> | 5 | 22 |
> | 10 | 42 |
> | 20 | 82 |
> | 100 | 402 |
>
> But I'm confused and can't see a pattern. Was this a good shortcut?
>
> Pat Turn

Crossing the River

Applying Skills

Suppose that a group of hikers with exactly two children and a number of adults must cross a river in a small boat. The boat can hold either one adult, one child, or two children. Anyone can row the boat.

How many one-way trips are needed to get everyone to the other side if the number of adults is:

1. 3?   **2.** 4?   **3.** 5?

4. Make a table that records the number of one-way trips needed for all numbers of adults from 1 to 8.

How many trips are needed if the number of adults is:

5. 11?   **6.** 37?

7. 93?   **8.** 124?

How many adults are in the group if the number of trips needed is:

9. 25?   **10.** 49?

11. 73?   **12.** 561?

Extending Concepts

13. Find the number of one-way trips that would be needed for a group of 4 adults and 3 children to cross the river. Use a recording method that keeps a running total of the number of trips and the number of adults and children on each side of the river.

14. Make a table showing the number of trips needed for 1 to 5 adults and 3 children to cross the river. Describe in words a general rule that you could use to find the number of trips needed for any number of adults and 3 children. How did your table help you to find the rule?

15. How many trips would it take for 82 adults and 3 children to cross?

16. How many adults are in the group if 47 trips are needed to get all the adults and 3 children across the river?

Making Connections

17. For transportation, the Hupa Indians of Northwestern California used canoes hollowed out of half of a redwood log. These canoes could carry up to 5 adults. If one adult could row the canoe, how many one-way trips would be needed for 17 adults to cross a river using one of these canoes?

Letter Shapes

Applying Skills

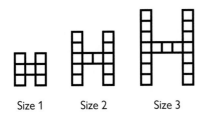

Size 1   Size 2   Size 3

1. Draw an *H* of size 4 and an *H* of size 5.

2. How many tiles are needed for each of the sizes 1 to 5 of the letter *H*?

3. How many tiles are added at each step to the letter *H*?

4. Which of these expressions tells how many tiles are needed for a letter *H*? The variable *s* stands for the size number.

$2s$ $5s$ $2s + 5$ $5s + 2$ $4s + 3$

5. Predict the number of tiles needed for a letter *H* of these sizes:

   a. 11   **b.** 19   **c.** 28

   d. 57   **e.** 129

6. What is the largest size of *H* you could make if you had:

   a. 42 tiles?   **b.** 52 tiles?

   c. 127 tiles?   **d.** 152 tiles?

Extending Concepts

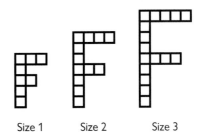

Size 1   Size 2   Size 3

7. a. Find how many tiles are needed for a letter *F* of sizes 1 to 5. Then describe in words a rule you could use to find the number of tiles needed for a letter *F* of any size.

   b. Write an expression to describe your rule in item **7a.** Use the letter *s* to stand for the size number.

   c. Explain why *s* is called a variable.

8. For a mystery letter, the number of tiles needed is $3s + 8$. The variable *s* stands for the size number. How many tiles are added at each step? How can you tell? Which letter grows faster, the mystery letter or the letter *F*?

Making Connections

9. The Celsius temperature scale uses the freezing point of water as 0 degrees Celsius and its boiling point as 100 degrees Celsius. If *c* stands for a known Celsius temperature, the expression $1.8c + 32$ can be used to find the Fahrenheit temperature. What Fahrenheit temperature corresponds to 16 degrees Celsius? to 25 degrees Celsius? How did you find your answers?

Tiling Garden Beds

Applying Skills

Find the value of these expressions if $l = 3$ and $w = 5$:

1. $6l$ **2.** $3l + w$ **3.** $4(l + w)$

4. $lw - 2$ **5.** $l(w - 2)$

For items **6–17**, assume that each garden is one square wide. Suppose you want to frame your garden with a single row of tiles like this:

Length 2,
10 border tiles needed

Find the number of border tiles needed for a garden of each length.

6. 4 **7.** 7 **8.** 13

9. 25 **10.** 57 **11.** 186

Find the length of the garden if the number of border tiles needed is:

12. 16 **13.** 38 **14.** 100

15. 370 **16.** 606

17. Which of these expressions could *not* be used to find the number of tiles needed to make a border around a garden with length l squares?

   a. $(l + 3) \times 2$ **b.** $(l + 2) \times 2 + 2$

   c. $2l + 6$ **d.** $(l + 2) \times 2$

   e. $(l + 1) \times 2 + 4$

Extending Concepts

18. a. Write two different expressions that both could be used to find the number of tiles needed to make a border around a garden whose width is 4 and whose length may vary. Use l to represent the length.

   b. Explain why each of the expressions makes sense by relating each part of the expression to the garden and the tiles.

   c. How many tiles are needed to make a border around a garden with a width of 4 and a length of 35?

19. Suppose that one length of the garden is along a wall like this:

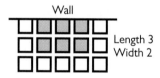

Length 3
Width 2

The length and the width may both vary. Write an expression for the number of tiles needed. Use l for the length and w for the width.

Making Connections

20. A Japanese garden is considered a place to contemplate nature. An enclosure such as a bamboo fence is often used to separate the garden from the everyday world outside and to create the feeling of a sanctuary. What length of fencing would be needed to enclose a rectangular garden 70 feet long and 30 feet wide?

Chocolates by the Box

Applying Skills

In a box of Choco Chocolates there is a light chocolate between each group of 4 dark chocolates as shown. The size of the box tells the number of columns and rows of dark chocolates.

3 by 4 size

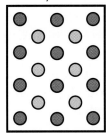

Find the number of dark chocolates and the number of light chocolates in boxes of these sizes:

1. 5 by 5   **2.** 8 by 10

3. 15 by 30   **4.** 40 by 75

Give the total number of chocolates in boxes of these sizes:

5. 3 by 5   **6.** 7 by 9

7. 18 by 20   **8.** 30 by 37

Extending Concepts

9. Either of the two equivalent expressions $lw + (l - 1) \times (w - 1)$ or $2lw - l - w + 1$ may be used to find the total number of chocolates in a box of Choco Chocolates.

  a. Verify that both expressions give the same result for a 16 by 6 box.

  b. Explain why the first expression makes sense.

10. Choco Chocolates wants to make new triangle-shaped boxes as shown. Write rules for finding the number of light chocolates, dark chocolates, and total chocolates in a triangular box of any size. How many dark and how many light chocolates are in a box of size 9? size 22?

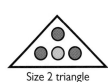

Size 2 triangle

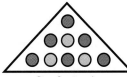

Size 3 triangle

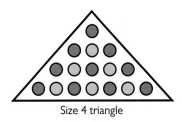

Size 4 triangle

Writing

11. Write a paragraph describing how you have used variables and expressions to describe patterns. Be sure to explain the meaning of the words *variable* and *expression*. Give some examples of using expressions to describe patterns.

Gridpoint Pictures

Applying Skills

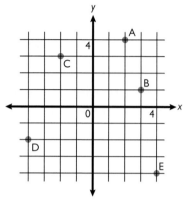

1. Give the coordinates of each of the five points shown on the coordinate plane.

2. Draw a grid and axes similar to those in item **1.** Place a dot at each point.

   a. $(1, 4)$ **b.** $(-3, 4)$ **c.** $(-1, 0)$

   d. $(-3, -2)$ **e.** $(1, -2)$

Tell whether each statement is true or false:

3. The y-coordinate of the point $(3, -5)$ is 3.

4. The x-coordinate of the point $(-9, 1)$ is -9.

5. The point $(0, -5)$ lies on the x-axis.

6. The point $(0, 4)$ lies on the y-axis.

7. The points $(2, 5)$ and $(-3, 5)$ lie on the same horizontal line.

Extending Concepts

8. Using coordinates, tell how to make this picture. You can include other directions but you may not use pictures.

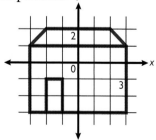

9. a. Give the coordinates of three points which lie on the x-axis. How can you tell if a point lies on the x-axis?

   b. Give the coordinates of two points which lie on the same vertical line. How can you tell if two points lie on the same vertical line?

Writing

10. Answer the letter to Dr. Math.

> Dear Dr. Math,
>
> Tom asked me to predict what I would get if I started at $(3, -5)$ on a coordinate plane and drew a line to $(3, 1)$, then another line to $(3, 7)$. I noticed right away that all the points have the same x-coordinate. I know that the x-axis is horizontal, so I figured that I would get a horizontal line. Is this good reasoning? I have to know for sure because Tom will really gloat if I get this wrong.
>
> K. O. R. Denate

Points, Plots, and Patterns

Applying Skills

Rule A: The *y*-coordinate is three times the *x*-coordinate.

Rule B: The *y*-coordinate is three more than the *x*-coordinate.

Read Rules A and B, then tell which of the ordered pairs below satisfy each rule.

1. $(2, 6)$ **2.** $(12, 4)$ **3.** $(3, 6)$

4. $(0, 3)$ **5.** $(-1, -3)$ **6.** $(5, 2)$

Read Rules C, D, and E, then answer items **7** and **8.**

Rule C: The *y*-coordinate is twice the *x*-coordinate.

Rule D: The *y*-coordinate is six more than the *x*-coordinate.

Rule E: The *y*-coordinate is five times the *x*-coordinate.

7. Of C, D, and E, which rule or rules produce a line passing through the origin?

8. Of C, D, and E, which rule produces the steepest line?

9. a. Copy and complete this table using **Rule F:** The *x*-coordinate is two less than the *y*-coordinate.

x	*y*
	4
	−2
3	
−1	

b. Plot the points from your table on a coordinate grid. Do the points lie on a straight line?

Extending Concepts

10. Make a table of points that fit this rule: The *y*-coordinate is twice the *x*-coordinate. Plot the points on a coordinate plane and draw a line through the points.

11. Pick a new point on the line you plotted in item **10.** What do you notice about its coordinates? Do you think that this would be true for any point on the line?

12. Make up two different number rules which would produce two parallel lines.

13. Make up a number rule which would produce a line that slopes downward from left to right.

Making Connections

In a *polygon,* the number of diagonals that can be drawn from one *vertex* is 3 fewer than the number of sides of the polygon.

6 sides, 3 diagonals

In the table below, *x* represents the number of sides of a polygon and *y* represents the number of diagonals that can be drawn from one vertex.

14. Complete the table and plot the points on a coordinate plane. What do you notice?

x	*y*
5	2
6	
9	
	8

Payday at Planet Adventure

Applying Skills

At Planet Adventure, Lisa works at the waterslide. Her rate of pay is $9 per hour. Joel works at the Mystery Ride and makes $5 per hour plus a one-time $12 bonus for dressing up in a clown costume.

1. Make a table to show the pay Lisa would receive for 1–7 hours of work.

2. How many hours would Lisa have to work to earn:

   a. $81?   **b.** $99?

   c. $31.50?   **d.** $58.50?

3. Make a table to show the pay Joel would receive for 1–7 hours of work.

4. How much will Joel earn if he works 8 hours? 4.5 hours? 7.5 hours?

5. How many hours would Joel have to work to earn:

   a. $57?   **b.** $67?

   c. $39.50?   **d.** $54.50?

6. Copy the axes shown. Make a graph of the data for Lisa's pay. On the same grid, make a graph of the data for Joel's pay.

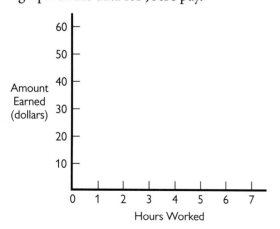

Extending Concepts

7. Write a rule that you could use to find the wage earned by Joel for any number of hours of work.

8. For what number of hours of work will Lisa and Joel earn the same amount? How can you figure this out using the graphs? without using the graphs?

9. In which hours will Joel earn more than Lisa?

10. Why is Lisa's graph steeper than Joel's?

11. Why does Joel's graph not pass through the origin?

12. If Joel works 4 hours, how much does he earn? How much *per hour*? If he works more than 4 hours, is his overall rate per hour higher or lower than this?

Writing

13. Answer the letter to Dr. Math.

> Dear Dr. Math,
>
> I've been offered two different jobs. The first one would pay $8 per hour. The second one would pay a fixed $24 each day plus $5 per hour. Which job should I take if I want to earn as much money as possible? How do I figure it out?
>
> Broke in Brokleton

Sneaking Up the Line

Applying Skills

Eric the Sheep is waiting in line to be shorn. Each time a sheep at the front of the line gets shorn, Eric sneaks up the line two places.

How many sheep will be shorn before Eric if the number of sheep in front of him is:

1. 5?   **2.** 8?

3. 15?   **4.** 42?

5. 112?   **6.** 572?

How many sheep could have been in line in front of Eric if the number of sheep shorn before him is:

7. 7?   **8.** 12?

9. 25?   **10.** 39?

Extending Concepts

For the following questions, suppose that each time a sheep at the front of the line gets shorn, Eric sneaks up *three* places instead of two.

11. Complete the table for this situation. Then graph the data.

Number of Sheep In Front of Eric	Number of Sheep Shorn Before Eric
4	
5	
6	
7	
8	
9	
10	
11	

12. How many sheep will be shorn before Eric if there are 66 sheep in front of him? How did you figure this out?

13. How could you find the number of sheep shorn before Eric for *any* number of sheep in front of him? Describe two different methods you could use and explain why each method works.

14. If 28 sheep are shorn before Eric, how many sheep could have been in front of him? How did you figure it out? Why is the answer not unique?

Writing

15. Describe a method you could use to find the number of sheep shorn before Eric for any number of sheep in front of him and for any number of sheep that Eric sneaks past.

Something Fishy

Applying Skills

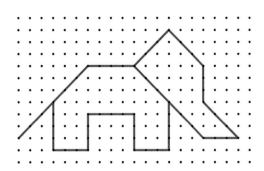

This elephant drawing in growth stage 3 has height 10, length 19, and body area (excluding the head) 49.

1. Figure out what the height, length, and body area would be for elephants in growth stages 1–6. Show your answers in a table.

2. Make graphs to show the height, length, and body area for elephant drawings in growth stages 1–6.

Use the patterns that you observe in your table to find the height, length, and body area for elephant drawings in each of these growth stages:

3. 12

4. 20

5. 72

6. 103

7. In what stage of growth is the elephant if its height is 28? 49? 76? 211?

8. In what stage of growth is the elephant if its length is 67? 133? 325?

Extending Concepts

9. Use words and expressions to describe rules you could use to find the height, length, and body area for elephant drawings in any growth stage.

10. What growth stage is an elephant in if its body area is 529? Explain how you figured out your answer.

11. Create your own "animal" and draw pictures to show how it grows in stages. Make sure you have a clear rule for the way it grows. Make a table to show stages 1–5 of your animal's growth. Describe in words a rule for its growth. Describe your rule using variables and expressions.

Writing

12. Do you think that in reality, the height of an actual elephant is likely to increase according to the pattern you described in item 9? Why or why not?

The Will

Applying Skills

Annie may receive money according to any one of three plans. The amounts of money that each plan would yield at the end of years 1, 2, 3, 4, and 5, respectively, are as follows:

Plan A: $100, $250, $400, $550, $700, and so on.

Plan B: $10, $40, $100, $190, $310, and so on.

Plan C: 1 cent, 3 cents, 9 cents, 27 cents, 81 cents, and so on.

1. Make a table showing the amount of money Annie would receive from each plan at the end of years 1–15.

2. For each plan, make a graph showing the amount of money Annie would receive at the end of years 1–10.

3. Which plan yields the most money at the end of year 8? 12? 17? 20?

4. Describe in words the growth pattern for each plan.

Extending Concepts

5. At the end of which year will Annie first receive more than $5,000 if she uses Plan A? Plan B? Plan C?

6. Which plan would you recommend to Annie? Why?

7. Figure out a pattern which gives more money at the end of the fifteenth year than Plan A but not as much as Plan B.

Making Connections

8. The **half-life** of a radioactive substance is the time required for one-half of any given amount of the substance to decay. Half-lives can be used to date events from the Earth's past. Uranium has a half-life of 4.5 billion years! Suppose that the half-life of a particular substance is 6 days and that 400 grams are present initially. Then the amount remaining will be 200 grams after 6 days, 100 grams after 12 days, and so on.

   a. What amount will remain after 18 days? after 24 days?

   b. When will the amount remaining reach 3.125 grams?

   c. Will the amount remaining ever reach zero? Why or why not?

STUDENT GALLERY

The Seeing and Thinking Mathematically project is based at Education Development Center, Inc. (EDC), Newton, MA, and was supported, in part, by the National Science Foundation Grant No. 9054677. Opinions expressed are those of the authors and not necessarily those of the National Science Foundation. ☀

CREDITS: Photographs: Chris Conroy • Beverley Harper (cover) • © Bruce Stromberg/Graphistock: pp. 3TC, 20–21 • © Jeremy Walker/Tony Stone Images: pp. 3TR, 28–29 • © Chad Ehlers/Photo Network: p. 27B • Illustrations: Manfred Geier: p. 33B • Bethann Thornburgh: pp. 2TL, 10B, 11B, 25B, 26B, 31B, 38BR

Creative Publications and MathScape are trademarks or registered trademarks of Creative Publications.

© 1998 Creative Publications
1300 Villa Street, Mountain View, California 94041

Printed in the United States of America.

0-7622-0215-7   1 2 3 4 5 6 7 8 9 10 . 02 01 00 99 98 97

INDEX